Art, Politics, and Will

ART, POLITICS, AND WILL

Essays in Honor of

LIONEL TRILLING

EDITED BY

QUENTIN ANDERSON

STEPHEN DONADIO

STEVEN MARCUS

Basic Books, Inc., Publishers   *New York*

909.08
A 784

Library of Congress Cataloging in Publication Data
Main entry under title:

Art, politics, and will.

    CONTENTS: Barzun, J. The imagination of the real.—
Himmelfarb, G. Social history and moral imagination—
Said, E. W. Renan's philological laboratory. [etc.]
    1. Civilization, Modern—Addresses, essays, lectures.
2. Trilling, Lionel—Criticism and interpretation—
Addresses, essays, lectures. I. Trilling, Lionel,
1905-1975. II. Anderson, Quentin, 1912-
III. Donadio, Stephen. IV. Marcus, Steven.
CB358.A74   909.08   76-48881
ISBN: 0-465-00448-2

CONTENTS

CONTENTS

FOREWORD

This volume was projected, and the contributors asked to undertake their work before Lionel Trilling's death on November 5, 1975, when it perforce became a memorial volume. This led the editors to include two brief essays on the work of the man we seek to honor. Our title refers to central, although not exclusive, preoccupations in the work of Lionel Trilling, preoccupations which the friends and admirers who have contributed to this book welcomed in him, and, in various ways and degrees, share themselves. Trilling found art, politics, and will inextricably related; he could not conceive of an art without political meaning, or an art which did not display will in all its energy and complexity of intention.

The occasion of this volume is not that of praise for the achievements of a specialist; to celebrate Lionel Trilling's work is not to advance any cause narrower than that of the cultivated literary and social intelligence addressed to the most generous conception of individual and social ends. Responsive as he was to the work of Freud, that fact no more defines him than does his allegiance to liberal democracy or his devotion to Wordsworth and Keats. If there is a characteristic mode of inquiry in his writing, it might be phrased: What, given the cultural situation with all its stresses, gaps, unarticulated oppositions, current shibboleths, are the appropriate objects of our attention at this moment? Among the foci he found revealing were the cultural fate of certain words, the shifts and permutations within a particular period of the significance attributed to certain books, poems, writers, social causes, human qualities, and—as in the notable essay, "The Fate of Pleasure," or his last book, *Sincerity and Authenticity*—the ways in which philosophy, history, and the arts recorded deep-running transformations in the culture in the course of the last two centuries.

When Trilling writes, he appears on each occasion to enter into the historical process as he conceives it, and by exposing the subject he has chosen for what it is and what it has become —for its contemporary resonance—asserts in the same breath our responsibility to facts and values of persisting importance and our responsibility to ourselves—readers who are tacitly urged to assume the implied burden of discrimination, judgment and action.

But the contents of this volume attest to the fact that to know and to cherish the work of our colleague and friend bore with it no implication that one was bound to agree with him—he would have found that stifling. We can happily report what will be evident to the reader: this book is a tribute without being in the least a chorus.

QUENTIN ANDERSON
STEPHEN DONADIO
STEVEN MARCUS

Art, Politics, and Will

THE IMAGINATION OF THE REAL,
OR IDEAS AND THEIR ENVIRONMENT

JACQUES BARZUN

Prologue on Origins

In the autumn of 1934 at Columbia College, two young in-
structors, who knew each other only slightly from undergraduate days, were set to teach together a seminar of upper-
classmen; or more exactly, to lead a colloquium on selected
great books of the modern period. One of the young men was
a student of history, the other of English literature. The latter
was deeply interested in the great deterministic systems of Marx
and Freud, which at that time were in the ascendant and still
wore a fresh, beckoning look. The other neophyte inclined to
the radical empiricism of William James. He was finding in
James, Nietzsche, Samuel Butler, Whitehead—the Pragmatic
Revolution generally—a set of ideas by which to reconcile respect for natural science with a watchful sense of its limitations, and to discern in all materialisms and determinisms the
illicit jump from empirical fact to arbitrary metaphysics.

There was at the outset no occasion for these unlikely class-
room partners to discuss politics, though they were alike aware
that political ideas are implied in literature and have links with
philosophy. Had they compared notes, the conclusion might
have emerged that the one bore the influence of his earlier

belief in the communist ideal, whereas the other was increasingly sure that after the "great" war (which he had experienced at first hand) anyone who was not simultaneously a liberal, a conservative, and a socialist was espousing futilities.

This ill-matched pair of dialecticians were 29 and 27 years old, but they must have lacked the dogmatism of youth, for despite the shocking discoveries they made about each other during the hot discussions with their students—over Hobbes and Rousseau, Milton and Goethe—they not only established a modus vivendi that soon turned into a deep friendship, but also developed a distinctive practice of joint teaching. Indeed, their unpremeditated rapprochement evolved into an original way of understanding both literature and history, and as things turned out, the joint practice continued to impart that understanding, through many courses on different topics, for more than a third of a century.

When I refer to Lionel Trilling's and my conception of our task as original, I mean that it was not consciously patterned on any model from the past and that when we set out it was not in use or favor. It is perhaps enough to say that we came to call it "cultural criticism"—a paradox, for in those days the "new" reigning criticisms, Southern and Marxist, were both scornful of what we thought of as culture; and the "old" criticism was wedded to a humdrum study of literary genres and lives. Among historians, "cultural history" was equated with German *Geistesgeschichte* and dismissed as misty generalizing. That left only the "history of ideas," which was cultivated by philosophical minds interested in the technical relations of pure ideas within the sequence of great systems.

Our peculiar outlook resembled none of these preferred or disallowed modes of study, nor was it an eclectic choice from among their parts. It arose rather from a lively sense of the force of circumstance, balanced by an equally strong sense of the free life that ideas lead when hatched. It seemed clear to us that in order to know what books and works of art, philosophies

4

and movements of opinion intend, one must learn their antecedents and concomitants *of whatever kind*; and to know how the ideas thrive and change, one must trace their consequences. Ideas cannot be reduced to simple products of the surroundings, or even to direct expressions of time and place; they are not resultants by necessity, like wind and tide. But—to follow the opposite extreme—ideas can be regarded as "pure" or unconditioned, and their meaning treated as self-contained, only by a temporary abstraction in thought. Making that abstraction may yield valuable findings, but they were not the object of our search.

To sum up, the road we took was not a via media between Marxist determinism and New-critical autonomy, nor between either of them and the then decaying "historical criticism," but a fresh path to be blazed through the jungle of historical, biographical, sociological, analytical, and philological circumstance—circumstance *of whatever kind*.

The effort was a work of the sturdiest imagination—the imagination which springs from fact and is hedged in by probability, the literal imagination, the imagination of the real. It is controlled divination. In such an inquiry no proof is possible, however thoroughly one delves. For "sources" also record only the divination (assumption, imputation) of the contemporary observer, himself usually less than controlled.

All this sounds obvious enough now, when as a result of many influences even then acting upon us, cultural history is an established genre widely read and popular with graduate students, and when criticism in the arts and historical sciences has absorbed much of the spirit of that genre. But the spread of this methodless method has brought with it misunderstandings and misleadings that we could perhaps more easily avoid before its accreditation, when we were groping toward uncertain ends and subjecting our thoughts to the test of academic distrust and pedagogic use.

The perennial difficulty, of course, is to choose from the

surrounding mass of "conditions" those that illuminate the subject, and once these are found, to avoid the fatal error of slipping into a new determinism. The activity of unearthing facts that spur the re-creative imagination tempts to taking these "conditions" as sufficient and compelling, when they are only limiting or suggestive; for the habit of thought based on linear causation and scientific correlation dies hard, and the common vocabulary of a technological age promotes the deceit. The whole question of "influence" is bedeviled by that error, and so is the practice of finding themes and significances by juxtaposing texts and events or texts and texts. Even in the so-called pure criticism that posits "autonomous" literary works, the interpretation of prose or poetic fiction suffers from the same rigidity and leads to those repetitious "problems" that impel the critics to discover, not so much the figure in the· carpet as the anatomy of the work and the pathology of its maker.

This urge the cultural critic resists. When coincidences between idea and circumstance strike him hard, he uses his skill to distinguish the quality of belief his findings deserve. He will believe to the full that John Locke in his essays on government was combating Sir Robert Filmer, because Locke takes issue with him by name and Filmer's presence visibly helps Locke to develop his ideas. But a different quality of belief possesses the critic when he assents to the usual statement about Locke's having "written to justify the Revolution of 1688." The critic remembers Locke's intellectual formation—long years of self-exile in Holland and France, where libertarian ideas similar to his own were flourishing before 1688; and there is Locke himself, speaking not *to* or *out of* circumstance, not as a party hack, but as an original fount of ideas.

The discipline of shading one's beliefs enables a student to regard as significant a miscellany of disparate conditions, not just a single series, and thus to escape the fate of the interpreter who is definable by an adjective: the cultural critic is not more psychological than class-conscious, not more structural than thematic. For him the mixture of elements classifiable under these and other heads varies with each case, and his internal assessment of their force is exact in the degree to which it is finally incommunicable. He can point and explain, but what is at work to give him understanding is, after all, *his* imagination; and in the nature of things he can only give an incomplete report of its contents.

The duty of the cultural critic, then, is to discover and sort out for himself the signs of the distant reality and in assembling them to be sensitive without being impressionable. In the colloquial French saying, *il ne faut pas croire que c'est arrivé.* This habit of judgment is not simple skepticism; on the contrary, it opposes its vision of the object not only to the conventional description, but also to its revisionist counterpart, each too often tolerant of large errors while stressing the details of its own parti pris.

What starts the work of imagining, that is, the transfer from the known or sensed to the imagined, is usually a fresh perception, conjunction, association, expectation, or objection. When it occurs it dislocates the contents of the mind, and out of the subsequent rearrangement comes the true novelty. When this common experience of self-review (it could be more common without harm) occurs by a sort of intellectual accident, a stumble over a hidden fact, one undergoes the very process by which circumstance affects ideas and in that situation the cultural critic finds warrant for studying ideas and facts as he means to do.

JACQUES BARZUN

The Critical Imagination

Subjects fitted to illustrate cultural criticism are not wanting; the difficulty is to avert the suspicion of using a predesigned case. Accordingly, I shall try an exercise in reverse: instead of starting from a work or a movement, begin with Circumstance and find what it inspired. The circumstance I have in mind is the advent of the railroad in the nineteenth century. What ideas and emotions did it set off, in the concentrated form of art as well as in the diffuse general mind? The familiar but abstract answers that the textbook absentmindedly recites—fear of change, pride in rapid transit—do not satisfy the historical imagination.

The full subject can claim a renewed novelty today, for in the past half-century several generations have grown up only distantly acquainted with the railroad, ignorant of its peculiar blend of power and romance. Now it looks impotent and drab, and neither the students of transportation nor the general historians seem aware of what happened to Western civilization when the railroad struck it.* Some writers, it is true, speak of "transportation revolution" without more. But the word revolution does duty is used nowadays about too many things imagined or actual, important or trivial. It often denotes no more than an irritable adjustment of our overstimulated sensorium. And compared with what assails us now, the change—the changes—brought about by the railroad were radical and fearful; they were unexampled and unrepeated; and unlike our restless shifts, they were permanent. Indeed, as I hope to show, they kindled the emotions we still find most disaffecting from life itself.

* For example, in G. R. Elton's excellent manual, *Modern Historians on British History*, apart from a railway bibliography described as useful for "specialist interests," only one entry out of 1351 touches on the railroads; it is a fourteen-page article about railway politics during the Peel Administration. *The Railway Age*, by Michael Robbins (London 1962), is an excellent essay, but much of its space is devoted to the history of railway development in various countries.

Students of literature, it is true, remember Wordsworth and Ruskin and others who from the first denounced the railroad for its desecration of natural beauty and psychic peace. But those outcries are now regarded as outworn romanticism. By our scale, their prescience of ecological damage seems feeble, and it is forgotten that the poetic-pastoral preoccupation with the railroad continued in conflicting forms to the very end of the century. The circle of spiritual and ethical effects kept widening and creating ambivalence even among the sharpest critics. In the end, unexpectedly, love and admiration overcame contempt and distrust, until in the first quarter of this century the glory, the poetry of the railroad was a fit subject for celebration by such men as Auden, Spender, and E. M. Forster. The earlier maledictions shifted to new agencies of evil: why?

In this state of imperfect public memory the shortest way to the truth is to begin at the beginning. It is significant in itself that the first railroad and its first journey can be precisely dated and described. September 15, 1830 was the day when the Liverpool and Manchester Railway, built by George Stephenson, was inaugurated by a trip on which also occurred the first fatal accident. Eight trains on a double track were carrying dignitaries and official guests to Manchester at a speed that once attained twenty-four miles an hour. In one train was the Duke of Wellington; in another, William Huskisson, the President of the Board of Trade. At Parkside, seventeen miles from Liverpool, a halt was made to water the engines, and many passengers took the opportunity to stretch their legs and exchange astonishments. Huskisson left his carriage to shake hands with the Duke and, returning, was flurried by the approach of an engine on the parallel track. Instead of standing still, he fumbled for protection behind the open carriage door. When it was struck by the oncoming engine he was knocked down and his upper leg run over. He knew he was mortally wounded and he died the next day.[1]

9

Greatly shaken, the Duke and his party wanted to return at once to Liverpool and cancel the large reception prepared for them at Manchester. But they were told that the waiting crowd there was at such a pitch of excitement that if the trains did not appear a riot might ensue. For civil peace and also for the prosperity of the line, the inaugural group overcame their emotion and sense of propriety and went on to receive the honors of the city and the plaudits of the mob.

Meanwhile, the impressions of the travelers had been these: bewildering speed, increased at will without seeming effort, along a path miraculously smooth. By contrast, sharp and sudden changes in the view—at one moment, the spread of sunny fields seen from the top of an embankment, and next, the darkness of a deep cutting, or worse, the noise and stifling sensation of a tunnel. Perhaps still more strange was the sense of being always on a flat road of almost undeviating straightness. For the ever-changing contours of the earth seen from horseback or stagecoach, travel by train substituted a narrow geometry. Only an occasional curve or bridge varied the margins of motion. Since all the early railroads were rural, man's sense of being suddenly detached from his native earth could not have been greater.

The cause of this first change of sensibility was neither the *rail way* as such nor the steam engine. The use of paired rails for wagon tracks had been used in English mining for two hundred years; the stationary steam engine in industry for a hundred. The revolutionary event was the conjunction of the two for land travel at unheard-of speeds. Already in 1830 the inaugural trains could have run at fifty miles an hour—the organization of safety alone was wanting.

And the change from the ancestral mode of transport by animal power had long been worked at. The great Darwin (Erasmus) had predicted success forty years earlier.* Steam-

---

* Soon shall thy arm, Unconquered Steam afar
Drag the slow barge, or drive the rapid car.
  —*The Botanic Garden* (1791)

ships and steam coaches were in use by the early 1800s, and while canals were multiplying for the shorter and cheaper carriage of goods, the new high roads and bridges built by the latest methods of McAdam and Telford permitted faster running by stagecoach. The service had so much improved since the 1780s that DeQuincey, looking back on it, could lyricize about "The English Mail Coach" as having first imparted to him "the glory of motion" and thereby helped to "develop the anarchies of his subsequent dreams."[2]

At the formation of the Liverpool and Manchester Railway, it was in fact expected that the motive power would be horses.* But Stephenson's genius, encouraged by the brilliant surveyor William James, devised and imposed the means by which the shock of true novelty was administered, the fact not of mere improvement or increase, but of experience transformed. When the poet Wilfrid Scawen Blunt took his first automobile ride in 1900, the breakneck rate of fifteen miles an hour made him exclaim in his diary: "Certainly an exhilarating experience!"[3] That great modern intoxicant, speed, clearly depends for its effect on surrounding conditions. DeQuincey succumbed to it when hurtling through the night at eight or nine miles an hour. On the early railroads, spurts at thirty were called "flights."[4] But equally thrilling to this day are a gallop on a horse, a steep descent on skis, and a surfboard skim, each at different low velocities, whereas a jet trip at enormously greater speed gives little or no DeQuinceyan "glory." Wind, noise, and bodily exposure; the mass, size, and solidity of the vehicle; the steadiness of its motion and the variation in the field of vision are what strikes our senses with pleasurable fear. If men could ever realize their insistent dream of flying, instead of merely boarding flying machines, their passage through the air at any modest speed or height would procure them the acme of motive and emotive satisfaction.

---

* As late as 1829 the *Quarterly Review* pronounced the steam railway to be "a visionary project unworthy of notice." (vol. 31, p. 361)

In 1830, man had not yet learned to move among moving machines. Unaccustomed to their size, force, noise, and blind relentlessness, he had to improvise new habits. He must judge distance and velocity on the instant, foresee the path of the vehicle and his relation to it, note the projection and interaction of mechanical parts, and be able to repress his bodily reactions of alarm.* Nothing had prepared the mere citizen on his travels for the confusion, smoke, whistles, signals, and incipient claustrophobia of railroading. Dealing with horse and carriage was traditional knowledge, learned from infancy as a common necessity. The scale was human and the power under harness was a sentient creature, rarely out of control, led by someone within range of sight and voice. The hand sufficed for every act, the will was free. But the machine—and even more the system—denied all these mitigations of Power. Its momentum coerced even those ostensibly in charge. It required, after thousands of years, a reeducation of the nervous system, indeed, a continuous adaptation ever more demanding and not yet ended.

Augmenting this deep and sudden disturbance was the effect of large crowds. One has only to look at the first paintings and lithographs of a railroad station to see the impression the new reality produced—that of a populace in panic, jammed together, desperate to save themselves, mouths open, as if screaming and straining toward the door of a theater on fire.† It is likely that the visual representation is false, but the emotional is true. Twelve years after Huskisson's death, English newspapers were still warning against letting the Queen take a train; Louis-Philippe, King of the French, was forbidden the rails by his ministers; and when Lady Holland risked a journey from London to Chippenham, she clung to the hand of the great civil engineer Brunel for the whole thirty-five miles.[5] In many countries the first users of trains were locked into their com-

---

* The workman in the factory had already learned to avoid injury from the loom or lathe; but action there was repetitious and predictable; its source was stationary.

† As late as 1862, Frith's famous documentary painting of Paddington Station still gives the impression of an abnormal huddling of displaced persons.

partments. The self-discipline of crowds, which has become a distinctive trait of Western man during the last one hundred years, was learned slowly and painfully from the new contraption.

It is no wonder that the most conscious spirits of the early days regarded the railroad as a monster and preeminently as a symbol of death. Dickens, who was haunted by the railroad till the end of his life, in a literal as well as symbolic fashion,* gave his first treatment of the subject in *Dombey and Son*; it is Mr. Dombey's stream of consciousness that we follow during his trip after the death of his son:

> He found no relief or pleasure in the journey. . . . The very speed at which the train was whirled along mocked the swift course of the young life that had been borne away so steadily and so inexorably to its fore-doomed end. The power that forced itself upon its iron way—its own—defiant of all paths and roads, piercing through the heart of every obstacle, and dragging living creatures of all classes, ages, and degrees behind it, was a type of the triumphant monster, Death.

This image is repeated through five more paragraphs, in antiphony with the refrain: "Away, with a shriek, and a roar, and a rattle," which introduces a rapid stream of visions and sensations: "burrowing among the dwellings of men . . . mining in through the damp earth, booming on in the darkness and heavy air . . . through the chalk, through the mould, through the clay . . . among objects close at hand and almost in the grasp, ever flying from the traveller, and a deceitful distance ever moving slowly within him: like as in the track of the remorseless monster, Death!

". . . sometimes pausing for a minute where a crowd of faces are, that in a minute more are not . . . . And now its way, still like the way of Death, is strewn with ashes thickly. . . . There

---

* He was in the boat train that was wrecked at Staplehurst on June 9, 1865. A manuscript part of *Our Mutual Friend* had then as narrow an escape as Dickens, who afterwards suffered dreams and waking anxiety patterned on his sensations during the accident. He died on its anniversary five years later.

are dark pools of water, muddy lanes, and miserable habitations far below. There are jagged walls and falling houses close at hand . . . battered roofs and broken windows . . . ; and deformity of brick and mortar penning up deformity of mind and body. . . . It was the journey's fitting end, and might have been the end of everything. . . ."[6]

This moving-picture sequence is predominantly hostile. Yet in the first outburst of poetry and prose, English and French, about the railroad, another voice is also heard. Fear and hatred are mixed with wonder and hope, and Dickens himself came to rhapsodize about "flights." Love and hate merged as often happens in fear. The monster was malign but might be mysteriously benevolent; it does bring terror and death but it might also bring unity and peace. This indecision was particularly noticeable among the French romanticist poets. True, Musset and Gautier scorned the engine of horror from the outset; but when Rachel the actress was compared to a locomotive for her tragic power, the similitude struck few of her contemporaries as ludicrous. Lamartine hoped for the "appeasement" of society through the quick satisfaction of material wants. To George Sand the socialist (not the artist in her, who expressed some doubts), the locomotive was the blessed force that would compel mankind into brotherhood and at last create "one world."

One writer among her revolutionary coterie, Maxime Du Camp, Flaubert's friend, wrote a volume of verse prefaced with a doctrine that divided literary Paris and earned Du Camp some rough words from Flaubert: "Watch yourself! You dish out in your Preface a bunch of absurdities that are tolerably disgraceful; you celebrate industry and sing paeans to steam, which is idiotic and altogether too Saint-Simonian."[7]

The battle was joined, but it was destined never to be won or lost. Other poets and critics—among them Hugo, Houssaye, and Vigny—believed that the new machinery got its soul by taking it from man and that the consequent spread of materialism would spell the end of poetry, morals, and the spiritual life. "We do not ride the railroad, it rides upon us," said Thoreau in *Walden*. Later still, Ruskin was as outraged as Wordsworth had been at the despoiling of the countryside, and he resented being "parted from the nobler characteristics of his humanity and transmuted from a traveller into a living parcel."[8]

Yet these same observers found in the experience something that stirred their souls against their will. The Versailles accident of 1842 called forth Vigny's "La Maison du Berger," a long philosophic brooding on the destruction of human love and the contemplative life by the reckless deployment of mechanical strength ("We have gambled with a power too strong for us"). Though generous impulses may benefit from the monster —free trade, for instance, and "love swiftly traversing two nations"—there will be left "No room for Chance./Each man henceforth will slide along his appointed track/Absorbed in his silent and cold calculation."

In Thoreau the balance is more even, though tendentious readings of *Walden* may overlook it. He versifies his scorn in "What's the railroad to me?" but he puts into hardly better poetic prose his contrary impression: ". . . when I hear the iron horse make the hills echo with his snort like thunder, shaking the earth with his feet and breathing fire and smoke with his nostrils, it seems as if the earth had got a race now worthy to inhabit it. . . . I watch the passage of the morning cars with the same feeling that I do the rising of the sun."[9]

What are we to make of these incoherent responses? They do not simply reflect the difference between esthetic and practical feeling in sensitive men taken by surprise. They mark rather the beginning of that dismay Western man has felt ever since, at the contrast between the grandly possible and the meanly actual: all this power reduced to these trivial uses! The profound disappointment is not so much with the machine as with mankind. Carlyle, Thoreau, Ruskin, Flaubert, Matthew Arnold were but a few of those who drove home the point that nothing in modern life justifies its effort, bustle, and speed.* The railroad fixed the moralist's gaze on man's responsibility for his lately acquired power. Industry making goods in abundance could be justified as a form of sharing; dashing about the earth at twenty-four miles an hour was only self-indulgence.

What began as moral questioning about "the monster" wound up as a controversy about its suitability as a subject for art. Moral and esthetic feelings fuse into a single force with which the war of the artist against society is carried on. The critics who saw life as a battle between art and utility, the champions of the genius and seer against the bourgeois, the appalled observers of the uglifying of life and the polluting of nature—all discharged their animus against the railroad, threat and symbol by turns.

This double role was plain. Before the motor car, the locomotive was the one fully public machine. Poets, artists, social philosophers did not then any more than now visit factories or live among their wage slaves. Industry was sparse; the articulate part of society could only imagine its evils. But in the railroad station the new breed of proletarians could be seen and smelt, just as the desolation of industrial life could almost be touched when the train carried its well-to-do passengers through the grim back doors of great cities.

The new crowds sent scurrying like beetles by the railroad were also an ambiguous phenomenon, like its mechanical cause. Sometimes they seemed a humanizing spectacle, the brotherhood of democracy advancing; at other times they were a repellent sight, begetting disgust as in Daumier's painting

---

* Carlyle, summing up in 1850, asks about the railway builders what their worth to mankind is: "I should say, Trifling if any worth." (*Latter-Day Pamphlets*, No. VII) Flaubert in his *Dictionary of Accepted Ideas* conveys through a philistine's remark the contempt that hundreds of other artists and social critics have uttered on the subject: "*Railways*: 'I, my dear sir, who am speaking to you now—this morning I was at X; I had taken the X train; I transacted my business there and by X o'clock I was back here.' " (Trans. by J. Barzun, 3rd ed., New York: New Directions, 1976)

"The Third Class Compartment."* Unquestionably, the chorus of hate denouncing modern life after the mid-century, the rancor piercing through the art of Baudelaire, Rimbaud, and the Symbolists, arise from contact with the unlovable multitude so recently set in motion. It was not a mob fired by an idea and rioting nobly for two or three days; it was the workingmen's train, the commuting clerks emptying into their burrows, the pell-mell excursionists with screaming children, all on their lawful occasions—DeQuincey's "fluctuating mobs"—forming and reforming daily and hourly.

The hope of separating them into classes, each with its waiting room, restaurant, and divinely ordained upholstery (or absence of it), persisted for decades; but it proved delusive almost from the start. Porters and other railway servants, by taking advantage of travelers' anxiety, soon democratized behavior, while the platform scrimmage and compartment togetherness automatically leveled ranks and pretensions. The railway could be no respecter of persons; its massive promiscuity was irreversible, making Ruskin rage at men herded like cattle and Tolstoy affirm that going by train was like frequenting a brothel.[10]

Nor were dignity and civility alone at stake; religious and sexual conventions were also being destroyed. Should trains operate on Sunday? The system that worked twenty-four hours a day could not stop in mid-flight for the Sabbath. As for the assumption that the unescorted woman in a public place was inviting advances, it had to be reversed: she must be treated with the greatest circumspection, for fear of immediate outcry and scandal.† By the late 1870s, when sleeping cars had been

* No less depressing is the same scene sentimentalized by Charles Rossiter in "To Brighton and Back for Three and Sixpence" (1859).

† In England carriages for ladies only were not much used, except on the Great Western, for a short time in the 1880s. In France, the "Dames Seules" compartments were maintained on some railroads as late as 1914. I remember traveling as a child with my mother in such a compartment in the Paris-Lyon-Méditerranée to Grenoble, but not on other lines. Having been given a plausible reason for the existence of such cars, I could not be brought to see why they were necessary on some lines and not on others.

introduced, "female independence" was well understood. The former prudery—a counterpart of male aggressiveness—became a subject for humorous irony, as one may see in Henry James's short story, "The Point of View."[11]

Before the horde of travelers could learn the new discipline, another large body of men had to acquire it at once, from the start. I mean the organized army of railway servants. The word army is hardly a metaphor. Among the managers, station-masters, inspectors, and others who ran the English railways, former soldiers were numerous. Railroading obviously depends on strict regimentation; its army is peculiar only in that officers and men are widely scattered and not subject to immediate command. In this they resemble the police, and it is no simple coincidence that the railroad and the Metropolitan Police were born within a year of each other. The traveling public needed policing quite apart from stopping theft or violence, and the first railway men who worked the signals (or gave them by hand), who inspected the road or dealt with train crowds were called—and were—policemen.

Soon all railway employees were put in uniforms copied from those of Peel's new police. Since that body was organized by a former officer imbued with the methods that General Sir John Moore had developed in the Peninsular War, it is not fanciful to see in the revolutionary era from 1792 to 1815 the conditions that prepared the European mind for the social regimentation of an industrial—and especially a railroading—community.* And since railroad men carried out their duties under the sanction of danger and death, they became, like soldiers, liable to uncommon penalties for common errors. Negligence became a crime; sleep and drunkenness, as on the sentry post, were heinous acts.† Thus was introduced the idea

---

* In the Chartist agitation of 1848, the 150,000 special constables sworn in to maintain order numbered many thousands of railwaymen. (J. R. Whitbread, *The Railway Policeman*, London, 1961, 35–6.)

† ". . . guilty of misdemeanor and liable to two years with hard labor if (any one)

of technical guilt, which now controls every man's behavior. Intention plays no part in it, only result—harm to one's fellowman, however indirectly caused.

Hidden in this changed view of responsibility is a new power, first embodied in railway working—remote control. This power, in turn, depends on symbolism. In dispatching trains the direct knowledge of successive situations is not possible or is not enough for safe operation. Whatever is must be read from signs. Hence the train order, the signal and switch thrown by lever and wire, the siding opened and shut at the exact times. The symbols for these realities (gestures, lights), the targets, numbers, boards for stop and slow, were not invented or agreed upon all at once. This organized "theology" was a laborious birth—just like the enforcement upon every town and hamlet of a common time, contrary to the visible noon.*

The peacetime, rational regimentation of Western man for workaday uses reached its high point in railroading;† and it was this spectacle of order and precision, the sureness of remote control and its fulfillment of prediction, that imparted to the railroad its unique "romance." The timetable prophesies a train at 4:12 p.m.; at 4:10 the home signal lifts and the starting signal drops; the engine, just within sight, can be heard whistling and decreasing speed; it steams into the station at exactly

---

employed as engine driver, guard, porter, or other servant of a railway company is found drunk or . . . wilfully, maliciously, or negligently does or omits to do any act whereby the life or limb of any person upon the railway shall or might be injured or the passage of engines, etc. impeded, or . . . aids or assists in such an offence." (J. F. Stephen, *Digest of the Criminal Law*, London, 1879, 201.)

* Some railroading injunctions now seem almost platitudinous, but others are far from obvious. They depend on many defined meanings, e.g., of "light engine" or "superior train."

Especially in the United States, common time was resisted until the 1880s as a violation of local autonomy. Dickens himself, though he saw the necessity well enough, resented the tyranny of the standardized time and synchronized clock. The feat of overcoming American prejudice was performed by Charles F. Dowd, the principal of the Seminary for Young Ladies at Saratoga Springs. (see C. N. Dowd, *C. F. Dowd: a Narrative of his Services*, etc., New York, 1930)

† But see *The Confessions of a Signalman* by James O. Fagan (Boston, 1908), which discusses the "free man's" stubborn resistance to rules and the correlation of this exercise of freedom with the frequency of accidents.

4:12, discharging its mixed cargo of objects and persons amid apparent confusion and the heightening of varied emotions. It is magical.*

DeQuincey knew the true source of our wonder: not the trappings of the vehicle, but ". . . the conscious presence of a central intellect, that, in the midst of vast distances—of storms, of darkness, of danger—overruled all obstacles into one steady cooperation to a national result."[12] The romance of the ship differs by being lived on board rather than beheld as the feat of a deployed army working by code and rule; nor can the sea ever be regimented by clock and signal. Again, the romance of the airplane was transient; it passed with the solo flights of a handful of pioneers. As for the precision that should bestow romance on orbitings and moon landings, it is as yet too exceptional. It evokes admiration but not wonder. And its creators are too well equipped. Their performance lacks the touch of man the maker, with hand and brain daily renewing order.

Organization, regimentation—the double aspect of one activity—were bound to put their mark on the formless crowd which the railroad drew to itself from town and countryside. The traveler learned to stop at the gate, line up at the window, speak and move in turn, watch the clock in patience;† in short, subdue his impulses to a level state of acquiescence in endless small servitudes. The constraints which in the end democratized him did so by rubbing off the edges and angles of the ego, and the fit symbol of this planing down was the ticket.‡

---

* This is what Kipling meant by the well-known lines in which he rebukes the unimaginative commuter who looks back to the stagecoach for "romance": ". . . And all unseen/Romance brought up the nine fifteen." ("The King" [1894] in Collected Verse of Rudyard Kipling, N.Y., 1907, p. 251.)

† See the painting by Nicol, "Irish Emigrants Waiting for the Train" (1846).

‡ The belief has sometimes been expressed that the railroad, by its three classes of seats (sometimes four), as well as by the opportunity it gave of living out of town in class-segregated suburbs, worked against rather than for democratic attitudes. This is to forget the social order that the railroad acted upon. Class-by-money is not the same as class-by-manners, and only lately has money become the sole definer of class—precisely as the result of the breakdown of distinctions which could not survive railway travel.

For at first, as seemed logical, the railroad passenger was "booked" like the traveler in a stagecoach; he gave his name and saw it written down in a book, with his address and destination. A copy of the waybill given to the driver of the small human group showed that the traveler was also a person. But in 1839 a clerk of the Newcastle and Carlisle Railway grew tired of writing out useless particulars and invented the ticket.* Printed and numbered ahead of time, and no longer filled with the traveler's description, the ticket recorded matters of interest only to the company. It was stamped and made good when sold. With the bang of the dating machine, the purchaser as individual was blotted out, becoming a ticketholder, a mere device to carry the ticket to its destination. He justified his continued existence by thrusting out the cardboard on demand and having little pieces taken out of its hide. If the words or the date were not what they should be, he was in trouble.

In the course of time, the ticket, the card of identity, the bare number became a substitute self more potent than the natural self, because validated, classified ahead of time, negotiable.† It need hardly be pointed out that in our present society. the basis of faith and credit, the proof of real existence is the unique number on the appropriate card; and the larger this denominator, the closer the self taken as *one* approaches zero.

The Victorians, who witnessed the beginnings of this diminution, also understood it. In the lively disputing that Meredith has his Diana of the Crossways carry on with her lover Redworth, the railroad magnate, Diana says: "You admit that your railways are rapidly 'polishing off' the individual."[13] In Russia a generation later, the aptly named Old Guard at Irkutsk sum-

---

* Or more exactly, reinvented; for in the middle of the thirteenth century, the pilgrims who sailed from Marseilles for the Holy Land were issued numbered tickets, and the names of travelers and sponsors were entered in a register. (Joan Evans, *Medieval France*, Oxford, 1925, 128.) In later centuries before the nineteenth, a (handwritten) slip of paper was occasionally used as an ad hoc mark of entitlement.
† In *Through the Looking Glass* (1871), Alice is asked for her ticket and says: "I'm afraid I haven't got one." In our day, only a person holding the right "ticket" among all those he is expected to carry can say that he is not afraid.

med up the issue in its objection to the proposed Transsiberian that was to come from Ekaterinburg: "We like better to travel by tarantass. . . . One leaves when one likes, stops where one likes, and at post stations of one's choice. With trains, you must board them at a fixed hour and ride in a carriage full of strange and unpleasant people; you are transported like a trunk, and you haven't the right to stop the train when you please."[14] Redworth's answer to Diana had been an evasion: "Railways will spread the metropolitan idea of comfort"; to which her riposte is: "I fear they will feed us on nothing but that big word."

The comfort was nevertheless undeniable. The railroad overcame not only distance but weather, and it introduced something peculiarly modern that differs from comfort and is often its opposite—convenience.* But this new freedom differed from the old and cannot readily be compared with it; the desires that each satisfies dwell in opposite quarters of the imagination. When facing natural obstacles, the will turns patient or inventive; it turns angry and frustrated when balked by hindrances that are—or seem—man-made. The man-made railroad having aroused utopian imaginings, men assumed that the new range of choices would simply be added to all the earlier forms of the pleasant and the possible. It was a shock to discover that the very conditions of "progress" meant only a substitution, that is, a general and painful deprivation. All revolutions, and not only the technological, proceed upon this same miscalculation.

* One has only to recall the obstacles to travel in the century of Bishop Berkeley (in Italy) and Arthur Young (in northern England) or, in our century, the condition of places without transport—such as the Congo when Gide went there—in order to measure the change of outlook on Possibility that was ushered in by steam travel. (See *The Works of George Berkeley*, London, 1820, I, xx; Arthur Young, quoted by F. S. Williams in *Our Iron Roads*, London, 1852, 6–7; André Gide, *Voyage au Congo*, Paris, 1927, *passim* and especially the notes dated December.)

A single example is enough to show the difference to culture with a big C of the advent of the railroad. In 1844, Berlioz answers an invitation to play his works in Italy with gratitude and good will, but he adds: "We must therefore give up this project until I am possessed of five or six millions, plus a railroad to transport to Milan my full Parisian orchestra." (To Alberto Mazzucato, May 19, 1844)

Every change in the modes of transportation has taken away something that man cherished. Already in the seventeenth century it was considered effeminate to ride in a coach instead of on horseback.[15] When the railroad came, manliness was threatened once again. The first riders were content, indeed proud, to stand up in boxlike cars exposed to the elements; and for a long time engine drivers and firemen on the bare footplate resisted offers of greater protection for themselves. Young men on excursions acted the daredevil by riding the roofs or the buffers, as still happens in the Middle East to this day.[16] The installation of the safety valve on the locomotive incensed some drivers, who turned it tight shut, to show they were not afraid of the boiler. In this country, brakemen who had to walk the roofs of freight cars cut off the warning ropes that indicated the nearness of a low bridge.

These irrationalities gradually dissipated, but in their day they were the signs of an image of man we can scarcely credit now—man defying nature by himself, individually, and therefore hating and fearing the safety that might weaken his fiber, the device that might cause others to impugn his self-sufficiency.* The modern conception of man collectively *defeating* nature and seeking "security" put in the place of the former heroic man the docile, apprehensive man, disciplined by his own mechanical creation, the "safety-first" man, who relies on the informed (and uniformed) official as his *guard*, his *conductor*, and who, when alone, would prefer, as in a famous Daumier lithograph of the timid bourgeois, to ride with the *dames seules*: "It's much safer."†

In time, all heroics gave way to method and system, union rules and government-imposed controls. Safe travel was finally achieved by the joint effect of invention and indignation after

* Compare the episode of the boys at Eton (1738), who broke the newly glazed windows of their sleeping rooms (formerly papered over), for fear that they should be thought soft.
† The English railway guard (U.S. conductor) derives his name from the armed guard who regularly rode the improved stagecoach as protection against highwaymen.

wrecks. As Charles Francis Adams pointed out apropos of the Westinghouse air brake, the victims of railroad disasters are an exception to the law of waste: they "do not lose their lives without great and immediate compensating benefits to mankind. After each new 'horror,' as it is called, the whole world travels with an appreciable increase of safety."[17] By 1890, sitting in a railway car at speeds close to 100 miles an hour had become the safest way not merely to travel, but to live and breathe on the planet.*

The cultural consequences of what the first railway promoters called "this important machine" cannot be fully inventoried, even in a long essay. The many unsuspected results I have collected would require detailed explanation; others are still to be found or surmised; it is a wide field of inquiry, hardly touched.† Nevertheless it is possible even now to hazard a few conclusions.

The first and clearest is that by causing a radical change in perception, the railway affected the measure of all cultural judgments—social, artistic, moral, and spiritual. Early in this century, the great archeologist, Flinders Petrie, surveying past and future in his *Janus in Modern Life*,[18] made an observation that gives a clue to this change of vision, and indeed of nature: "We shall no longer find men of high quality leading simple lives in remote districts. The gain to the whole community is clear, but we lose the most interesting types of natural character." In that contrast with the world we have lost we may read the beginning of the statistical view of life, the life of

---

* The risk of murder on a train has been surprisingly low, considering the tempting privacy of the European compartment. In England, only eight murders on trains were recorded during the first century of trains. (Colin Wilson and Patricia Pitman, *Encyclopedia of Murder*, N.Y., 1962, 182; and *Great Unsolved Crimes*, ed. anon., London, 1934, 161.) At the same time, suicide was facilitated and its drama increased, as witness the fictional use of this means, almost simultaneously, by Tolstoy and Trollope in *Anna Karenina* and *The Prime Minister*.

† The original version of this sketch took up a number of these original topics but exceeded the available space by many pages, which must await another opportunity of publication.

calculation, which seeks always the *collective* advantage. We still talk of individualism, and our political institutions take the individual for granted, counting his vote, but where is he, the natural character leading a simple life of high quality?

To raise this question does not mean that intellectual resistance to the collectivizing machine has lessened. The opposition is still divided, yet stronger than before. One branch of it denounces all industry and, like the old alchemists, believes that speed is from Satan: their doctrine is a radical primitivism. Other opponents look back to the railroad with longing and press its claims to elegance and ecological purity against present-day pollutions and indignities. For these, who reason from history, the techniques of matter can be bent to the service of man, the evolution of railroading being itself a prime example of such domestication. The third and strongest army of dissent shares the century-old outlook of the embattled artists and is led by them. Not interested in reforming or administering, they embody the New Inconsistency; for—it is manifest—speed, functionalism, glass and concrete, cinema, L.S.D., the visual products of science and the plastic products of *techne*, all entrance the artistic imagination, even while the artistic mind assails their source as dehumanizing.

It follows from this spectacle of continuing struggle that the railroad has imposed on culture not a necessary but a contingent set of consequences. We saw how diversely men "took" the railway at first. The outcome of all their "takings" depended on *those* men in their numerical proportions and the influence of their shifting opinions.* In great cultural changes that result from new techniques, as Peter Drucker has shown about the transformation of the Middle East by irrigation 7,000 years ago, the new conditions set new limits, just as they open

---

* Even Ruskin came to speak of "a divine railway journey." (*Diary*. Sept. 10, 1880, and again Nov. 13, 1882; in *Complete Works*, 1908, v. 33, xxiv and xliii). And modern poets, unlike their predecessors, readily accept trains and rails as symbols adaptable to the poetic expression of life-enhancing ideas. See Auden, Spender, Hardy, Sassoon, Eliot, *passim*.

new choices, but the purposes achieved are "largely within human control. The bony structure of a society is prescribed by the tasks it has to accomplish. But the ethos . . . is in man's hands. . . ."[19]

The great new constraint imposed by the railroad was that of unremitting discipline, ever more complex—the most exacting ever maintained on land in peacetime. The machine was more demanding than nature, the rewards of serving it less satisfying than those of hand labor. Remembering all the sweated, unheroic devotion to inanimate matter and abstract purpose which the nineteenth century took on, one can see why, after the kindred discipline endured by millions during the First World War, mankind in our time has acquired by cultural contagion a great weariness. Much can be understood about the twentieth century by reflecting that it was born to the promise of enjoyment, whereas its inheritance has been the Great Fatigue, coupled with the permanent hope and fear of System.

I have repeated in these pages my belief that any cultural change since the one brought on by the railroad between 1840 and 1860—"the deliberate earthquake," in Ruskin's phrase—has been a change not of essence but of size. Particularly since 1914, little has taken place in the Western world that was not done or shown or thought of before. But for all our angry, subconscious awareness of repetition and nonaccomplishment, we must remind ourselves of the conclusion just drawn about fact and idea. The railroad and its offshoots, despite all their power, neither deadened the mind to further changes of a like sort nor prevented anybody—early or late, poet or simple—from taking the world around him with the same freedom that men have ever had: the ways are blocked or open in different places but judgment remains sovereign. It is then for the imagination of the real, fashioning practice after it has found understanding, to work with what is and what was, and so make its way toward what it would.

NOTES

1. *The Times* (London), Sept. 17, 1830.

2. "The Glory of Motion" in *Blackwood's Magazine* for October 1849 was followed by another fragment in December, and both were later supplemented to form the well-known essay, "The English Mail Coach."

3. W. S. Blunt, *Diaries* (New York, 1922), Part One, Sept. 8, 1900, p. 371.

4. L. A. G. Strong, *The Rolling Road* (London, 1956), p. 76.

5. O. S. Nock, *The Railways of Britain*, 2nd ed. (London, 1949), p. 77.

6. Charles Dickens, *Dombey and Son*, chap. 20. In the Gadshill ed. of *The Works of Charles Dickens*, ed. Andrew Lang, vol. 8, pp. 341–43.

7. Du Camp, *Souvenirs Littéraires* (Paris, 1883), vol. 2, p. 417. *George Sand, sa vie et ses oeuvres* (Paris, 1912), vol. 3, p. 292 ff., and Victor Hugo, *En Voyage: France et Belgique* (the section on Normandy).

8. *The Seven Lamps of Architecture*, chap. 4, sec. 21 in *The Complete Works of John Ruskin*, Library ed., 1904, vol. 7, p. 159.

9. Henry David Thoreau, *Walden*, "Sounds," *ad init.*

10. John Ruskin, *Modern Painters*, chap. 16; *Complete Works*, vol. 5, p. 570; Tolstoy: this reference, once verified, now eludes me.

11. *The Siege of London*, etc. (Boston, 1883), p. 259.

12. "The English Mail Coach," sec. 1, p. 1 (Everyman ed., p. 3).

13. George Meredith, *Diana of the Crossways*, chap. 11, *ad init.*

14. Harmon Tupper, *To the Great Ocean* (Boston, 1965), p. 69.

15. Henry A. Talon quoting David Ogg in *Bunyan* (London, 1956), p. 10.

16. See, for example, the UPI dispatch on a derailment in Egypt, *The New York Times*, Jan. 19, 1975.

17. *Notes on Railroad Accidents* (New York, 1879), p. 2.

18. Flinders Petrie, *Janus in Modern Life* (London, 1907), p. 57.

19. "The First Technological Revolution and Its Lessons," *Technology and Culture*, vol. 7, No. 2, Spring 1966, p. 150.

SOCIAL HISTORY AND THE
MORAL IMAGINATION

GERTRUDE HIMMELFARB

There was a dramatic moment in a symposium a few years ago on "New Trends in History." Frank Manuel was contrasting his own mode of writing history to that of Charles Tilly: where Tilly would do an exhaustive quantitative study of strikes and strikers in nineteenth-century France, Manuel would analyze the personalities of the strikers and the values prevalent at the time. There was no meeting ground between them, he concluded, only the tolerant understanding that each be allowed to do his own thing in his own way. Lawrence Stone was moved to protest: "If this is true, I think it is tragic. It is appalling if two men studying a single phenomenon just walk past each other and have nothing to say to each other."[1]

Stone was describing an experience that is becoming all too familiar—among historians most dramatically, with the development of quantitative and psychoanalytic history, but in other disciplines as well. For all of the brave talk about interdisciplinary studies, scholarship has never been as factionalized and polarized as it is today. Two scholars working on the French Revolution are apt to produce books so disparate one can hardly recognize in them the same subject; they might be dealing with events centuries and continents apart. This has come about not, as was once feared, because of a fragmentation of learning, a division of labor with each scholar intensively cultivating his own small piece of the turf. Nor is it because the "two cultures" have created disciplines so specialized and recondite that their practitioners can no longer understand each other. In spite of the technical apparatus of the "new" methods, the quantifiers and psychoanalyzers of history can still understand each other, and the traditional historian can understand them both. In one respect they understand one another all too well. This, indeed, is the difficulty. For what they understand is that each school is staking out for itself not a part but the whole of the subject, each is laying claim to the deepest level of understanding, each thinks it has exclusive access to the truth. If they agree to tolerate each other, as Manuel suggests, it is out of sheer civility. But they do not really communicate with each other because they insist upon speaking different languages, with different vocabularies, different rules of syntax, different intonations and gestures—all reflecting profoundly different interpretations of reality.

The situation would be harmless if it applied only to such relatively limited topics as strikes in nineteenth-century France. What makes it serious, and what Stone was properly exercised about, is the fact that the largest, most comprehensive, and most crucial themes are treated in the same disparate manner. Take, for example, a subject that has been said to be at the heart of all history, that to some degree impinges upon most human activities—the subject of class. There are periods and events in history which are unintelligible without reference to the phenomenon of class, centuries of literature and entire genres (the novel, most notably) which have drawn sustenance from it, philosophies and ideologies of the greatest practical as well as theoretical import which make of it the central fact of life. When this subject is treated as diversely as it has been in recent years, to the point where serious scholars "walk past each other and have nothing to say to each other," we may well be disturbed.

The problem has only recently become acute. Twenty-five years ago, when *The Liberal Imagination* was published, the historian, no less than the literary critic, could read that book as a testament of his own faith. When Lionel Trilling spoke of the social reality that was the substance of the novel, when he deplored the misguided liberalism that thought it enlightened to ignore the fact of class, as if that fact were demeaning to the critic and belittling to the individual, the historian took heart, recognizing that social reality as the stuff of history. But if the historian was emboldened by this message, he was also forewarned by Trilling's admonition to avoid the opposite extreme, the philistine pretense that facts had nothing to do with ideas, that social reality stood apart from and independent of the exercise of mind. In Trilling's concept of "the moral imagination," the historian, as much as the literary critic, could find his own mission: to examine the assumptions and preconceptions, the attitudes, beliefs, and ideas which are as much the facts of history as of culture. And the facts of history in both senses of "history"; if the moral imagination shaped the past, it must to the same degree shape our thinking and writing about the past.[2]

But that was twenty-five years ago. Today a generation of historians is being trained to write a kind of history that is as nearly devoid of moral imagination as the computer can make it. It was one of Trilling's heroes, Matthew Arnold, who characterized as "barbarians" and "philistines" those in his own day who were "inaccessible to ideas" and therefore obsessively concerned with the "machinery" of life. But neither Arnold nor Trilling could have anticipated the mechanization of ideas that is even more insidious than the mere use of computers.

In place of the moral imagination, we are more and more confronted with something that might be called the sociological imagination. The sociologist *cum* historian assimilates history to the social or behavioral sciences. He prides himself on using only "hard" data, precise and unambiguous, the kind that can be counted, sorted, added, weighed, and arranged in tables, charts, graphs. In a more sophisticated variant of this method, he goes beyond the empirical, quantitative method and constructs models intended to represent the abstract essence of the data.

Model-building has recently emerged as the *ne plus ultra* of the sociological imagination. The model seems to have all the advantages of the quantitative method and more. It is abstract as well as precise; it lends itself readily to comparative analysis; it is scientific, objective, and "value-free"; it makes explicit what might otherwise remain implicit; it evokes the largest statements, generalizations, and theories. Most important, as one disciple of the method has said, it liberates history from the conventional, undisciplined, "impressionistic" historian who, instead of defining and theorizing, takes refuge in "literary grace," in "paradox, antithesis, innuendo, and gratuitous irony."[3]

Although any aspect of history is amenable to quantification and model-building (it has become a measure of the ingenuity of the sociological historian to apply his methods to political, diplomatic, military, even religious history), social history is the special province of the sociological historian. And within social history, the subject he has staked out for himself is that of class. In reading the recent literature on this subject one can easily get the impression that the sociological historian invented, or at the very least discovered, the phenomenon of class. One is tempted to forget that the consciousness of class was as old as class itself, and that in some periods, in nineteenth-century England most notably, contemporaries spoke of class with a candor and clarity that may come as a shock to some latter-day historians.

The most ambitious attempt to build a class model for early nineteenth-century England may be found in an article by R.S. Neale originally published in 1968 and recently reprinted.[4]

Dissatisfied with the conventional three classes, Neale proposes a five-part division: upper class, middle class, middling class, working class A, and working class B. To the unsophisticated eye, this may look like the familiar distinctions of upper, upper-middle, lower-middle, upper-lower, and lower-lower. But Neale intends to signify by his divisions not more or less of the same thing but different things; thus he distinguishes his classes in terms of the distinctive sources of their income, their professions or occupations, their attitudes towards themselves, and their relations with each other.

So far, Neale concedes, his five-class model is essentially static and therefore inappropriate for an England where the only certainty was the fact of change. To convey the dynamic nature of the model, the classes are visualized not as separate boxes in the usual manner, but as pools of water:

> . . . Think of the five classes, each embracing a number of social strata, as separate pools of water linked together by streams of water and located on a convex but asymmetrical hill with the Middling Class on the summit exposed to all the elements. The Upper and Middle Class pools lie on the sheltered sunny side of the hill and both Working Class pools lie on the higher and more exposed northern slope. The stream linking the summit or Middling Class pool to the Middle and Upper Class pools is controlled by traditional sluices between each pool. The two Working Class pools are linked to each other and the Middling Class pool by more sluggish streams but there are no obstacles to the downward flow of water although eddies will result in water moving backwards and forwards between any two pools.[5]

But even this verbal account cannot describe the model in all its precision, abstraction, and complexity. Only the diagram (see Fig. 1*) can do justice to it.

Neale has taken us far from an old-fashioned "impressionism"

° Reprinted by permission from: R. S. *Neal, Class and Ideology in the 19th Century* (Boston: Routledge and Kegan Paul, Ltd., 1975), p. 31.

FIGURE 1

Diagram of the Five-Class Model

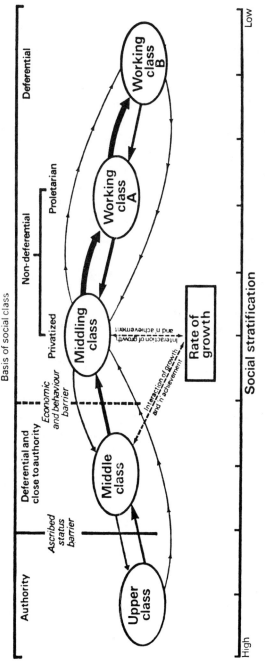

Arrows indicate direction of flow. Thickness of line indicates guessed probability of moving from one class to another circa 1800 (probabilities will vary with rate of growth, "n" achievement, time, population growth, and the strength of barriers). Given sustained growth the probabilities of moving from low to high increase, the probabilities of moving from high to low decrease.

(the quantifier's invidious term for conventional history), or even an old-fashioned mode of quantification. The language of the model suggests a high order of sociological sophistication: "authority" and "deferential" levels, "social stratification," "status" and "behavior" barriers, "ascribed" and "privatized." And these concepts are presented in such a manner as to connote a correspondingly high degree of precision: lines are solid or broken, of varying thicknesses, graduated in equal parts, pointing in one or another direction. The model even contains something resembling a formula: "Interaction of growth and 'n' achievement." And a note appears to give directions for calculating the "probability" of movement from one class to another: "Probabilities will vary with rate of growth, 'n' achievement, time, population growth, and the strength of barriers."

It may seem churlish, after all this, to complain that one does not know what it all means or what it all adds up to. What good is a formula in which some of the variables cannot be quantified because the historian lacks the necessary data (the "rate of growth" at any particular time), and in which other of the variables are by their nature unquantifiable ("the strength of barriers")? If the formula is only intended to point to the presence of these factors, does one need either a formula or a diagram to do that? Is a "guessed probability"indicated by the "thickness of line" a better guess, more exactly "indicated," than that which might be conveyed verbally by such notoriously inexact words as "more" and "less"? Does the whole of this elaborate diagram really tell us anything more than the admittedly imprecise accounts of the conventional historian?

The diagram does have one important virtue: it offers an alternative to the traditional three-class model. But that alternative emerges earlier in the article without benefit of diagrams, charts, or even statistics. It is on the basis of the usual kinds of literary, "impressionistic" evidence—excerpts from commission reports, articles, memoirs, letters, buttressed by an occasional reference to a secondary source—that the author was moved to challenge the traditional three-class model. But if he finds three classes insufficient to account for the complexities of the social reality, why stop at five? Would it not be more precise to separate some of the disparate groups lumped together in the "Middling Class"—"petit bourgeois, aspiring professional men, other literates, and artisans"—or the motley assortment comprising "Working Class B"—"agricultural laborers, other low-paid nonfactory urban laborers, domestic servants, urban poor, most working-class women whether from Working Class A or B households"?[6] Why not, for the sake of greater precision, assign each of these groups a pool of its own, with its own streams, sluices, barriers, and all the rest?

Neale is undoubtedly right to be dissatisfied with the conventional class trinity, especially with the category of the middle class. (George Kitson Clark put the matter well when he said that the concept of the middle class has "done more to stultify thought about Victorian England than anything else."[7]) And there is much in his article that is suggestive and valuable. The question is whether the model helps or hurts his case, whether it does not, for all its curves rather than straight lines and arrows pointing in both directions, make for new crudities and rigidities, whether a misplaced or spurious precision is better than an avowed imprecision. A five-class (or seven- or eight- or 'n'-class) pool-model is not, after all, the only alternative to a three-class box-model. Another alternative is a well-reasoned, well-documented argument in which the nuances of language, rather than the number and thickness of lines, bear the burden of conveying the complexities and subtleties of the social reality.

To the sociological historian, however, language is a "burden" in the worst sense. Having made a great virtue of precise and explicit definitions, he often proceeds to formulate definitions that are either so obtuse as to be incomprehensible or so tautological as to be useless. For the sociologist, there may be

35

some meaning or utility in the definition of social classes as "conflict groups arising out of the authority structure of imperatively coordinated associations";[8] its abstractness may be appropriate to his purpose, which is to describe the phenomenon of class in its most general, universal, abstract sense. But for the historian, interested in the particularity of a historical situation (or in the particularities of a number of related situations), such a definition can hardly be helpful. At best it plays no part in his research; at worst it distracts him from attending to the actualities of the historical situation. What it does do is give him the illusion that by virtue of some such definition, he has "objectively identified"[9] the concept of class. It is this illusion, this claim of objectivity, that is the driving force behind the enterprise of sociological history.

The historian, any historian, may properly be accused of hubris, of professing to know more about a historical event, to understand it better, more objectively, than those contemporaries who lived through it. It is an inescapable occupational hazard. For all his wariness of the "Whig fallacy"—the history of hindsight in which the past is read in terms of the present—for all his attempts to avoid that fallacy by immersing himself in contemporary sources, it remains his eternal temptation and besetting sin. But where the traditional historian is abashed by his presumptuousness, the sociological historian flaunts it; it is his pride and distinction. He invents a language that he claims conveys the social reality better than the language of contemporaries; he freely reorders and remodels the experiences of contemporaries; he abstracts, generalizes, theorizes for whatever purposes he deems proper, to elicit whatever categories or postulates he deems important. At every point he is asserting his independence of and his superiority over those contemporaries who provide his material. In the currently fashionable phrase, they are his "objects"; he alone can see them "objectively," scientifically.

Yet even as objects contemporaries have a limited interest for the sociological historian, whole dimensions of their experiences being denied or belittled by him. The only parts of their experience he can recognize, because they are the only parts he can use, are those that manifest themselves externally, that are visible, measurable, quantifiable. Their ideas, attitudes, beliefs, perceptions enter into his tables and models only when they express themselves behaviorally—in riots, or elections, or church attendance, or production and consumption.

It is often said that this kind of sociological history is the only democratic form of history; it is the history of the "anonymous" masses instead of "great men," the politicians, writers, leaders of one sort or another who emerged in their own time as identifiable individuals. There is no question but that sociological history has had the effect of suppressing these notable individuals. The question is whether it has succeeded in bringing to life the anonymous masses, whether it has not "upstaged" the masses just as it has the leaders, whether it does not display towards the masses the same condescension, the same sense of superiority, it does towards all contemporaries.

It is true, of course, that individual contemporaries, contemporaries who distinguished themselves in one fashion or another, cannot be presumed to speak for the anonymous masses. But if distinguished contemporaries are thus disqualified, surely a historian, generations removed from those masses, familiar with them only through certain kinds of records that happen to have been preserved, must be immodest indeed to think that he can understand them better than the wisest men of their time. Surely, he cannot afford to ignore the considered judgments of these contemporaries. Nor can he afford to confine himself to their private letters and memoirs in preference to their essays and books, on the assumption that truth is best revealed—exposed, "given away"—at the level of least consciousness, that greater consciousness brings with it more of the delusions of "false consciousness." There is something slanderous about this assumption. It implies that a great contemporary, precisely when he is at his greatest, expressing himself most carefully and deliberately, is least to be trusted to tell the truth. And if the great men of the time are thus defamed, so also are all those anonymous people who bought their books, listened to their speeches, or otherwise accorded them the title of greatness. What purports to be democratic history may well prove to be the most insidious kind of "elitist" history.

When the discussion of class is returned to contemporaries, one discovers quite different conceptions from those found in the tables and models of the "new" historians. One also discovers why these historians cannot readily incorporate the contemporary concepts into their own models. Contemporaries, it appears, were not only acutely class-conscious; their class-consciousness was a highly charged moral affair. Over and above all those economic, legal, and social distinctions that can be quantified and diagrammed, there is an order of facts that defies the sociological imagination: men's perceptions of themselves in relation to others, and their conceptions of what is proper and improper, just and unjust, right and wrong about those relations. The most ingenious sociologist cannot translate these perceptions and conceptions into the language—the models, abstractions, and quantifications—of sociology. They were rendered at the time, and they are still only intelligible, in literary language, the discourse of ordinary people as well as the learned, a language thoroughly, ineradicably penetrated by moral nuances.

If we refuse to indulge the current prejudice against greatness, we may choose to consult, on the subject of class, one of the great commentators on Victorian England, Thomas Carlyle. Carlyle was great not only in himself but in his influence, and in his influence not only upon readers of all classes but also upon some of the greatest and most influential of his own contemporaries—Mill, Arnold, Dickens, Eliot, Disraeli, Kingsley, Ruskin, Swinburne, Thackeray.[10] Some of these, Mill most notably, were eventually put off by the blatantly undemocratic tone of Carlyle's later writings. But the younger Carlyle helped shape the moral, intellectual, and social consciousness of early Victorian England as perhaps no other single figure did. And even when he provoked criticism, he confronted his critics with an alternative vision of society they could not ignore.

What is remarkable is that Carlyle had the effect he did in spite of a rhetoric so extraordinary that today it tends to repel all but the staunchest devotee. We think of the nineteenth century as an age of great conformity, repressive of all individuality, enthusiasm, passion. We also think of it as an age of great complacency and hypocrisy, in which the realities of life were obscured by polite euphemisms and a mindless adherence to convention. If anything could put such myths to rest, a reading of Carlyle would do so.

He was the most individualistic, indeed eccentric of writers, and the most outspoken. He denounced the false "gospels" of the age, the "foul and vile and soul-murdering Mud-gods," with all the fervor of a Jeremiah.[11] His invectives are famous: utilitarianism was "pig philosophy"; laissez-fairism was the freedom of apes; parliamentary reform was "constitution-mongering"; material progress was "mammonism"; rationalism was "dilettantism." And the more he denounced these false idols, and the more intemperately and idiosyncratically he did so, presenting his ideas in the guise of a newly published work of German philosophy or the chronicle of a twelfth-century monk, using elaborate metaphors and obscure references, the more attentively he was read. It is perhaps just as well that much of his audience did not understand all his allusions; Professor Teufelsdröckh, the hero, or anti-hero, of *Sartor Resartus*, translates, in its most refined version, as Professor Devil's Dung.

But those who did know German, including Mill and Arnold, were not disconcerted by his pungent language, perhaps because they respected the moral passion inspiring it.

It is ironic—but only because of what historians have since made of it—that Carlyle should have coined the phrase, "Condition-of-England Question." Today this is generally interpreted as the "standard-of-living question," which is taken as an invitation to quantification, the amassing of statistics relating to wages and prices, production and consumption, birth and death rates. Carlyle understood it quite otherwise. Having opened his book, *Chartism*, with the "Condition-of-England Question," he followed it with an extremely skeptical chapter on "Statistics."

> Tables are like cobwebs, like the sieve of the Danaides; beautifully reticulated, orderly to look upon, but which will hold no conclusion. Tables are abstractions, and the object a most concrete one, so difficult to read the essence of. There are innumerable circumstances; and one circumstance left out may be the vital one on which all turned. Statistics is a science which ought to be honourable, the basis of many most important sciences; but it is not to be carried on by steam, this science, any more than others are; a wise head is requisite for carrying it on. Conclusive facts are inseparable from inconclusive except by a head that already understands and knows.[12]

To "understand" and to "know," Carlyle said, was to ask the right questions, questions that could not be answered with the most comprehensive figures and charts. The opening sentence of his book defined the condition-of-England question as the "condition and disposition of the Working Classes." If we are inclined to forget the second of these terms, Carlyle never was. What gave Chartism its enduring strength, he explained, was the fact that it was only a new name for an age-old phenomenon: it meant "the bitter discontent grown fierce and mad, the wrong condition therefore, or the wrong disposition, of the Working Classes of England." The question "What is the condition of the working classes?" had as its corollary: "Is the condition of the English working people wrong; so wrong that rational working men cannot, will not, and even should not rest quiet under it?" And this raised the further question: "Is the discontent itself mad, like the shape it took? Not the condition of the working people that is wrong; but their disposition, their own thoughts, beliefs and feelings that are wrong?" The answers to these questions were not quantifiable because the condition of people depended not upon their material goods but upon their moral disposition. "It is not what a man outwardly has or wants that constitutes the happiness or misery of him. Nakedness, hunger, distress of all kinds, death itself have been cheerfully suffered, when the heart was right. It is the feeling of *injustice* that is insupportable to all men."[13]

Carlyle's other famous invention, the phrase "cash payment the sole nexus," derived from the same moral impulse.[14] He attributed to the economists the deplorable idea that men were subject to the principle of supply and demand as surely as material goods were, that human relations were best left to the impersonal forces of the marketplace, that cash payment was the sole nexus between man and man. What outraged him was not only that men were reduced to this inhuman condition—although that would be outrage enough—but that this condition should be represented as perfectly natural, a God-given law of nature. This was blasphemous as well as inhuman, a mockery of God and of man.

If the relations of individual men were tainted by this modern heresy, so were the relations of classes. Like most of his contemporaries, Carlyle had a simple view of the class structure of England: there was an upper class and a lower class, a class of the rich and a class of the poor. Generally, again like most of his contemporaries, he pluralized each of these, making them the "upper classes" and "lower classes"; sometimes he gave them a special Carlylean twist, as when he spoke of the "Under Class." But his special contribution to the nomenclature—and to the conception—of classes was his distinction between the "Toiling Classes" and the "Untoiling."[15] It was here that the two classes, so far from being simple descriptive terms, became morally charged.

And it was here that Carlyle parted company from Marx and Engels, who were happy to borrow his aphorism about the cash nexus and to quote him on the condition of the lower classes. For what Carlyle meant by Toiling and Untoiling was not at all what Marx or Engels meant by what might seem to be their equivalents: Labor and Capital. His Toiling Classes included those members of the upper classes who did in fact work; and his Untoiling Classes included those of the working who did not work. Thus the rich comprised "rich master-workers" and "rich master-idlers" (or "Master Unworkers").[16] And among the poor too there were "Unworkers," made so by the monstrous Poor Law which created "houses for idling" under the euphemism of "workhouses."

The implications of Carlyle's distinctions were momentous, for they made him something very different from the primitive or crypto-socialist that some present-day socialists would make of him. Socialists can share Carlyle's outrage at the condition of the poor, his condemnation of the idle rich, his detestation of laissez-faire economics. They can find in him premonitions of the evils of dehumanization, desocialization, and alienation. They can even share his respect for work, under certain ideal conditions; the young Marx might have said, as Carlyle did: "Labour is not a devil, even while encased in Mammonism; Labour is ever an imprisoned god, writhing unconsciously or consciously to escape out of Mammonism!"[17]

What the Marxist cannot do, however, and what Carlyle insisted upon doing, was to make of work an ennobling quality for the capitalist as well as the laborer—provided only that the capitalist was a "master-worker" rather than a "master-idler." "*Laborare est orare*": this was the true gospel according to

Carlyle.[18] "All work . . . is noble; work is alone noble."[19] And this dictum redeemed the capitalist, the working capitalist, the "Mill-ocracy," as Carlyle put it, as much as the working-man.[20] Just as in the Marxist schema the concept of surplus value, or exploitation, illegitimized, so to speak, the capitalist, made him the villain of that particular morality play, so the concept of work legitimized him for Carlyle—made of him a "Captain of Industry," a natural leader and a true hero.

This is why the struggle between rich and poor, between the upper and lower classes, was not, for Carlyle, the same inexorable, fatal war-to-the-death that the class struggle was for Marx. Indeed for Carlyle, a symptom and also a cause of the prevailing misery and discontent was the fact that there was such a struggle. The idle aristocracy, abdicating its natural political role, made the process of government seem artificial, the fortuitous product of competition and struggle. This was the true perversion of political economy. Denying the proper function of government, the laissez-fairists also subverted the proper relationship of the governed and the governors. And without this relationship, cash payment became the sole nexus connecting the rich and the poor.

After reading the reviews of *Chartism*, Carlyle remarked: "The people are beginning to discover that I am not a Tory. Ah, no! but one of the deepest, though perhaps the quietest, of all the Radicals now extant in the world."[21] Carlyle's radicalism may not be ours. Nor was it that of all radicals at the time.[22] But it was a form of radicalism that most contemporaries recognized as such. One reader of *Past and Present* quipped that the book would be very dangerous if it were ever "turned into the vernacular."[23]

Carlyle's radicalism consisted not in the answers he gave to the condition-of-England question but in putting the question itself, and in putting it in such a form that it raised the most fundamental doubts about the legitimacy of prevailing doctrines and class relations. Nothing is more banal than the idea that

43

England, that any country, is divided into an upper and a lower class, into rich and poor. What Carlyle did was to raise the idea of class to a new level of consciousness by giving it a new moral urgency. In Victorian England the idea of work was a powerful moral concept, a cogent instrument of legitimization and illegitimization. By associating it with the idea of class, Carlyle made problematic—"dangerous," as one reader said—what had previously been the most natural and innocent of propositions, that England was divided into two classes.

In *Sartor Resartus*, Carlyle described the extremes to which those two classes were being pushed. The book is an elaborate play upon a treatise, *Die Kleider, ihr Werden and Wirken*, by the ubiquitous Herr Teufelsdröckh, Professor of Allerlei Wissenschaft at the University of Weissnichtwo. The clothes metaphor inspired Carlyle to invent two sects, Dandies and Drudges, the first worshipping money and the trappings of gentlemanliness, the second slaving to keep barely clothed and fed.

> Such are the two Sects which, at this moment, divide the more unsettled portion of the British People, and agitate that ever-vexed country. . . . In their roots and subterranean ramifications, they extend through the entire structure of Society, and work unweariedly in the secret depths of English national Existence, striving to separate and isolate it into two contradictory, un-communicating masses. . . . To me it seems probable that the two Sects will one day part England between them, each re-cruiting itself from the intermediate ranks, till there be none left to enlist on either side.[24]

If Carlyle's final words remind us of Marx, with his predictions of the polarization of classes—the increasing concentration of wealth on the one hand, the increasing proletarianization and pauperization on the other—the rest of the passage recalls Disraeli's famous phrase, "the two nations." I would not go so far as some historians who have claimed that Disraeli made of that expression a "household word."[25] Nor would I make too much of the fact that others used it before him.[26] It is enough to say that Disraeli dramatized and popularized a concept that was, as we say, "in the air."

Disraeli also dramatized, perhaps romanticized as well, the condition-of-England question. In *Coningsby*, published in 1844, five years after Carlyle's *Chartism*, Disraeli referred to the "Condition-of-England Question of which our generation hears so much."[27] A few months later, in an address to his constituents, he claimed some priority for that concept: "Long before what is called the 'condition of the people question' was discussed in the House of Commons, I had employed my pen on the subject."[28] He had already begun writing *Sybil* and was evidently anticipating a criticism that was to be leveled against that book: that parts of it sound like a transcript of Royal Commission reports and parliamentary debates. Since he had in fact been listening to those debates (a Factory Bill had been introduced in that very session of parliament) and was actually inserting verbatim into his novel portions of one of those reports (the second report of the Children's Employment Commission which had been released in 1842), Disraeli had reason to be sensitive on this account.[29]

The message of *Sybil* is too familiar to require much discussion. It is also perfectly clear and explicit. Unlike Carlyle, with his extended metaphors and heavy irony, Disraeli, even when writing fiction, was engaged in a not very subtle form of political indoctrination. If parts of *Sybil* read like transcripts of the blue books (which they were), other parts sound like extracts from a *Short Course in the History of England, by a Young Englander*, or from penny pamphlets on "the social problem." In the novel the crucial passages announced themselves, so to speak, by the presence of capitals. Thus the first mention of the two nations theme appeared in a dialogue between Egremont, the good aristocrat (one is tempted to capitalize these identifications, as in a morality play), and "the stranger," later identified as Stephen Morley, an Owenite who has joined forces with the Chartists.

> "Say what you like, our Queen reigns over the greatest nation that ever existed."
>
> "Which nation?" asked the younger stranger, "for she reigns over two."
>
> The stranger paused; Egremont was silent, but looked inquiringly.
>
> "Yes," resumed the stranger. "Two nations; between whom there is no intercourse and no sympathy; who are as ignorant of each other's habits, thoughts, and feelings, as if they were dwellers in different zones, or inhabitants of different planets; who are as formed by a different breeding, are fed by a different food, are ordered by different manners, and are not governed by the same laws.'
>
> "You speak of—" said Egremont, hesitatingly.
>
> "THE RICH AND THE POOR."

This final line of bold type was followed by a fade-out scene worthy of a grade C movie: The grey ruins were suffused by a "sudden flush of rosy light," and the voice of Sybil was heard singing the evening hymn to the Virgin—"a single voice; but tones of almost supernatural sweetness; tender and solemn, yet flexible and thrilling."[30] This was Disraeli prose at its worst, blatantly tendentious and mawkishly romantic. Most of it was very much better —tendentious, to be sure, but cleverly so—sharp, acerbic, witty, and surprisingly often conveying some provocative thought. And even the romantic interludes were redeemed by a latent irony that made for a slightly off-beat, campy effect. *Sybil* was, in fact, an eminently readable book, and although the literary strategy was obvious enough—the contrast between high society and the life of the lowliest poor, between parliamentary intrigue and Chartist conspiracy—there were memorable episodes satirizing the upper classes and dramatiz-

ing the lower. The opening scene, for example, in the fashionable club, found a group of rich, blasé, and rather effete young
men chatting idly about the forthcoming Derby races, with
one man confessing that he rather liked bad wine because, you
know, "one gets so bored with good wine."[31] In the same
mood were scenes featuring the ladies of the great houses who
thought they were wielding political power (perhaps they
were wielding power—Disraeli left the matter ambiguous) by
extending or withholding invitations to their dinner parties;
they vainly attempted to extract information from dim-witted
lords who did not know that they were being pumped, for the
very good reason that they knew nothing at all.

On the other side of the social spectrum was the reality that
these fashionable men and women were so abysmally ignorant
of: the reality of THE PEOPLE, or THE POOR—terms
which Disraeli used interchangeably. Disraeli has been criticized, and properly so, for overdramatizing the condition of
England in the nineteenth century and over idealizing the condition of England in the good old days.

> When I remember [says Sybil, as if she were recalling her own
> youth in pre-Reformation times] what this English people once
> was; the truest, the freest, and the bravest, the best-natured
> and the best-looking, the happiest and most religious race upon
> the surface of this globe; and think of them now, with all their
> crimes and all their slavish sufferings, their soured spirits and
> their stunted forms; their lives without enjoyment, and their
> deaths without hope; I may well feel for them, even if I were
> not the daughter of their blood.[32]

Even if the extravagant rhetoric, with all those superlatives—
the truest, the freest, the bravest—did not forewarn us that
Disraeli intended us to take this mythically and allegorically,
the last sentence should surely alert us to that possibility; for
at this point in the story we know that Sybil was not, in fact,
"the daughter of their blood," that far from being one of the

people, she was the purest descendant of one of the oldest and noblest families.

But apart from such mythicized representations of past and present (intentionally mythicized, as I read Disraeli), there were scenes which, however exaggerated, revealed important and frequently ignored aspects of social reality. For all his fantasies and extravagances, Disraeli had a clear perception of different varieties of conditions and different kinds of poverty. He distinguished, for example, between rural and industrial poverty, between manufacturing and mining towns, between the ordinary working poor and an underclass that was almost a race apart, brutalized, uncivilized, living in a virtual state of nature. There was a precision in these distinctions the historian may well respect.

The historian may also profitably read the exchange between the good aristocrat Egremont and the Chartist Gerard in which each cited statistics about the condition of England, the one proving that it was much better, the other much worse, than ever before, with Gerard concluding (like Carlyle before him) that in any event it was not so much material conditions that were at issue as the relations of men with each other.[33] Earlier the Owenite Morley had made the same point: "There is no community in England; there is aggregation, but aggregation under circumstances which make it rather a dissociating than a uniting principle."[34]

When sociologists make this distinction, under the labels of "gemeinschaft" and "gesellschaft," historians listen respectfully. When Disraeli did it, he was dismissed as a medievalist and romantic. Yet Disraeli was careful to assign this speech about community not to Sybil, who *was* a medievalist and romantic, but to the Owenite, who believed that "the railways will do as much for mankind as the monasteries ever did."[35] Neither Morley nor Gerard had any hankering for a pre-industrial age; both wanted only to humanize and socialize relations under the conditions of industrialism. The one character in the novel whose occupation it was to exalt and perpetuate the past was a fraud, if a kindly one; this was the antiquarian Hatton, who made his fortune by tracing—inventing, if need be—the lineage of noble and would-be-noble families, and who himself turned out to be the brother of the vilest and lowest of the rabble.

If Disraeli's cast of characters included good aristocrats as well as bad, so it also included good factory owners as well as bad ones. To be sure, the best of these factory owners happened to be a younger son of an old, impoverished landed family. And it was this heritage that made him so exemplary a character: "With gentle blood in his veins, and old English feelings, he imbibed, at an early period of his career, a correct conception of the relations which should subsist between the employer and the employed. He felt that between them there should be other ties than the payment and the receipt of wages."[36] (If the last sentence was not a conscious echo of Clarlyle's "cash nexus," it testified to the prevalence of that sentiment at the time.) Disraeli's account of this model factory town was more than a little idyllic; everyone was happy, healthy, moral, and content. But it is also noteworthy that what Disraeli was idealizing, contrary to the conventional image of him, was a *factory* town. (In the same spirit, in his earlier novel *Coningsby*, he had Sidonia interrupt Coningsby's reveries about the glories of Athens. "The Age of Ruins is past," Sidonia reminded him. "Have you seen Manchester?")[37]

Disraeli's two nations, like Carlyle's two classes, were more complicated than they appear at first sight—and again, because they were moral as well as descriptive categories. Just as Carlyle's upper classes contained a toiling and an idle class, so Disraeli's rich contained a responsible and an irresponsible element. For the indolent club-lounger titillated by the idea of drinking bad wine, or the ladies of the salons who looked upon politics, like matrimony, as a game devised for the exercise of their female wiles, Disraeli had nothing but contempt. Riches, position, power had "only one duty—to secure the social welfare of the PEOPLE."[38] Just as work was the legitimizing principle for Carlyle, so duty was the legitimizing principle for Disraeli. Where Carlyle, putting a premium upon work, found most of his heroes among the "Mill-ocracy," the "Captains of Industry," Disraeli looked primarily to the landed aristocracy who, in his mythical rendition of English history, traditionally functioned in this responsible, moral fashion.

If Carlyle and Disraeli chose to eulogize and mythicize different groups among the upper classes, they were in agreement that it was the responsibility of the upper class to rule—humanely, justly, compassionately, but rule—and the obligation of the lower classes to be ruled. The main plot of *Sybil* centered about the attempt of the lower classes to find salvation in themselves, to try to cure their condition with their own resources, by developing leaders of their own and seeking power on their own behalf. This was the aspiration of the Chartists and, according to Disraeli, the lesson of its failure. In spite of the fact that Gerard was the purest, noblest, wisest of men, the movement degenerated into an illegal conspiracy and finally into a wild, bloody, pointless rampage, as a result of which both Morley and Gerard died and Sybil was disabused of her illusions—her "phantoms," as Egremont delicately put it. These phantoms included her faith in the people as the means of their own salvation, her belief that the poor could do no wrong and the rich no right, and her conviction that between the two "the gulf is impassable."[39]

Sybil has generally been taken as the heroine of the book. But if so she was a distinctly flawed character—the heroine, perhaps, but not the hero. Even her final aggrandizement came not from her being the true heir to Mowbray—with her father's death the title went to another claimant—but from her marriage to Egremont, who had just come into his own title and whose fortune, as the gossiping ladies noted, was equaled by only "three peers in the kingdom."[40] It was Egremont, the good aristocrat, who bore the moral burden of the book. It was he who wanted to obtain, as he said, "the results of the Charter without the intervention of its machinery," a somewhat cryptic statement that bewildered some characters in the novel and that others interpreted as "sheer Radicalism," "the most really democratic speech that I ever read."[41] What Egremont meant, of course, was that the welfare of the people could best be ensured not by transferring power to them, as the Chartists advised, but by exercising power on their behalf. Elsewhere, less cryptically, Egremont declared that "the rights of labour were as sacred as those of property; that if a difference were to be established, the interests of the living wealth ought to be preferred; . . . that the social happiness of the millions should be the first object of a statesman, and that, if this were not achieved, thrones and dominions, the pomp and power of courts and empires, were alike worthless."[42]

Contemporaries did not always know what to make of Disraeli, and historians know still less. The distinguished historian, G. M. Young, who was old-fashioned enough (and old enough) to draw upon his own memories and those of his acquaintances, asked one elderly Gladstonian why his generation had been so profoundly distrustful of Disraeli. The answer surprised Young. It was, the old man said, because of "his early Radicalism."[43] Whatever one may think of the practicality of Disraeli's kind of radicalism, or of its desirability, or whether it was radical at all, or even whether Disraeli was entirely serious in propounding it, one cannot deny that it did color his own thinking and the thinking of contemporaries about him.

More important, however, than Disraeli's solution of the social problem—the nation unified under the direction of a "natural" aristocracy dedicated to the "social welfare"—was his conception of the problem itself: a society in which the two classes were diverging so rapidly that they were perilously close to becoming "two nations." Many contemporaries who did not subscribe to his ideology, who found him too radical or insufficiently radical, shared his view of the social condition.

And it was this view—this class model, so to speak—that was enormously influential, that made the "two nations" a graphic image of the social reality and a powerful symbol of discontent.

Disraeli and Carlyle are only two of the many Victorians whose vision of the social reality helped shape that reality as well as reflect it. If one is looking for class models, surely their two-nation and two-sect models are as worthy of consideration as any the historian may devise. Or one might contemplate the three-class model reluctantly advanced by James Mill—reluctantly because utilitarianism was a profoundly individualistic theory loath to assign any reality to such "fictions" as society or class. Yet even Mill could not entirely dispense with some idea of class, although he did shun the word; in his schema the people were divided into an "aristocratical body," a "democratical body," and a "middle rank," the latter being the repository of virtue, intelligence, and leadership. Matthew Arnold's three classes were substantively the same as James Mill's, but his characterizations of them made for a radically different conception of society. Positing an aristocracy of "barbarians," a middle class of "philistines," and a populace combining the worst features of both, he obviously had to look elsewhere for virtue, intelligence, and leadership—to a state capable of transcending these classes. Without his class "model," one cannot begin to comprehend either his idea of the state or his analysis of the social reality.

There are obviously other ways of drawing upon the contemporary consciousness of class, not only by inquiring into all the eminent and not so eminent men who had occasion, in books, articles, speeches, or memoirs, to reflect upon their times and experiences, but also by consulting a variety of other sources that dealt with the same issue more obliquely, less self-consciously: novels, tracts, newspaper accounts, parliamentary debates, Royal Commission reports, legislative acts, and administrative measures. A few obvious models emerge from these sources—two or three classes, for the most part, often with each class pluralized ("working classes," for example), suggesting an acute sense of the fluidity and complexity of social relations. But whatever the model, it almost invariably contained a strong moral component. The classes themselves were described in moral terms, and the relations among them were presumed to have a moral character (or criticized for failing to exhibit the proper moral character, which was itself a moral judgment). Just as we would not today (or most of us would not, even today) define familial relations in purely behavioral terms—age, sex, physical condition, economic circumstances, social status—so the Victorians would have found inadequate any purely behavioral description of social relations that did not take into account men's sense of duty and obligation, propriety and responsibility, right and wrong.

This is where much of recent social history goes grievously astray. Even those works that avoid the more egregious fallacies of misplaced precision, excessive abstraction, and obfuscatory language are insufficiently attentive to the quality of mind that permeated nineteenth-century England. It may seem odd that historians should fail to avail themselves of such obvious sources of evidence as the ideas and beliefs of contemporaries, of the great men of the time as well as the ordinary men—until one realizes that to take seriously that evidence would be to jeopardize the enterprise of social history as it is generally conceived. Intent upon creating a scientific, objective history, these historians think it necessary to purge the social reality of the values that interfere with this "value free" ideal.

It is not only this ideal of a positivist science that is inimical to the moral imagination. It is also a distaste for the particular kind of moral imagination that prevailed in nineteenth-century England. Today all moral concepts are to some degree suspect; they strike the modern ear as condescending, subjective, arbitrary. And they are all the more disagreeable applied to classes—when the poor were described, as they habitually were in the nineteenth century, as "deserving" or "undeserving," or when the working classes were divided into the "respectable" and the "unrespectable," or when reformers announced their intention of fostering among the lower classes the virtues of thrift, temperance, cleanliness, and good character.

To the latter-day historian this moral temper suggests a failure not only of compassion but also of understanding. One recent author characterized it as an ideological "deformation" produced by the "distorting lens" of the middle class, a deformation so pervasive it even affected the consciousness of the working classes themselves.[44] From this perspective the moral imagination of the Victorians is not something to be understood and described as an essential part of the social reality, but something to be exposed and criticized from the vantage point of the historian's superior understanding of the reality. And the reality itself is assumed to be best understood in "objective" —which is to say, economic—terms without reference to such subjective ideas as moral character.

To call for a restoration of moral imagination in the writing of social history—in the writing of all history, indeed, but it is in the realm of social history that it is most sadly lacking—is not to give license to the historian to impose his own moral conceptions upon history. This has been the impulse behind yet another fashionable school of thought, that of the "engaged" or "committed" historian. In this view, all pretensions of objectivity are suspect, the only honest history being that which candidly expresses the moral, political, and personal beliefs of the historian. At the opposite pole, in one sense, from the sociological mode, this kind of "engaged" history shares with sociological history a contempt for the experiences and beliefs of contemporaries and an overweening regard for the superior wisdom and judgment of the historian.

What is wanted is not so much the exercise of the historian's moral imagination as a proper respect for the moral imagination of those contemporaries he is professing to describe. This, to be sure, takes an exercise of imagination on the historian's part—a sensitivity to moral ideas, a tolerance for ideas that may not be his own, above all a respect for moral principles as such, so that he will not dismiss them too readily as rationalizations of interest, or deformations of vision, or evidence of an intellectual obtuseness that conceals from contemporaries those simple economic facts which are so obvious to the historian.

It is a modest undertaking that is called for, indeed an exercise in modesty. It asks for nothing more than that moral data —the ideas, beliefs, principles, perceptions, and opinions of contemporaries—be taken as seriously, be assigned the same reality, as facts about the distribution of income, consumption of meat, or growth of population. The historian is in the fortunate position of being able to do what the sociologist cannot do; he can transcend the fact-value dichotomy that has so plagued sociological thought. The values of the past are the historian's facts. He should make the most of them, as the great Victorians did.

NOTES

1. "New Trends in History," *Daedalus*, Fall 1969, p. 894.
2. In a memorable passage of the *Reflections on the Revolution in France*, Edmund Burke attacked those rationalists who would strip the "moral imagination" of its authority, leaving the individual and the polity exposed to the brute facts of power:

> All the pleasing illusions, which made power gentle, and obedience liberal, which harmonized the different shades of life, and which, by a bland assimilation, incorporated into politics the sentiments which beautify and soften private society, are to be dissolved by this new conquering empire of light and reason. All the decent drapery of life is to be rudely torn off. All the superadded ideas, furnished from the wardrobe of a moral imagination, which the

heart owns, and the understanding ratifies, as necessary to cover the defects of our naked shivering nature, and to raise it to dignity in our own estimation, are to be exploded as a ridiculous, absurd, and antiquated fashion. (World's Classics ed., p. 84.)

3. S. G. Checkland, "The Historian as Model Builder," *Philosophical Journal*, 7 (Jan. 1969): 37.

4. R. S. Neale, "Class-Consciousness in Early Nineteenth-Century England: Three Classes or Five?" *Victorian Studies*, 12 (Sept. 1968): 5-32; reprinted in *Class and Ideology in the Nineteenth Century* [London, 1972].

5. Ibid., pp. 23-24.

6. Ibid., p. 23.

7. G. Kitson Clark, *The Making of Victorian England* (Cambridge, Mass., 1962), p. 5.

8. Neale, p. 9.

9. Ibid., p. 10.

10. A typical testimonial to Carlyle's influence was expressed by George Eliot in 1855:

> It is an idle question to ask whether his books will be read a century hence: if they were all burnt as the grandest suttees on his funeral pyre, it would only be like cutting down an oak after its acorns have sewn a forest. For there is hardly a superior or active mind of this generation that has not been modified by Carlyle's writings; there has hardly been an English book written for the last ten or twelve years that would not have been different if Carlyle had not lived. The character of his influence is best seen in the fact that many of the men who have the least agreement with his opinions are those to whom the reading of "Sartor Resartus" was an epoch in the history of their minds. (*The Leader*, Oct. 1855, quoted by John Mander, *Our German Cousins* [London, 1974], p. 84.)

11. Thomas Carlyle, *Reminiscences*, ed. J. A. Froude (New York, 1881), p. 226.

12. Carlyle, "Chartism," in *English and Other Critical Essays* (Everyman's ed.), p. 170.

13. Ibid., pp. 165-67, 188. (Carlyle's italics.)

14. Ibid., p. 208.

15. Ibid.

16. *Past and Present* (Everyman's ed.), pp. 1, 5.

17. Ibid., p. 199.

18. Ibid., p. 193.

19. Ibid., p. 147.

20. Ibid., p. 166.

21. James Anthony Froude, *Thomas Carlyle: A History of His Life in London, 1834–1881* (London, 1884), 1: 174 (Feb. 11, 1840).

22. In his review of *Past and Present* in the *Deutsch-Französische Jarhbücher* in 1844, Engels opened on a kindly note: Of all the books published in England the preceding year, *Past and Present* was the only one "worth reading"; and of all the learned men of England, Carlyle was the only one to be concerned with the "social condition of England." But the review became progressively sterner, with Engels taking Carlyle to task for not realizing that the cause of the social evil was private property. The bulk of the review, however, consisted of a critique of Carlyle's religious views, which Engels characterized as a form of "pantheism." The old question, "What is God?" Engels reported (paraphrasing Feuerbach), had finally been answered by German philosophy: "God is Man." (*Marx-Engels Gesamtausgabe*, ed. D. Riazanov [Berlin, 1930], Part I, vol. II, 405–31.) The following year, in *The Condition of the Working Class in England*, Engels quoted approvingly the "cash nexus" statement. (He used the expression twice, the first time without attribution.) (Ed. W. O. Henderson and W. H. Chaloner [Oxford, 1958], pp. 138, 312.)

23. James Pope-Hennessy, *Monckton Milnes: The Years of Promise, 1809–1851* (London, 1949), p. 184. Milnes was passing off as his own a comment Harriet Martineau had earlier made in a letter to him.

24. *Sartor Resartus* (Everyman ed.), pp. 214–15.

25. Kathleen Tillotson, *Novels of the Eighteen-Forties* (Oxford, 1965), p. 80; Robert Blake, *Disraeli* (London, 1966), p. 201.

26. Asa Briggs quotes one of several such usages. In 1841, the famous American preacher William Channing wrote: "In most large cities there may be said to be two nations, understanding as little of one another, having as little intercourse, as if they lived in different lands." (Briggs, "The Language of 'Class' in Early Nineteenth-Century England," in *Essays in Labor History*, ed. A. Briggs and J. Saville [New York, 1960], p. 48.)

27. Benjamin Disraeli, *Coningsby: or The New Generation* (London, 1948), p. 78.

28. W. F. Monypenny and G. E. Buckle, *The Life of Benjamin Disraeli Earl of Beaconsfield* (London, 1929), I, 629. The allusion, his biographers tells us, was to his novel, *The Voyage of Captain Popanilla*, published in 1828. But neither the term nor the subject in the usual sense appears in that novel.

29. For an analysis of his indebtedness to the Commission Report, see Sheila M. Smith, "Willenhall and Wodgate: Disraeli's Use of Blue Book Evidence," *Review of English Studies*, 1962.

30. Disraeli, *Sybil, or The Two Nations* (London: Penguin Books, 1954), pp. 72–73.

31. Ibid., p. 15.

32. Ibid., p. 126.

33. Ibid., p. 171.

34. Ibid., p. 71. On one occasion Morley goes so far in urging the principle of "association" as to declare the home to be "obsolete." "Home is a barbarous idea; the method of a rude age; home is isolation; therefore antisocial. What we want is Community." Gerard, the Chartist, benignly but firmly puts him down: "It is all very fine, . . . and I dare say you are right, Stephen; but I like stretching my feet on my own hearth." (p. 190)

35. Ibid., p. 88.

36. Ibid., p. 179.

37. *Coningsby*, p. 116.

38. *Sybil*, p. 264.

39. Ibid., p. 270.

40. Ibid., p. 398.

41. Ibid., p. 272.

42. Ibid., p. 281.

43. G. M. Young, *Victorian Essays* (London, 1962), p. 163.

44. Gareth Stedman Jones, *Outcast London: A Study in the Relationship between Classes in Victorian Society* (Oxford, 1971), pp. 16, 196, 344.

RENAN'S PHILOLOGICAL LABORATORY

EDWARD W. SAID

> Quel beau livre ne composerait-on pas en racontant la
> vie et les aventures d'un mot? sans doute il a reçu
> diverses impressions des événements auxquels il a servi;
> selon les lieux il a reveillé des idées différentes; mais
> n'est-il pas plus grand encore à considérer sous le
> triple aspect de l'âme, du corps, et du mouvement?
> Balzac, *Louis Lambert*

> Toute révélation vient d'Orient, et, transmise à l'Occi-
> dent, s'appelle tradition. L'Asie a les prophètes,
> L'Europe a les docteurs; tantôt ces deux mondes, echos
> de la meme parole, ont entre eux un meme esprit; ils
> s'attirent, ils se confirment l'un l'autre, et gardent le
> souvenir de la filiation commune; tantôt leurs génies
> se repoussent comme deux sectes; leurs rivages semblent
> se fuir, du moins ils s'oublient, pour se retrouver et se
> confondre plus tard; et jamais l'accord ne se rétablit
> entre l'un et l'autre que de cette harmonie ne naisse
> avec un dogme nouveau, pour ainsi dire, un dieu
> nouveau. Edgar Quinet, *Le Génie des religions*

I

Amongst Renan's discriminating and later English admirers
Oscar Wilde and James Frazer saw him as critic, scientist and
skeptic. A generation earlier, Matthew Arnold had praised
Renan in the Preface to *Culture and Anarchy* (1869) as a
"friend of reason and the simple natural truth of things,"[1] among
which were (presumably) the underlying racial difference between Indo-European Hellenism and Semitic Hebraism; since
Renan's earliest professional reputation was based on his *Histoire Générale et système comparé des langues sémitiques*
(completed in 1848, first published in 1855), it was from that

work in particular that Arnold was soliciting Renan's authority for his polemical division of English life into two types of behavior.[2] Yet Arnold's references to Renan here and there in his work refer generally to Renan's stature as a French, even European public figure whose specialized professional work was behind him, but whose presence in the general culture of his time was that of a moral sage concerned with contemporary issues—intellectual and institutional reform, national, religious and cultural questions of high priority.

In *The Soul of Man Under Socialism* (1891), Wilde puts Renan in the company of Darwin ("a great man of science"), Keats ("a great poet"), Flaubert ("a supreme artist"). Renan is only slightly less eminent, "a fine critical spirit."[3] The vagueness of Wilde's praise is somewhat dissipated when we read in "The Critic as Artist" (originally written in 1885, but revised for publication in *Intentions*, 1891) that far from "Criticism" being a sterile thing, it is "Criticism" that has made the nineteenth century "a turning point in history." How?

> . . . on account of the work of two men, Darwin and Renan, the one the critic of the Book of Nature, the other the critic of the books of God. Not to recognize this is to miss the meaning of one of the most important eras in the progress of the world. Creation is always behind the age. It is Criticism that leads us. The Critical Spirit and the World Spirit are one.[4]

The parallel that Wilde draws between the scientist and the textual or philological critic is impressive, not only because he herds them together under the rubric of Criticism, but also because Wilde uses the metaphor of a text to portray the domains the two work in. This portrayal is less like Mallarmé's *Livre* than it is, I think, like Renan's well-known attempt to draw distinctions and similarities between "les sciences de la nature" and "les sciences historiques." Wilde may have read, there in the public letter of 1863 to Marcellin Berthelot, Renan's enthusiastic reduction of zoological species and the secret of their formation to "morphology" understood in the linguistic sense; "animal forms," Renan said, "are a hieroglyphic language to which we do not have the key; moreover, the explanation of the past is there in its entirety in facts which we have before our eyes and which we cannot yet read."[5] In placing natural and historical sciences together Renan was actually containing them both inside a framework, an imprecise and later form of which Wilde was to employ using the word *Criticism*, that allowed the interchange of linguistic science with biological science. At any rate to Wilde, Renan is now less the moralist than he was to Arnold and more the scientific critic.

While Wilde may have had some stray knowledge of Renan's own predilection from time to time to move from comparative grammar to comparative anatomy and back again, and therefore to gain the reputation of a scientist, he characterized Renan as a "Critic" in a more general manner than Frazer did. The latter had been invited in 1920 to address the Societé Ernest Renan in Paris, and could therefore use the occasion to draw connections between his own work and Renan; hence his title, "Ernest Renan et la méthode de l'histoire des religions." Having already cited, in a preface written for the text of his speech, the French inability to produce poets like Shakespeare or Virgil (the French have "un esprit plutôt prosaïque que poètique"[6]), Frazer could then dole out praise on other grounds than imaginative ones. Renan, he said, had the Celtic love for enigmas, silence, mournful spaces; but more important he possessed a special capacity, shared only by Voltaire, to understand science and to appreciate beauty.[7] This gift was of special importance to the study of religion as a historical phenomenon. Frazer then went on to outline the main principles of such history, whose origins he locates in the methods of comparative biology used by Darwin.[8] The anachronism tells us something about Frazer's striking ignorance of comparative methods and their history, which extends further back than he knows; Frazer is accurate, however, in remarking how comparative studies, whether in science or in history, were often cross-bred. But Renan's importance, Frazer goes on to add, is that he understood development not as unilinear and simply progressive but as uneven, discontinuous, and unexpectedly erratic. Therefore the exemplary value to Renan (and to Frazer) of "savage" and "unequal" societies. In them, and here Frazer becomes elegaic, one can discern both the inconstant habits of barbaric cultures as well as the constant values of world-civilization; he pays Renan the high compliment of borrowing for the end of *The Golden Bough* an anti-Germanic passage from Renan's study of Feuerbach in which the bells of Rome resound (as a symbol of Latinity) across the Campagna and the ages.[9]

Frazer's Renan, even with Franco-Celtic doubts, reservations, hesitations admitted to frankly by the British scholar, is still a "savant" with a method; perhaps more like Wilde than Arnold, Frazer sensed that the cumbersome prestige with which Renan's name as a frowning public man (who had a message of positive reform) had been associated was no longer very serviceable. A more precise, even limited estimate was required, and hence the effort Frazer made to put Renan and *The Golden Bough* in some relationship of filiation. But only, I think, a supremely gifted literary stylist could understand the peculiar and *scriptive* phenomenon that was Renan, and this stylist is Proust, a contemporary of both Wilde and Frazer. Steeped in the late-nineteenth-century Parisian atmosphere that was composed of rarefied versions of the Restoration and Second Empire culture in which Renan first flourished, Proust caught hold of Renan as a fact of *style*, not so much either a fact of method or of subject matter. By style here I mean an orderly field of references, themes, motifs, figures, produced by writing, a field that could, if one had the requisite genius, be reproduced with distinction and quintessential clarity as an "air de chanson."

Dès que je lisais un auteur, je distinguais bien vite sous les paroles l'air de chanson qui en chaque auteur est différent de ce qu'il est chez tous les autres et, tout en lisant, sans m'en rendre compte, je le chantonnais, je pressais les mots ou les ralentissais ou les interrompais tout à fait, comme on fait quand on chante où on attend souvent longtemps, selon le mesure de l'air, avant de dire la fin d'un mot.[10]*

For such a project Proust's vehicle was the pastiche, or literary imitation; he practiced this method mainly as a way of demonstrating that he had a finer and more correct ear than most others,[11] but also as a way of preparing for that re-creative stylistic commemoration of the past, specific, embroiled in the reflective and fleshly circumstances of time and place, that was to become *A la recherche du temps perdu*. In 1919 Proust collected together a group of imitations that dated back to the winter of 1908 when, partly because he owned stock in the De Beers diamond enterprises, he followed the ins and outs of what was known as L'Affaire Lemoine. Lemoine was a confidence man who had proclaimed a method for manufacturing diamonds, and had also managed to obtain a large sum of money from Sir Julius Wernher, managing director of De Beers. Later it was revealed that Lemoine's game was to bring down the price of De Beers stock enough for him to purchase them cheaply because of his highly touted process; then when the process was revealed to be unsuccessful Lemoine intended to realize a handsome profit on the shares as their price shot back up. For Proust the occasion was an opportunity to treat L'Affaire Lemoine in the manner of variations on a constant subject: he rewrote the details in nine different pastiches, doing the story as it might appear in a Balzac novel, in a Flaubert novel, in an article by Sainte-Beuve, and in pieces by

---

* "No sooner do I begin to read an author, then very quickly I distinguish underneath the words the song melody which, in each author, is different from every other author and, while reading, without being aware of it, I sing, I hurry, slow down, or interrupt the words altogether, as one does when one sings, where frequently one waits for a long period of time, in time with the melody's rhythm, before pronouncing the last syllable of a word."

Henri de Regnier, Michelet and Saint-Simon. There are also pastiches of the Goncourt journal and of dramatic criticism by Émile Faguet. The eighth and longest is a pastiche of Renan.

There is little affinity between what Proust does and what Joyce was to do in the "Oxen of the Sun" episode in *Ulysses*. Proust's range is deliberately limited to nineteenth-century French styles; consequently his pastiches are more painstakingly exact (they are also a good deal longer), and because he is dealing with actual events, they are examples of style understood not as parody or caricature but as an extended way of being in and seeing a specific history. In both Proust and Joyce, however, the apprehension of style as mannerism is inevitable, as is also the tendency to view style as an exorbitant distillation, mainly comic, of antecedent masters of style. But Proust is concerned with the historical perspective sense delivered as an aspect of style by the writers he imitates. Each writer, he had said, has a *chanson* truly his own; translated into the technique of pastiche this meant that each writer has a very precise verbal *range*, which is as much a matter of the writer's references (to early Church history, for example, in Renan's case; to characters in *La Comédie humaine* in Balzac's; to details of atmosphere and corporeality in Flaubert's) as of his deployment of pronouns, adjectives, excursuses, his recurrent figures of speech, his embellishment (or suppression) of circumstances in Lemoine's adventures.

This technique is not only literary criticism of a very high order, whether for the student of Proust or of Proust's chosen authors; it is also an importantly valuable way of dealing with such authors as Renan whose precise status in culture history is difficult to fix. For if we remember that Renan was primarily a man of letters whose role in French and European intellectual life touched variously on the types of writing we would call history, philology, moral and cultural criticism, politics, humanistic speculation, personal memoirs, as well as several others, we will find it difficult to confine him exactly either to a genre or to a set of ideas. Proust's notion is to apply to Renan neither a schematic history of ideas nor a purely parodistic representation; rather it is to see him as what I have been calling a range of expression, a dynamic style, a highly nuanced verbal field of representation and incorporation. Accordingly then, Proust's way is to *open* his ears to Renan's *chanson*, rather than to close down the features of Renan's style to a few simplified, though easily recognizable, features.

Before discussing the unique relevance of such an approach to Renan, who in my opinion occupies a privileged position in the study of nineteenth-century European intellectual culture, let me try to give some idea of what it is that Proust does in his pastiche of Renan. From the beginning "Renan" feels obliged to connect Lemoine's exploits with humanity's history, and its conflicting impulses towards spirituality and materiality. Whether or not Lemoine actually succeeded in manufacturing diamonds is, for "Renan," more interesting as a speculation equal to proof (or not) of the supernatural; Proust's recollection is clearly that of the issues around which the *Vie de Jésus* was written, in which matters of faith are treated as matters of fact, and in which there is—as in the pastiche—an obvious savoring both of the skeptic's dilemma (should one or should one not believe?) and of the historian's power to grasp, even to experience, facts positivistically. Soon "Renan" expands his vision, first by the use of an unctuous "nous," then by the unsubtle decoration of simple facts either with analogues or with a riot of material details. Hence a description of Lemoine's alleged factory recalls an account given by Ruskin of the factory's locale set amongst poplar trees, which is then followed by details of flora, fauna, ambiance of a sort to be done to death by the Flaubert of *Salammbô* but perfected as historical detail given "naturally" in Renan's volumes on the rise of Christianity. Yet all this is as a prelude to the central portion of the pastiche. Suddenly "Renan" starts a learned meditation on Lemoine's name: philology, regional history, literature, gratuitous recollection, learned irrelevance make their appearance. All, however, are subservient to "Renan's" intention to connect Lemoine with the history of his own time, and with the history of Christian Europe. Soon we are back into an analysis of the Hebrew Bible, and that leads in turn to fond reminiscences of Henriette (*ma soeur Henriette*) Renan, Renan's teacher Le Hir, and "mon oncle Pierre" done in the manner of *Souvenirs d'enfance et de jeunesse*.

Proust's imitation now predictably ropes in the requisite references to Renan's *va-et-vient* relations with the Collège de France, the exhortations to humanity at large, the hopelessly obscure but urbane-sounding references to Latin passages and, finally, the characteristic muddling of imaginative freethinking and liberal reform with the problems of religious belief. "Renan's" final paragraph is a dazzling *tour de force* of Renanisms, which it is virtually impossible to describe, so dense and amusing—and so uncannily accurate—the style. By the last line "Renan" has become virtually incomprehensible as reflections on Job, Beranger and Emerson jostle references to the Emperor Decius (done in the autumnal manner of *Marc-Aurèle*) and the Comtesse de Noailles. All this seemingly indiscriminate variety is legitimized by the historico-scientific *non sequitur* that "we are all as sketches used by the genius of an epoch for the prelude to a masterpiece it will probably never execute."[12] Science, history, faith, personal musing, moral commentary—these intermingle in the foreground of "Renan's" style, less like a series of objects than like a sort of screen on which miscellaneous thoughts are projected with divine ease. It is the aura and tone of generality in Renan's writing that Proust captures perfectly, that is, the general envelope his writing seems everywhere to fling out, inside which, as a form of regularized presence denoting "Ernest Renan," a wide variety of subjects can be contained. One is reminded here of how Renan drew sustenance for his general world view from Malebranche, for whom the divine was manifested neither in individual human will nor in miracles, but in pattern and general order.[13]

It would be wrong, I believe, to say merely that Proust "did" Renan and that this doing has an evident critical, or literary historical, value. There is that and more. What Proust conveys with the kind of precision that neither Arnold, Wilde nor Frazer could manage is the exact *element*, whose chief feature is a type of achieved confidence, out of which Renan's style is composed. Proust's "Renan" can say something as patently comic as the following, with absolute fidelity to Renan's own style.

> Patience donc! Humanité, patience! Rallume encore demain le four éteint mille fois déjà d'où sortira peut-être un jour le diamant! Perfectionne, avec une bonne humeur que peut t'envier L'Eternal, le creuset où tu porteras le carbone à des températures inconnues de Lemoine et de Berthelot. Répète inlassablement le *sto ad ostium et pulso*, sans savoir si jamais une voix te répondera: "*Veni, veni, coronaberis.*"[14]*

What Proust in fact sees is that there must in both cases be a place, or a sense of place, created in the style allowing Renan to stand and address his audience with self-conviction. I choose the spatial metaphor advisedly here and elsewhere in preference to the rhetorical terms *tone* or *persona* customary in such designations. By place I mean that as Proust sees him Renan inhabits a verbal environment, or element, which allows certain things to be brought together, and discussed, and from which an audience can repeatedly be addressed with authority.

And indeed Proust is especially correct, I think. What he understands is that Renan was a figure neither of total originality nor of absolute derivativeness. As a cultural force he cannot

---

* "Have patience therefore! Humanity, have patience! Re-kindle again tomorrow the already-thousand-fold-extinguished oven out of which, someday perhaps, a diamond will emerge. Perfect, with a good humor which even the Étern 1 might envy you, the crucible in which you will take carbon up to temperatures unknown either to Lemoine or to Berthelot. Indefatigably repeat the *sto ad ostium et pulso*, without knowing whether a voice will ever respond: '*Veni, veni, coronaberis.*' "

be reduced simply to his personality nor to a set of schematic ideas in which he believed. Rather Renan is best grasped as a dynamic force whose opportunities were created for him by specialized institutions in the culture as a kind of currency which he circulated and recirculated with (to force the image a little further) his own unmistakable re-currency. Renan is a figure who must be grasped, in short, as a type of cultural *praxis*, as a style for making discursive statements within what Michel Foucault would call the *archive* of his time.[15] What matters is not only the things that Renan says, but also how he says them: what, given his background and training, he chooses to use in his subject matter; what to combine with what, and so forth. Renan's relations with his subject matter, with his time and audience, even with his own work, can be described then without resorting to formulae that depend on an unexamined assumption of ontological stability (e.g., the *Zeitgeist*, history of ideas, life-and-times). Instead we will be able to read Renan as a writer *doing* something describable, *in a place* defined temporally, spatially and culturally (hence archivally), for an audience and, no less important, for the furtherance of his own position in the archive of his era. Let us attempt now to detail *this* Renan.

II

For anyone to whom the word *philology* suggests dry-as-dust and inconsequential word-study, Nietzsche's proclamations that along with the greatest minds of the nineteenth century he is a philologist will come as some surprise.[16] What is the category that includes himself, Wagner, Schopenhauer, Leopardi, all as philologists? The term seems to include both a gift for exceptional spiritual insight into language and the ability to produce work whose *articulation* is of aesthetic and historical power. Although the profession of philology was born the day in 1777 "when F. A. Wolf invented for himself the name of *stud. philol.*,"[17] Nietzsche is nevertheless at pains to show that professional students of the Greek and Roman classics are commonly incapable of understanding their discipline: "they never reach the *roots of the matter*: they never adduce philology as a problem."[18] For simply "as knowledge of the ancient world philology cannot, of course, last forever; its material is exhaustible." It is this that the herd of philologists cannot understand. But what distinguishes the few exceptional spirits whom Nietzsche entitles to praise—not unambiguously, and not in the cursory way that I am now describing—is their profound relation to modernity, a relation that is given them by their practice of philology. This is how he puts it as he continues his description of philology's exhaustibility:

> What cannot be exhausted is the always new adjustment every age makes to the classical world, of measuring ourselves against it. If we set the philologist the task of better understanding *his own age* by means of antiquity, then his task is eternal.— This is the antinomy of philology. *The ancient world* has in fact always been understood only *in terms of the present*—and should *the present* now be understood *in terms of the ancient world?*[19]

The answer is yes, but only if the philologist is a man with experience, which means that he must be of his time and place as intensely and as seriously as possible. Philology problematizes—itself, its practitioner, the present. It embodies a peculiar condition of being modern and European, since neither of those two categories has true meaning without being related to an earlier alien culture and time. What Nietzsche also sees is philology as something *born, made* in the Vichian sense as a sign of human enterprise, created as a category of human discovery, self-discovery, and originality. Philology is a way of historically setting oneself off, as great artists do, from one's time and an immediate past even as, paradoxically and anti-nomically, one actually characterizes one's modernity by so doing.

Between the Friedrich August Wolf of 1777 and the Nietzsche of 1875 there is Ernest Renan, also a philologist, also a man with a complex and interesting sense of the way philology and modern culture are involved in each other. In *L'Avenir de la science*, written in 1848 but not published till 1890, he wrote that "the founders of modern mind are philologists." And what is modern mind, he said in the preceding sentence, if not "rationalism, criticism, liberalism, [all of which] were founded on the same day as philology?"[20] Philology, he goes on to say, is both a *comparative* discipline possessed only by moderns, and a symbol of modern (and European) superiority; every advance made by humanity since the fifteenth century can be attributed to minds we should call philological.[21] The job of philology in modern culture (a culture Renan calls philological) is to continue to see reality and nature clearly, thus driving out supernaturalism, and to continue to keep pace with discoveries in the physical sciences.[22] But more than all this, philology enables a general view of human life and of the system of things: "Me, being there at the centre, inhaling the perfume of everything, judging, comparing, combining, inducing,—in this way I shall arrive to the very system of things."[23] There is an unmistakable aura of *power* about the philologist. And Renan makes his point about philology and the natural sciences:

> To practice philosophy is to know things; following Cuvier's nice phrase, philosophy is *instructing the world in theory*. Like Kant I believe that every purely speculative demonstration has no more validity than a mathematical demonstration, and can teach us nothing about existing reality. Philology is the *exact science* of mental objects (La philologie est la *science exacte* des choses de l'esprit). It is to the sciences of humanity what physics and chemistry are to the philosophic sciences of bodies.[24]

70

I shall return to Renan's citation from Cuvier, as well as the constant references to natural science, a little later. For the time being, we should remark that the whole middle section of *L'Avenir de la science* is taken up with Renan's admiring accounts of philology, a science he depicts as being at once the most difficult of all human endeavors to characterize, as well as the most precise of all disciplines. In the aspirations of philology to a veritable science of humanity, Renan associates himself explicitly with Vico, Herder, Wolf, Montesquieu, as well as with such philological near-contemporaries as Wilhelm von Humboldt, Bopp, and Eugene Burnouf (to whom the volume is dedicated). Renan locates philology centrally within what he everywhere refers to as the march of knowledge, and indeed the book itself is a manifesto of humanistic meliorism, which considering its subtitle ("Pensées de 1848") and other books of 1848 like *Bouvard and Pecuchet* and *The Eighteenth Brumaire of Louis Bonaparte* is no mean irony. In a sense then, the manifesto generally and Renan's accounts of philology particularly—he had by then already written a first version of the massive philological treatise on Semitic languages that had earned him the Prix Volney in 1848—were designed to place Renan as an intellectual in a clearly perceptible relationship to the great social issues raised by 1848. That he should choose to fashion such a relationship on the basis of the *least* immediate of all intellectual disciplines (philology), the one with the least degree of apparent *popular* relevance, the most conservative and the most traditional, suggests the extreme deliberateness of Renan's position. For he did not really speak as one man to all men but rather as a reflective specialized voice that took, as he put it in the 1890 preface, the inequality of races and the necessary domination of the many by the few for granted as an antidemocratic law of nature and society.[25]

But how was it possible for Renan to hold himself and what he was saying in such a paradoxical position? For what was

philology on the one hand if not a science of all humanity, a
science premised on the unity of the human species and the
worth of every human detail; and yet what was the philologist
on the other hand if not—as Renan himself proved with his
notorious race-prejudice against the very Semites whose study
had made his professional name[26]—a harsh divider of men into
superior and inferior races, a liberal critic whose work harbored
the most esoteric notions of temporality, origins, development,
relationship and human worth? Part of the answer to this question is that, as his early letters of philological intent to Victor
Cousin, Michelet and Alexander von Humboldt show,[27] Renan
had a strong guild sense as a professional scholar, a sense that
put distance between himself and the masses. But more important, I think, is Renan's own conception of his role as a
philologist within the discipline's history, development and ob-
jectives, as he saw them. In other words, what may to us seem
like paradox was the expected result of how Renan perceived
his dynastic position within philology, its history and inaugural
discoveries, and what he, Renan, did within it. Therefore
Renan should be characterized not as speaking *about* philology,
but rather as *speaking philologically* with all the force of an
initiate using the encoded language of a new prestigious science
none of whose pronouncements about language itself could
therefore be construed either directly or naively.

As Renan understood, received, and was instructed in philology, the discipline imposed a set of doxological rules upon
him. To be a philologist meant to be governed in one's activity
first of all by a set of recent revaluative discoveries which
effectively *began* the *science* of philology and gave it a distinctive epistemology of its own: I am speaking here of the
period roughly from the 1780s to the mid-1830s, which coin-
cides with the beginning of Renan's education. His memoirs
record how the crisis of religious faith that culminated in the
loss of that faith led him in 1845 into a life of scholarship: this
was his initiation into philology, its world view, crises, and

style. His life he believed reflected on a personal level the institutional life of philology. In his life, however, he determined to be as Christian as he once was, only now without Christianity and with what he called "la science laïque" (lay science).[28]

The best example of what a lay science could and could not do was provided years later by Renan in a lecture given at the Sorbonne in 1878, "On the Services Rendered by Philology to the Historical Sciences." What is revealing about this text is the way Renan clearly had religion in mind when he spoke about philology—for example, in what philology, like religion, teaches us about the origins of humanity, civilization, language —only to make it evident to his hearers that philology could deliver a far less coherent, less knitted-together and positive message than religion.[29] Since Renan was irremediably historic and, as he once put it, morphological in his outlook, it stood to reason therefore that the only way in which as a very young man he could move out of religion into philological scholarship was to retain there in the new lay science a historical world view he had gained from religion. Hence "one occupation alone seemed to me to be worthy of filling my life; and that was to pursue my critical research [an allusion to Renan's major scholarly project on the history and origins of Christianity] into Christianity using those far ampler means offered me by lay science."[30] Renan had assimilated himself to philology according to his own post-Christian fashion.

The difference between the history offered internally by Christianity and the history offered by philology, a relatively new discipline, is precisely what made modern philology possible, and this Renan knew perfectly. For whenever "philology" is spoken of around the end of the eighteenth century and the beginning of the nineteenth, we are to understand the *new* philology, whose major successes include comparative grammar, the reclassification of languages into families, and the final rejection of the divine origins of language. It is no exaggeration to say that these accomplishments were a more or less direct consequence of the view that held language to be an entirely human phenomenon. And this view became current once it was discovered empirically that the so-called sacred languages (Hebrew primarily) were neither of primordial antiquity nor of divine provenance. What Foucault has called the discovery of language is therefore a secular event that displaced a religious conception of how God delivered language to man in Eden.[31] Indeed one of the consequences of this change, by which an etymological, dynastic notion of linguistic filiation was pushed aside by the view of language as a domain all of its own held together with jagged internal structures and coherences, is the dramatic subsidence of interest in the problem of the origins of language. Whereas in the 1770s it was all the rage to discuss the origins of language (Herder's essay on the origin of language won the 1772 Medal from the Berlin Academy), by the first decade of the new century the subject was all but banned as a topic for learned dispute in Europe.

On all sides, and in many different ways, what William Jones stated in his *Anniversary Discourses* (1785–92), or what Franz Bopp put forward in his *Vergleichende Grammatik* (1832), is that the divine dynasty of language was ruptured definitively and discredited as an idea. A new historical conception, in short, was needed, since Christianity seemed unable to survive the empirical evidence that reduced the divine status of its major text. For some, as Chateaubriand put it, faith was unshakable despite new knowledge of how Sanskrit outdated Hebrew: "Hélas! il est arrivé qu'une connaissance plus approfondie de la langue savante de l'Inde a fait rentrer ces siècles innombrables dans le cercle etroit de la Bible. Bien m'en a pris d'être redevenue croyant, avant d'avoir eprouvé cette mortification."[32]* For others, especially philologists like the pioneering Bopp himself, the study of language entailed its

---

* "Alas! it has happened that a deeper knowledge of the learned language of India has forced innumerable centuries into the narrow circle of the Bible. How lucky for me that I have become a believer again before having had to experience this mortification."

own history, philosophy and learning, all of which did away with any notion of a primal language given by the Godhead to man in Eden. As study of Sanskrit seemed to have moved the earliest beginnings of civilization very far east of the Biblical lands, so too language became less of a continuity between an outside power and the human speaker than an internal field created and *accomplished* by language users among themselves. There was no first language just as, except by a method I shall be discussing presently, there was no simple language.

The legacy of these first-generation philologists was, to Renan, of the highest importance. Whenever he discussed language and philology, whether at the beginning, middle, or end of his long career, he repeats the lessons of the new philology, of which the antidynastic, anticontinuous tenets of a *technical* (as opposed to divine) linguistic practice are the major pillar. Bopp, who is the great figure of the early group, makes these antidynastic points on the first page of his introduction to the *Comparative Grammar*.[33] Friedrich Schlegel's Dresden lectures of 1828-29, *Philosophie der Sprache und des Wortes*, dismiss all attempts to comprehend any such thing as a first language spoken in Paradise; such attempts, he says, involve a complete misconstruing of the huge distance in time separating us from an essentially unknowable first beginning and origin of the world.[34] In one of his French essays, August Wilhelm Schlegel devotes a great deal of time to limiting the uses of etymology, especially those etymologies that try to trace words back to some first origin given either in or even outside Eden.[35] Even the redoubtable Lord Mondoddo in his *Ancient Metaphysics* (1795) had tried desperately to accommodate Sanskrit to the scheme he had adumbrated in *The Origin and Progress of Language*; as it turned out, he had not really changed his mind that language was divine, but the important thing is that he tried to. Fabre D'Olivet wrote an unusual, now neglected book called *La Langue hébraïque restituée* (1815-16) showing how Hebrew was not at all the first language nor even one of the *langue-mères* because of Sanskrit, but rather—as he says—one among many other languages expressing the character of a powerful, wise and religious people; Hebrew, he adds simply, "devint l'idiome particulier du peuple hebreu." That was all.[36]

One could give many more examples, all among writers, poets, philosophers, philologists in what we would recognize as the central romantic tradition, all of them belonging to the generation of Renan's philological and secular precursors. For them language cannot be pictured as the result of force emanating unilaterally from God. As Coleridge put it, "Language is the armory of the human mind; and at once contains the trophies of its past and the weapons of its future conquests."[37] The idea of a first edenic language gives way to the heuristic notion of a protolanguage (Indo-European, Semitic, etc.) whose existence is never a subject of debate, since it is acknowledged that no such language can be recaptured, it can only be reconstituted in the philological process. To the extent that *one* language serves, again heuristically, as a touchstone for all the others, it is Sanskrit in its earliest Indo-European form. The terminology also shifts: there are now *families* of languages (the analogy with species and anatomical classifications is marked); there is *perfect* linguistic form which need not correspond with any "real" language; and there are original languages only as a function of the philological discourse, not because of nature. By the mid-1830s Wilhelm von Humboldt could put the new position as follows:

> That an extant linguistic family or simply an individual language of such family coincides completely with the perfect linguistic form cannot be expected, and we have not encountered one within the scope of our experience. However the Sanskritic languages approach this form to the highest degree and are also those in which the intellectual progress of the human race has developed through the longest series of progressions and in the most fortunate manner. Thus we can regard them as a fixed point of comparison for all remaining tongues.[38]

Humboldt's approbation for Sanskrit was symptomatic of a general excess of zeal where Sanskrit was concerned. Some writers shrewdly commented on how it was that Sanskrit and things Indian in general simply took the place of Hebrew and the edenic fallacy. As early as 1804 Benjamin Constant noted in his *Journal Intime* that he was not about to discuss India in his *De la religion* because the English who owned the place and the Germans who studied it indefatigably had made India the *fons et origo* of everything; and then there were the French who had decided after Napoleon and Champollion that everything originated in Egypt.[39] These teleological enthusiasms were fueled after 1808 by Friedrich Schlegel's celebrated *Ueber die Sprache und Weisheit der Inder*, which seemed to confirm Schlegel's pronouncement made in 1800, *"Im Orient muessen wir das höchste Romantische suchen."*

What Renan's generation—educated from the mid-thirties to the late forties—retained from all this enthusiasm about the Orient is the *necessity* of the Orient for the Occidental scholar of languages, cultures and religions. Here the key text is Edgar Quinet's *Le Génie des religions* (1832), a work that announced the Oriental Renaissance and placed the Orient and the West in a functional relationship with each other. The vast meaning of this relationship has been analyzed comprehensively by Raymond Schwab in *La Renaissance orientale*;[40] my concern with it here is only to note specific aspects of it that bear upon Renan's vocation as a philologist and as an Orientalist. Quinet's association with Michelet, their interest in Herder and Vico respectively, impressed on them the need for the scholar-historian to confront, almost in the manner of an audience seeing a dramatic event unfold, or a believer witnessing a revelation, the different, the strange, the distant. Quinet's formulation was that the Orient proposes and the West disposes: Asia has its prophets, Europe its doctors (its learned men, its scientists: the pun is intended). Out of this encounter, a new dogma or god is born, but Quinet's point is that both East and West fulfill their destinies and confirm their identities in the encounter. As a scholarly attitude the picture of a learned Westerner surveying as if from a peculiarly suited vantage-point the passive, seminal, feminine, even silent and supine East, going on then to *articulate* the East, making the Orient deliver up its secrets under the learned authority of a philologist whose power derives from the ability to unlock secret, esoteric languages—this will persist in Renan. What does not persist in Renan during the forties, when he serves his apprenticeship as a philologist, is the dramatic attitude: that is replaced by the scientific attitude.

For Quinet and Michelet, history was a drama. Quinet suggestively describes the whole world as a temple, and human history as a sort of religious rite. Both Michelet and Quinet *saw* the world they discussed. The origin of human history was something they could describe in the same splendid and impassioned and dramatic terms used by Vico and Rousseau to portray life on earth in primitive times. For Michelet and Quinet there is no doubt that they belong to the communal European romantic undertaking "either in epic or some other major genre—in drama, in prose romance, or in the visionary 'greater Ode'—radically to recast into terms appropriate to the historical and intellectual circumstances of their own age, the Christian pattern of the fall, the redemption, and the emergence of a new earth which will constitute a restored paradise."[41] I think that for Quinet the idea of a new god being born is tantamount to the filling of the place left by the old god; for Renan, however, being a philologist means the severance of any and all connections with the old Christian god, so that instead a new *doctrine*—probably science—will stand free and in a new place, as it were. Renan's whole career was devoted to the fleshing out of this progress, and so we should turn to it immediately.

He put it very plainly at the end of his undistinguished essay on the origins of language: man is no longer an inventor, and the age of creation is definitely over.[42] There was a period, at which we can only guess, when man was literally *transported* from silence into words. After that there was language, and for the true scientist the task is to examine how language *is*, not how it came about. Yet if Renan dispels the passionate creation of primitive times (which had excited Herder, Vico, Rousseau, even Quinet and Michelet) he instates a new and deliberate type of artificial creation, one that is performed as a result of scientific analysis. In his Leçon Inaugurale at the Collège de France (February 21, 1862), Renan proclaimed his lectures open to the public so that it might see at first hand "le laboratoire même de la science philologique" (the very laboratory of philological science).[43] Any reader of Renan would have understood that such a statement was meant also to carry a typical, if rather limp, irony, one less intended to shock than passively to delight. For Renan was succeeding to the Chair of Hebrew, and his lecture was on the contribution of the Semitic peoples to the history of civilization. What more subtle affront could there be to "sacred" history than the substitution of a philological laboratory for divine intervention in history; and what more telling way was there of declaring the Orient's contemporary relevance to be simply material for *European* investigation?[44]

The stirring peroration with which Renan concluded his *leçon* had another function than simply to connect Semitic philology with the future and with science. Etienne Quatremère, who immediately preceded Renan in the Chair of Hebrew, was a scholar who seemed to exemplify the popular caricature of what a scholar was like. A man of prodigiously industrious and dry habits, he went about his work, Renan said in a relatively unfeeling memorial minute for the *Journal des Débats* in October 1857, like a laborious worker who even in rendering immense services nevertheless could not see the whole edifice being constructed. The edifice was nothing less than "la science historique de l'esprit humaine," now in the

79

process of being built stone by stone.[45] Just as Quatremère was not of *this* age, so Renan in *his* work was determined to be of it. Moreover, if the Orient had been identified exclusively and indiscriminately with India and China, Renan's ambition was to carve out a new Oriental province for himself, in this case the Semitic Orient. He had no doubt remarked the casual, and surely current, confusion of Arabic with Sanskrit (as in Balzac's *La Peau de Chagrin*, where the fateful talisman's Arabic script is described as Sanskrit),[46] and he made it his job accordingly to do for the Semitic languages what Bopp had done for the Indo-European: so he said in the 1855 Preface to the comparative Semitic treatise.[47] Therefore Renan's plans were to bring the Semitic languages into sharp and glamorous focus à la Bopp, and in addition to elevate the study of these neglected inferior languages to the level of a passionate new science of mind à la Louis Lambert.

On more than one occasion Renan was quite explicit in his assertions that Semites and Semitic were *creations* of philological study.[48] Since he was the man who did the study there was meant to be little ambiguity about the centrality of his role in this new, artificial creation. But how did Renan mean the word *creation* in these instances? And how was this creation connected with either natural creation or the creation ascribed by Renan and others to the laboratory, classificatory and natural sciences, principally what was called philosophical anatomy? Here we must speculate a little. Throughout his career Renan seemed to imagine the role of science in human life as (and I quote in translation as literally as I can) *telling*, speaking to, or articulating for man the word (logos?) of things.[49] Science gives speech to things; better yet, science brings out, causes to be pronounced, a potential speech within things. The special value then of linguistics (as the new philology was then often called) is not that natural science resembled it, but rather that it treated words as natural, otherwise silent objects, which were made to give up their secrets.

Remember that the major breakthrough in the study of inscriptions and hieroglyphs was the discovery by Champollion that the symbols on the Rosetta stone had a *phonetic* as well as a semantic component.[50] To make objects speak was like making words speak, giving them circumstantial value and a precise place in a rule-governed order of regularity. In its first sense *creation*, as Renan used the word, signified the articulation by which an object like *Semitic* could be seen as a creature of sorts. Second, creation also signified the setting—in the case of Semitic it meant history, culture, race, mind—illuminated and brought forward from its reticence by the scientist. Finally, creation was the formulation of a system of classification by which it was possible to see the object in question *comparatively* with other like objects; and by comparatively Renan intended a complex network of paradigmatic relations that obtained between Semitic and Indo-European languages.

If in what I have so far said, and what I will be saying, I have insisted so much on Renan's study of Semitic languages, I do so for several important reasons, which I should list immediately. Semitic was the scientific study to which Renan turned right after the loss of his Christian faith; I described above how he came to see the study of Semitic as replacing his faith and enabling a critical future relation with it. The study of Semitic was Renan's first full-length scientific study (finished in 1847, published first in 1855), which was as much a part of his late major works on the origins of Christianity and the history of the Jews as it was a propaedeutic for them. In intention, if not perhaps in achievement—interestingly, none of the standard or contemporary works in either linguistic history or the history of Orientalism cites Renan with anything more than cursory attention[51]—his Semitic opus was proposed as a philological breakthrough, from which in later years he was always to draw retrospective authority for his deeply reactionary and ethnocentric positions on religion, race, and nationalism.[52] Whenever Renan wished to make a statement about either the Jews or the Moslems, for example, it was always with his remarkably harsh (and unfounded, except according to the science he was practicing) strictures on the Semites in mind. Furthermore, Renan's Semitic was meant as a contribution both to the development of Indo-European linguistics and to the differentiation of *Orientalisms*. To the former, Semitic was a degraded form, degraded both in the moral and biological sense, whereas to the latter Semitic was a, if not *the*, stable form of cultural decadence. Lastly, Semitic was Renan's first creation, a fiction invented by him in the philological laboratory to satisfy his sense of public place and mission. It should by no means be lost on us that Semitic was for Renan's ego the symbol of European (and consequently his) dominion over the Orient, and over his own era.

Therefore Semitic was not fully a *natural* object, like a species of monkey for instance, nor fully an unnatural or divine object, as it had once been considered. Instead, Semitic occupied a median position, legitimated in its oddities (regularity being defined by Indo-European) by an *inverse* relation with normal languages, comprehended as an eccentric quasi-monstrous phenomenon partly because libraries, laboratories, and museums could serve as its place of exhibition and analysis. In his treatise therefore, Renan adopted a tone of voice and a method of exposition that drew the maximum from book-learning and from natural observation as practiced by men like Cuvier and the Geoffroy Saint-Hilaires, *pére et fils*. This is an important stylistic achievement I think, for it allowed Renan consistently to avail himself of the *library*, rather than either primitivity or divine fiat, as a conceptual framework in which to understand language, together with the *museum*, which is where the results of laboratory observation are delivered for exhibition, study, and teaching.[53] That these two institutions should lurk behind the effectiveness of Renan's novel style tells us much of the story hinted at in what I called the *range* of Proust's pastiche of it. Everywhere Renan treats of normal

human facts—language, history, culture, mind, imagination—
as transformed into something else, something peculiarly devi-
ant, because they are Semitic. Thus the Semites are rabid
monotheists who produced no mythology, no art, no commerce, no civilization; their consciousness is a narrow and
rigid one; all in all they represent "une combinaison inférieure
de la nature humaine."[54] At the same time Renan wants it
understood that he speaks of a prototype, not a real Semitic
type with actual existence (although he violated this too by
discussing present-day Jews and Moslems with less than scientific detachment in many places in his writings).[55] So on the
one hand we have the transformation of the human into the
specimen, and on the other the comparative judgment rendered by which the specimen remains a specimen and a subject
for philological, scientific study.

Scattered throughout the *Histoire Générale et système comparé des langues sémitiques* are reflections on the links between
linguistics and anatomy, and—for Renan this is equally important—remarks on how these links could be employed to do
human history (*les sciences historiques*). But first we should
consider the *implicit* links. I do not think it wrong or an exaggeration to say that a typical page of Renan's *Histoire
Générale* was constructed typographically and structurally
with a page of comparative philosophical anatomy, in the style
of Cuvier or Geoffroy Saint-Hilaire, kept in mind. Both
linguists and anatomists purport to be speaking about matters
not directly obtainable or observable in nature; a skeleton, or a
detailed line drawing of a muscle, as much as paradigms constituted by the linguists out of a purely hypothetical proto-
Semitic or proto-Indo-European, are similarly products of the
laboratory and of the library. The text of a linguistic or an
anatomical work bears the same general relation to nature (or
actuality) that a museum case exhibiting a specimen mammal
or organ does. What is given on the page and in the museum
case is a truncated exaggeration whose purpose is to exhibit a

relationship between the science (or scientist) and the object, not one between the object and nature. Read almost any page by Renan on Arabic, Hebrew, Aramaic and proto-Semitic and you read a fact of power, by which the philologist's authority summons out of the library at will examples of man's speech, and ranges them there surrounded by a suave European prose that points out defects, virtues, barbarism, and shortcomings in the language, the people, and the civilization. The tone and the tense of the exhibition are done almost uniformly in the contemporary present, so that one is given an impression of a pedagogical demonstration during which the scholar-scientist stands at a lecture-laboratory platform, creating, confining and judging the material he discusses before our eyes.

This anxiety on Renan's part to convey the sense of a demonstration actually taking place is heightened when he remarks explicitly that whereas anatomy employs stable and visible signs by which to consign objects to classes, linguistics does not.[56] Therefore the philologist must make a given linguistic fact correspond in some way with a historical period, and hence the possibility of a classification; yet, as Renan was often to say, linguistic temporality and history are full of lacunae, enormous discontinuities, hypothetical periods. Therefore linguistic events occur in a nonlinear and essentially discontinuous temporal dimension controlled by the linguist in a very particular way. That way, as Renan's whole treatise on the Semitic languages goes very far to show, is comparative: Indo-European is taken as the living, *organic* norm, and Semitic languages are seen comparatively to be *inorganic*.[57] Time is transformed into the space of comparative classification, which at bottom is based on a rigid binary opposition between organic and inorganic languages. So on the one hand there is the organic, biologically generative process represented by Indo-European, while on the other there is an inorganic, essentially unregenerative process, ossified into Semitic; most important, Renan makes it absolutely clear that such an imperious judg-

84

ment is *made* by the philologist in his laboratory, for distinctions of the kind he is concerned with are neither possible nor available for anyone except the trained professional. "Nous refusons donc aux langues sémitiques la faculté de se régénérer, toute en reconnaissant qu'elles n'échappent pas plus que les autres oeuvres de la conscience humaine à la nécessité du changement et des modifications successives."[58]*

Yet behind even this radical opposition, there is another one working in Renan's mind, and for several pages in the first chapter of Book V he exposes his position quite candidly to the reader. This occurs when he introduces Saint-Hilaire's views on the "degradation of types."[59] Although Renan does not specify which Saint-Hilaire he refers to, ambiguous though it is, the reference is clear enough. For both Etienne and his son Isidore were biological speculators of extraordinary fame and influence, particularly among literary intellectuals during the first half of the nineteenth century in France. Balzac, for instance, dedicated a major portion of the preface to *La Comédie humaine* to Etienne's achievement and there is much evidence available to prove that Flaubert read the two, and used their views in his work.[60] Not only were Etienne and Isidore legatees of the tradition of "romantic" biology passed down by Goethe among others, with their strong interest in analogy, homology, and organic Ur-form among species, but they were also specialists in the philosophy and anatomy of monstrosity, teratology as Isidore called it, in which the most horrendous physiological aberrations were considered to be a function of internal degradation within the species-life.[61] I cannot here go into the intricacies (as well as the macabre fascination) of teratology, thought it is enough to mention that both Etienne and Isidore exploit the theoretical power of the linguistic paradigm to explain the deviations possible within a biological system. Thus

---

* "Therefore we refuse to allow that the Semitic languages have the capacity to regenerate themselves, even while recognizing that they—any more than other products of human consciousness—do not escape the necessity of change or of successive modifications."

Etienne's notion is that a monster is an *anomaly*, in the same sense that in language words exist in analogical as well as anomalous relations with each other: in linguistics the idea is at least as old as Varro's *De Lingua Latina*. No anomaly can be considered simply as a gratuitous exception; rather anomalies confirm the regular structure binding together all members of the same class. Such a view is quite daring in anatomy. At one moment in the "Préliminaire" to his *Philosophie Anatomique* Etienne says:

> Et, en effet, tel est la caractère de notre époque, qu'il devient impossible aujourd'hui de se renfermer sévèrement dans la cadre d'une simple monographie. Etudiez un object isolé, vous ne pouvez le rapporter qu'à lui-même, et par conséquent vous n'en aurez jamais qu'une connaissance parfaite. Mais voyez-le au milieu d'êtres qui s'en rapprochent sous plusieurs rapports, et qui s'en éloignent à quelques autres, vous lui découvrirez des relations plus étendues. D'abord vous le connaitrez mieux, même dans sa specialité: mais de plus, le considerant dans le centre da sa sphére d'activité, vous saurez comment il se conduit dans son monde éxterieur, et tout ce que lui-même reçoit de qualités par la réaction du milieu ambiant.[62]*

Not only is Saint-Hilaire saying that it is the specific character of contemporary study (he was writing in 1822) to examine phenomena comparatively; he is also saying that for the scientist there is no such thing as a phenomenon, no matter how aberrant and exceptional, that cannot be explained with reference to other phenomena. Note also how Saint-Hilaire employs the metaphor of centrality (*le centre de sa sphére*

---

* "And, in effect, such is the character of our epoch that it becomes impossible today to enclose oneself strictly within the framework of a simple monograph. Study an object in isolation and you will only be able to bring it back to itself; consequently you can never have perfect knowledge of it. But see it in the midst of beings who are connected with each other in many different ways, and which are isolated from each other in different ways, and you will discover for this object a wider scope of relationships. First of all you will know it better, even in its specificity: but more important, by considering it in the very center of its own sphere of activity, you will know precisely how it behaves in its own exterior world, and you will also know how its own features are constituted in reaction to its surrounding milieu."

d'activité) used by Renan in *L'Avenir de la science* to describe the position occupied by any object in nature—including the philologist—once the object is scientifically *placed* there by the examining scientist. Thereafter between the object and the scientist a bond of sympathy is established. Of course this can only take place during the laboratory experience, and not elsewhere. The point being made is that a scientist has at his disposal a sort of leverage by which even the totally unusual occurrence can be seen naturally and known scientifically, which in this case means without recourse to the supernatural, and with recourse only to an enveloping environment constituted by the scientist. As a result nature itself can be re-perceived as continuous, harmoniously coherent and fundamentally intelligible. *Natura non facit saltus, non datur hiatus formarum.*

Thus for Renan Semitic is a phenomenon of arrested development in comparison with the mature languages and cultures of the Indo-European group.[63] The paradox that Renan sustains, however, is that even as he encourages us to see languages as in some way corresponding with *êtres vivants de la nature*, he is everywhere else proving that the Semitic languages are inorganic, arrested, totally ossified, incapable of self-regeneration; in other words, Semitic is not a live language, and for that matter neither are Semites live creatures. Moreover Indo-European language and culture is alive and organic *because* of the laboratory, not despite it. But far from this being a marginal issue in Renan's work, the paradox stands I believe at the very center of his entire work, his style, and his archival existence in the culture of his time, a culture to which—as people like Arnold, Wilde, Frazer, Proust assented—he was a very important contributor. To be able to sustain a vision that incorporates and holds together life and quasi-living creatures (Indo-European, European culture) as well as quasi-monstrous, parallel inorganic phenomena (Semitic, Semitic culture) is precisely the achievement of the European scientist in his laboratory. He *constructs*, and the very act of construction is a sign of imperial power over recalcitrant phenomena, as well as a confirmation of the dominating culture and its "naturalization." Indeed it is not too much to say that Renan's philological laboratory is the actual locale of his European ethnocentrism; but what needs emphasis here, is that the philological laboratory has no existence outside the discourse, the writing by which it is constantly produced and experienced. Thus even the culture he calls organic and alive—Europe's—is also a *creature being created* in the laboratory and by philology. This is what Proust saw.

Renan's entire later career is European and cultural. Its accomplishments were varied and celebrated. Whatever authority his style possessed, I think, can be traced back to his technique for *constructing* the inorganic (or the missing), and for giving it the appearance of life. He was most famous of course for his *Vie de Jésus*, the work that inaugurated his monumental histories of Christianity and the Jewish people. Yet we must realize that the *Vie* was exactly the same type of feat that the *Histoire Générale* was, a construction enabled by the historian's capacity for skillfully crafting a rather lifeless (lifeless for Renan in the double sense of his dead Christian faith and a lost, hence dead, historical period) biography—and the paradox is immediately apparent—*as if it were* the truthful narrative of a natural life. Whatever Renan *said* had first passed through the philological laboratory; when it appeared in print woven through the text, there in it was the life-giving force of a contemporary cultural signature, which drew from modernity all its scientific power and all its uncritical self-approbation. For such a culture such genealogies as dynasty, tradition, religion, ethnic communities were all simply functions of a theory whose job was to instruct the world. In borrowing this latter phrase from Cuvier, Renan was circumspectly placing scientific demonstration over experience; temporality was relegated to the scientifically useless realm of ordinary experience, while to the special periodicity of culture and cultural comparativism (which spawned ethnocentrism, racial theory, and economic oppression) were given powers far in advance of moral vision.

III

Renan's style, his career, the circumstances of the meaning he communicates, his peculiarly intimate relationship with the European scholarly and general culture of his time—liberal, exclusivist, imperious, antihuman except in a very conditional sense—all these are what I would call *celibate* and scientific. Generation for him is consigned to the realm of *l'avenir* which in his famous manifesto he associated with science. Although as a historian of culture he belongs to the school of men like Turgot, Condorcet, Guizot, Cousin, Jouffroy, and Ballanche, and as a scholar to the school of Sylvestre de Sacy, Caussin de Perceval, Ozanam, Fauriel and Burnouf, Renan's is a peculiarly ravaged, ravagingly masculine world of history and learning; it is indeed the world not of fathers, mothers and children,[64] but of men like his Jesus, his Marcus Aurelius, his Caliban, his solar god (as described in "Rêves" of the *Dialogues Philosophiques*).[65] He cherished the power of science, he sought its insights and its techniques, he used it to intervene, often with considerable effectiveness, in the life of his epoch. And yet his ideal role was that of the spectator. In 1854 he wrote:

Quelle vie charmante que celle des philologues, quand ils savent comprendre leur bonheur et ne l'échangent pas contre les décevantes jouissances de l'ambition! Réchargés du plus rude, souci qui soit imposé à l'homme ici-bas, celui d'avoir une opinion exprimée sur les choses divines et humaines, ils joucent dans ce monde le plus commode des rôles, celui de spectateurs. Étrangers aux passions de secte ou de parti, ouverts à la vérité, de quelque part qu'elle vienne, ils voient tout aboutir à leur tribunal, et eux-mêmes ne relèvent de personne. Le bien, le mal, le beau, le laid, le médiocre même, tout les intéresse; car toute chose a son prix, quand on l'envisage comme partie intégrante de cet univers.[66]*

A philologist ought to choose *bonheur* over *jouissances*: the preference expresses a choice of elevated, if sterile, happiness over worldly pleasure. Words belong to the realm of *bonheur*, as does the study of words, ideally speaking. To my knowledge, there are very few moments in all of Renan's public writing where a beneficent and *instrumental* role is assigned to women. One occurs when Renan opines that foreign women (nurses, maids) must have instructed the conquering Normans' children, and hence caused the changes that take place in their language.[67] Note how productivity and dissemination are not the functions aided, but rather internal change, and a subsidiary one at that. "Man," he said at the end of the same essay, "belongs neither to his language nor to his race; he belongs to himself before all, since before all he is a free being and a moral one."[68] Man was free and moral, but enchained by race, history and science as Renan saw them, conditions imposed by the scholar on man.

The study of words took Renan to the heart of these conditions, and philology made it concretely apparent that knowledge of man was (to paraphrase from Cassirer) poetically transfiguring[69] only if it had been previously severed from raw actuality and then put into a doxological strait-jacket. By be-

---

* "How charming is the life of philologists when they can understand their happiness and not exchange it for the deceitful pleasures of ambition! Disabused of the hardest worry imposed on man in this world, the anxiety of having an expressed opinion on things divine and human, they play in this world the most convenient of roles, that of spectators. Strangers to the passions of either sect or party, open to the truth—from whatever quarter it comes—they see everything end up before their tribunal, although they themselves are dependent on no one. The good, the evil, the beautiful, the ugly, even the mediocre—all these concern philologists; for everything has its price when it is conceived of as an integral part of this universe."

coming *philology*, the study of words as once practiced by Vico, Herder, Rousseau, Michelet and Quinet, lost its plot and its dramatic presentational quality, as Schelling once called it. Instead philology became epistemologically complex; *Sprachgefühl* was no longer enough since words themselves pertained less to the senses or the body (as they had for Vico) and more to a sightless, imageless, and abstract realm ruled over by such hothouse judgments as race, mind, culture and nation. In that realm, which was discursively constructed, certain kinds of assertion could be made, all of them possessing the same powerful generality and cultural validity.

This essay has been concerned with *where* that generality and validity first took place, *where* (to use a poignantly inappropriate metaphor) they were born. For all of Renan's effort was to deny culture the right to be generated, except artificially, in the philological laboratory. A man was not a child of the culture: that dynastic conception had been too effectively challenged by philology. Philology taught one how culture is a construct, an *articulation* (in the sense that Dickens used the word for Mr. Venus's profession in *Our Mutual Friend*), even a creation, but not anything more than a quasiorganic structure. Thus the line from Renan's conception of the philologist, or *Wortkünstler*, to Mann's Leverkuhn, the *Tonkünstler*, is a direct one, via Nietzsche of course. Culture leaps from human actuality to demonic transhumanity, from the community to the technocratic situation room, from drama to commanding abstract games—with what human expense and at what exorbitant price paid we know only too well.

What is specially interesting in Renan is how much he knew himself to be a creature of his time and of his ethnocentric culture. On the occasion of an academic response to a speech made by Ferdinand de Lesseps in 1885 Renan averred how "it was so sad to be a wiser man than one's nation. . . . One cannot feel bitterness towards one's homeland. Better to be

mistaken along with the nation than to be too right with those
who tell it hard truths."[70] Such a statement applies almost too
perfectly to Renan himself. For does not the old Renan say that
the best relationship is one of parity with the culture, morality,
and ethos of the time, that and not a dynastic relation by which
one is either the child of his times or their parent? And here
we return to the laboratory, for it is there—as Renan thought
of it—that filial, and ultimately social responsibilities cease,
and scientific ones take over. The laboratory is then the platform from which one addresses the world; it mediates the
statements one makes, gives them confidence and general precision, as well as continuity. Thus the philological laboratory
as Renan understood it redefined not only his epoch and his
culture, dating and shaping them in new ways; it *made* his
subject matter, and more, it made him into the *cultural* figure
he then became. We may well wonder whether this new
autonomy within the culture was the freedom Renan hoped
science would bring or, so far as the contemporary student of
culture is concerned, if it was a complex affiliation between culture and the human subject that we are still trying to unravel.

NOTES

1. Matthew Arnold, *Culture and Anarchy*, ed. J. Dover Wilson (Cambridge: Cambridge University Press, 1969), p. 17.

2. Ibid., p. 141. For a later, but fundamentally unchanged, account of
Renan by Arnold see his review in 1872 of Renan's *La Reforme intel-
lectuelle et morale* collected in Arnold's *Complete Prose Works*, the
volume entitled *God and the Bible*, ed. R. H. Super (Ann Arbor: University of Michigan Press, 1970), pp. 40–50. See also Lewis F. Mott,
"Renan and Matthew Arnold," *Modern Language Notes* 32, 2 (February 1918): 65–73, as well as Flavia M. Alaya, "Arnold and Renan on
the Popular Use of History," *Journal of the History of Ideas* 28, 4
(October-December 1967): 551–576. For an excellent account of the
"race-theory" employed culturally by Arnold (and Renan among

others) see Lionel Trilling, *Matthew Arnold* (New York: Meridian Books, 1955), pp. 212–222.

3. Oscar Wilde, *The Artist as Critic: Critical Writings of Oscar Wilde*, ed. Richard Ellmann (New York: Vintage Books, 1969), p. 255. For a detailed study see Brian Nichols, "Two Nineteenth Century Utopias: The Influence of Renan's *L'Avenir de la science* on Wilde's *The Soul of Man Under Socialism*," *Modern Language Review* 59, 3 (July, 1964), 361–370.

4. *The Artist as Critic*, p. 407.

5. Ernest Renan, "Les Sciences de la nature et les sciences historiques: Lettre à M. Marcellin Berthelot," in *Oeuvres Complètes*, ed. Henriette Psichari, vol. 1 (Paris: Calmann-Lévy, 1947–1961), pp. 636–7. (Hereafter all citations from this edition will be referred to as *OC*, with the volume number following. All translations from Renan are my own.) For an interesting description of how Renan's German Romantic predecessors viewed nature as a language see Marianne Thalmann, *Zeichensprache der Romantik* (Heidelberg: Lothar Stiehm Verlag, 1967).

6. James Frazer, *Sur Ernest Renan* (Paris: Claude Aveline, 1923), p. 17.

7. Ibid., p. 37.

8. Ibid., p. 47.

9. Ibid., pp. 64–68.

10. Marcel Proust, *Contre Sainte-Beuve, précédé de Pastiches et mélanges, et suivi de Essais et articles*, ed. Pierre Clarac and Yves Sandre (Paris: Gallimard, 1971), p. 303.

11. Ibid., p. 303.

12. Ibid., p. 37.

13. Henri Peyre, *Renan* (Paris: Presses Universitaires de France, 1969), pp. 40–41.

14. Proust, *Contre Sainte-Beuve*, p. 36. In 1920 Proust wrote an explicitly savage attack on Renan's style: see *Contre Sainte-Beuve*, pp. 607–8. Elsewhere, however, Proust seems to admire Renan.

15. Foucault's characterization of an archive is to be found in his *The Archeology of Knowledge and The Discourse on Language*, trans. A. M. Sheridan Smith and Rupert Swyer (New York: Pantheon Books, 1972), pp. 79–131. Gabriel Monod, one of Renan's younger and very perspicacious contemporaries, remarks that Renan was by no means a revolutionary in linguistics, archeology or exegesis, yet because he had the widest and the most precise learning of anyone in his period he was its most eminent representative: *Renan, Taine, Michelet* (Paris: Calmann-Lévy, 1894), pp. 40–41. See also Jean-Louis Dumas, "La Philosophie de l'histoire de Renan," *Revue de Metaphysique et Morale* 77, 1 (January-March 1972), 100–128.

16. Nietzsche's remarks on philology are everywhere throughout his works. See principally his notes for "Wir Philologen" taken from his notebooks for the period January-July, 1875, translated by William Arrowsmith as "Notes for 'We Philologists,'" *Arion*, New Series 1/2

(1974), 279–380; also the passages on language and perspectivism in *The Will to Power*, trans. Walter Kaufmann and R. J. Hollingdale (New York: Vintage Books, 1968).

17. Nietzsche, "We Philologists," p. 281.

18. Ibid., p. 332.

19. Ibid., p. 296.

20. Renan, *L'Avenir de la science: Pensées de 1848*, 4th edition (Paris: Calmann-Lévy, 1890), p. 141.

21. Ibid., pp. 142–145.

22. Ibid., p. 146.

23. Ibid., p. 148.

24. Ibid., p. 149.

25. Ibid., p. xiv and *passim*.

26. The entire opening chapter—Book One, Chapter One—of the *Histoire Générale et système comparé des langues sémitiques* in *OC*, vol. 8, pp. 143–163 is a virtual encyclopedia of race prejudice directed against Semites (i.e., Moslems and Jews). The rest of the treatise is sprinkled generously with the same notions, as are many of Renan's other works, including *L'Avenir de la science*, especially Renan's notes.

27. Ernest Renan, *Correspondance; 1846–1871*, Vol. I (Paris: Calmann-Lévy, 1926), pp. 7–12.

28. Renan, *Souvenirs d'enfance et de jeunesse* in *OC*, vol. 2, p. 892. Two works by Jean Pommier treat Renan's meditation between religion and philology in valuable detail: *Renan, d'aprés des documents inédits* (Paris: Perrin, 1923), pp. 48–68, and *La Jeunesse clericale d'Ernest Renan* (Strasbourg, 1933). There is a more recent account in J. Chaix-Ruy, *Ernest Renan* (Paris: Emmanuel Vitte, 1956), pp. 89–111. The standard description—done more in terms of Renan's religious vocation—is still valuable also: Pierre Lasserre, *La Jeunesse d'Ernest Renan: Histoire de la crise religieuse au XIX siècle*, in 3 volumes (Paris: Garnier, 1925). In volume 2, pp. 50–166, 265–298 are useful on the relations between philology, philosophy, and science.

29. Renan, "Des Services rendus aux sciences historiques par la philologie," in *OC*, vol. 8, p. 1228.

30. Renan, *Souvenirs*, in *OC*, vol. 2, p. 892.

31. Foucault, *The Order of Things: An Archeology of the Human Sciences*, trans. anonymous (New York: Pantheon Books, 1970), pp. 290–300. Along with the discrediting of the Edenic origins of language, a number of other events—the Deluge, the results of the building of Babel—also were discredited as methods for explaining language. The most comprehensive history of theories of linguistic origin is Arno Borst, *Der Turmbau von Babel: Geschichte der Meinungen uber Ursprung und Vielfalt der Sprachen und Volker*, 6 volumes (Stuttgart: Anton Hiersemann, 1957–1963).

32. Quoted by Raymond Schwab, *La Renaissance orientale* (Paris: Payot, 1950), p. 69. On the dangers of too quickly succumbing to gen-

eralities about Oriental discoveries, see the reflections of the distinguished contemporary Sinologist Abel Remusat, *Mélanges Posthumes d'histoire et littèrature orientales* (Paris: Imprimerie Royale, 1843), p. 226, and *passim*.

33. Franz Bopp, *Vergleichende Grammatik*, 3rd edition (Berlin: Dummler's Verlagsbuchhandlung, 1868), p. iii.

34. Schlegel, *Kritische Friedrich-Schlegel-Ausgabe*, vol. 10, ed. Ernst Behler (Munich: Verlag Ferdinand Schoningh, 1969), pp. 361–2.

35. "De l'étymologie en general," in *Oeuvres de M. Auguste-Guillaume de Schlegel*, vol. 2, ed. Edouard Böcking (Leipzig: Weidmann, 1846), pp. 103–141.

36. Fabre D'Olivet, *La Langue hébraique restituée* (reprinted, Paris: Editions de la Tête de Feuille, 1971), p. xvi.

37. Coleridge, *Biographia Literaria*, Chapter XVI, in *Selected Poetry and Prose of Coleridge*, ed. Donald A. Stauffer (New York: Random House, 1951), pp. 276–7.

38. Humboldt, *Linguistic Variability and Intellectual Development*, trans. George C. Buck and Frithjof A. Raven (Coral Gables: University of Miami Press, 1971), p. 194.

39. Constant, *Oeuvres*, ed, Alfred Roulin (Paris: Gallimard, 1957), p. 78.

40. It is only very recently that the extraordinary value of Schwab's book for cultural study of the nineteenth century has become a bit better known. As an instance of the kind of light Schwab can shed on a major author see Jean Bruneau's *Le "Conte Oriental" de Flaubert* (Paris: Denoel, 1973), which draws heavily on Schwab.

41. M. H. Abrams, *Natural Supernaturalism: Tradition and Revolution in Romantic Literature* (New York: W. W. Norton, 1971), p. 29.

42. Renan, *De l'Origine du langage* in *OC*, vol. 8, p. 122.

43. Renan, "De la part des peuples sémitiques dans l'histoire de la civilisation," in *OC*, vol. 2, p. 320.

44. Ibid., p. 333.

45. Renan, "Trois Professeurs au Collège de France: Etienne Quatremère," in *OC*, vol. 1, p. 129. Renan is not wrong about Quatremère, who had a talent for picking interesting subjects to study, and then making them quite uninteresting. See his essays "Le Gout des livres chez les orientaux" and "Des Sciences chez les arabes," in his *Mélanges d'Histoire et de philologie orientale* (Paris: E. Ducrocq, 1861), pp. 1–57.

46. Balzac, *La Peau de chagrin*, vol. 9 (*Etudes Philosophiques*, I) of *La Comédie humaine*, ed. Marcel Bouteron (Paris: Gallimard, 1950), p. 39.

47. Renan, *Histoire Générale des langues sémitiques, OC*, vol. 8, p. 134.

48. See, for instance, *De l'Origine du langage*, p. 102 and *Histoire Générale*, p. 180, both in *OC*, vol. 8.

49. Renan, *L'Avenir de la science*, p. 23. The whole passage reads as follows: "Pour moi, je ne connais qu'un seul resultat à la science, c'est

de resoudre l'énigme, c'est de dire définitivement à l'homme le mot des choses, c'est de l'expliquer a lui-même, c'est de lui donner, au nom de la seule autorité légitime qui est la nature humaine toute entière, le symbole que les religions lui donnaient tout fait et qu'ils ne peut plus accepter."

50. See Madeleine V.-David, *Le Débat sur les écritures et l'hiéroglyphe aux XVIIe et XVIIIe siècles et l'application de la notion de déchiffrement aux écritures mortes* (Paris: S.E.V.P.E.N., 1965), p. 130.

51. Renan is mentioned only in passing in Schwab's *La Renaissance orientale*, not at all in Foucault's *The Order of Things*, and only somewhat disparagingly in Holger Pedersen's *The Discovery of Language: Linguistic Science in the 19th Century*, trans. John Webster Spargo (1931; repr. Bloomington: Indiana University Press, 1972). Max Muller in his *Lectures on the Science of Language* (reprint ed., New York: Scribner, Armstrong, and Co., 1875) and Gustave Dugat in his *Histoire des orientalistes de l'Europe du XIIe au XIXe siècle*, 2 vols. (Paris: Maisonneuve, 1868–70) do not mention Renan at all. James Darmesteter's *Essaix Orientaux*—whose first item is a history, "L'Orientalisme en France"—(Paris: A. Lévy, 1883) is dedicated to Renan but does not mention his contribution. There are half a dozen short notices of Renan's production in Jules Mohl's encyclopedic (and extremely valuable quasi-logbook) *Etudes Orientales*, 2 vols. (Paris: Reinwald, 1879–80). See also the guarded praise of Renan as Semiticist in William Wright: *Lectures on the Comparative Grammar of the Semitic Languages* (1890; reprinted Amsterdam: Philo Press, 1966), p. 3.

52. In works dealing with race and racism Renan occupies a position of some importance. He is treated in the following: Ernest Seillière, *La Philosophie de l'impérialisme*, 4 vols. (Paris: Plon, 1903–1908); Theophile Simar, *Etude Critique sur la formation de la doctrine des races au XVIIIe siècle et son expansion au XIXe siècle* (Brussels: Hayez, 1922); Erich Voegelin, *Rasse und Staat* (Tubingen: J. C. B. Mohr, 1933), and here one must also mention his *Die Rassenidee in der Geistesgeschichte von Ray bis Carus* (Berlin: Junker und Dunnhaupt, 1933) which, although it does not deal with Renan's period, is an important complement to *Rasse und Staat*; Jacques Barzun, *Race: A Study in Modern Superstition* (New York: Harcourt, Brace, 1937).

53. In *La Renaissance orientale* Schwab has some brilliant pages on the museum, on the parallelism between biology and linguistics, and on Cuvier, Balzac and others: see pp. 323 and *passim*. On the *library* and its importance for mid-nineteenth century culture see Foucault, "La Bibliothèque fantastique" which is his Preface to Flaubert's *La Tentation de Saint Antoine* (Paris: Gallimard, 1971), pp. 7–33. I am indebted to Professor Eugenio Donato for drawing my attention to these matters. See his "A Mere Labyrinth of Letters: Flaubert and the Quest for Fiction," *MLN* 89, 6 (December, 1974): 885–910.

54. Renan, *Histoire Générale*, *OC*, vol. 8, pp. 145–6.

55. See *L'Avenir de la science*, p. 508 and *passim*.

56. Renan, *Histoire Générale*, p. 214.

57. Ibid., p. 527. This idea goes back to Friedrich Schlegel's distinction between organic and agglutinative languages, of which Semitic is an instance. Humboldt makes the same distinction, as have most Orientalists since Renan.

58. Ibid., pp. 531–2.

59. Ibid., p. 515 and *passim*.

60. See Jean Seznec, *Nouvelles Etudes sur La Tentation de Saint Antoine* (London: Warburg Institute, 1949), p. 80.

61. See Etienne Goeffroy Saint-Hilaire, *Philosophie Anatomique: Des Monstruosités humaines* (Paris: published by the author, 1822). His son was Isidore Geoffroy Saint-Hilaire and the complete title of his work, in 3 volumes, is: *Histoire Générale et particulière des anomalies de l'organization chez l'homme et les animaux, ouvrage comprenente des recherches sur les caractères, la classification, l'influence physiologique et pathologique, les rapports généraux, les lois et les causes des monstruosités, des varietés et vices de conformation, ou traité de teratologie* (Paris: J.-B. Baillière, 1832–1836). There are some valuable pages on Goethe's biological ideas in Erich Heller, *The Disinherited Mind* (New York: Meridian Books, 1959), pp. 3–34. See also François Jacob, *La Logique du vivant: une histoire de l'hérédité* (Paris: Gallimard, 1970) and Georges Canguihelm, *La Connaissance de la vie* (Paris: J. Vrin, 1969), pp. 171–184 for very interesting accounts of the Saint-Hilarires' place in the development of the life-sciences.

62. Saint-Hilaire, *Philosophie Anatomique*, pp. xxij–xxiij.

63. Renan, *Histoire Générale*, *OC*, vol. 8, p. 156.

64. See H. W. Wardman, *Ernest Renan: A Critical Biography* (London: Athlone Press, 1964), pp. 66 and *passim*, for a subtle description of Renan's domestic life; although one would not wish to force a parallel between Renan's biography and what I have called his "masculine" world, Wardman's descriptions here are suggestive indeed—at least to me.

65. Renan, *OC*, vol. 1, pp. 621–2 and *passim*.

66. Renan, "Souvenirs d'un vieux professeur allemand," in *OC*, vol. 2, p. 226.

67. Renan, "Des services rendus au sciences historiques par la philologie," *OC*, vol. 8, p. 1228.

68. Ibid., p. 1232.

69. Ernst Cassirer, *The Problem of Knowledge: Philosophy, Science, and History since Hegel*, trans. William H. Woglom and Charles W. Hendel (New Haven: Yale University Press, 1950), p. 307.

70. Renan, "Response au discours de reception de M. de Lesseps (23 Avril 1885)," *OC*, vol. 1, p. 817. Yet the value of being truly con-

temporary was best shown with reference to Renan by Sainte-Beuve in his articles of June 1862. See also D. G. Charlton, *Positivist Thought in France during the Second Empire* (Oxford: Clarendon Press, 1959) and his *Secular Religion in France, 1815–1870* (London: Oxford University Press, 1963). Also Richard M. Chadbourne, "Renan and Sainte-Beuve," *Romantic Review* 44, 2 (April, 1953): 126–135.

EMERSON, CHRISTIAN IDENTITY, AND THE DISSOLUTION OF THE SOCIAL ORDER*

STEPHEN DONADIO

Although it has been cited less frequently and with less nodding assent in recent years than D. H. Lawrence's pronouncement that "the essential American soul is hard, isolate, stoic, and a killer," for generations readers of American literature have been similarly captivated—one might almost say hypnotized—by that passage in Henry James's book on Hawthorne (first published in 1879) in which James catalogues a few of the virtually indispensable elements lacking in the American life of the nineteenth century. "Indeed," James writes, "with a little ingenuity . . . one might enumerate the items of high civilization, as it exists in other countries, which are absent from the texture of American life, until it should become a wonder to know what was left." And mustering the ingenuity required, he begins the famous litany:

> No State, in the European sense of the word, and indeed barely a specific national name. No sovereign, no court, no personal loyalty, no aristocracy, no church, no clergy, no army, no diplo-

* An earlier version of this essay was presented under the title "Emerson and the Christian Imagination" at The English Institute, Harvard University, September 4, 1973.

matic service, no country gentlemen, no palaces, no castles, nor manors, nor old country houses, nor parsonages, nor thatched cottages, nor ivied ruins; no cathedrals, nor abbeys, nor little Norman churches; no great Universities or public schools—no Oxford, nor Eton, nor Harrow; no literature, no novels, no museums, no pictures, no political society, no sporting class—no Epsom nor Ascot! Some such list as that might be drawn up of the absent things in American life—especially in the American life of forty years ago. . . .

As a result of such cultural deprivation, James argues, Hawthorne's artistic development was inevitably arrested in the prenovelistic phase: without entrenched social realities to cut its teeth on, his art eventually languished in the empty American environment.

Interestingly enough, Hawthorne's own view of his predicament was just the reverse. As he makes clear in the "Custom-House" essay, it was not the paucity of materials that frustrated his art, but his own persistent inability to master the abundant (and abundantly complex) materials available to him. "The fault was mine," he tells us: "The page of life that was spread out before me seemed dull and commonplace, only because I had not fathomed its deeper import. A better book than I shall ever write was there; leaf after leaf presenting itself to me, just as it was written out by the reality of the flitting hour, and vanishing as fast as written, only because my brain wanted the insight and my hand the cunning to transcribe it." And far from lamenting the absence of a dense tissue of circumstances and associations, Hawthorne makes it plain that such circumstances crowd his consciousness, and that if anything he finds the weight of his surroundings oppressive. In view of such difficulties, the author of *The Scarlet Letter* confesses that he regards that book (generally held to be the most adequately realized of his longer fictions) as an essentially evasive, weak, and misbegotten effort, the product of an anxious escapist impulse: "I might readily have found a more serious task," he observes. "It was a folly, with the materiality of this daily life pressing so intrusively upon me, to attempt to fling myself back into another age; or to insist on creating the semblance of a world out of airy matter, when, at every moment, the impalpable beauty of my soap-bubble was broken by the rude contact of some actual circumstance."

What Hawthorne is acknowledging here is that the realities actually confronting him are stronger than the works of his imagination. This seems a positively shameless admission for any American writer to make, and it is precisely because such a possibility is unthinkable to James that he fails to credit it in Hawthorne's case. Indeed, the greatest value of James's understanding of Hawthorne lies in what it tells us about the extraordinary degree to which the commanding literary figures who preceded James had succeeded in clearing away all obstacles to their imaginative power, had dispelled all doubts about the authority of the artist. "The literary man in this country has no critic," Emerson wrote in his journal in 1836, and the ambiguity of the declaration barely conceals the sense of power from which it derives. Implicit in James's observations on Hawthorne is the settled conviction that no reality, however intractable, is strong enough to withstand the sustained pressure of the imagination, to resist rendering in form. This was a conviction which he had inherited from a generation of writers—of whom Emerson occupies the central position—whose works actually seemed to stand in the place of history. What James's catalogue finally tells us, then, is just how little weight the existing social arrangements had come to have in the minds of the nation's most sensitive citizens, how little the presence of institutions had come to figure in the formation and validation of identity. For James, preeminently "a citizen of the James family," as his brother said, there seemed to be nothing substantial enough in American society to require serious acknowledgment, much less imaginative allegiance.

Like his Transcendentalist forebears, James has a tendency

to "see through" society, dissolving mundane appearances to reveal the more fundamental spiritual realities which they signify. Hence, it never really mattered where James actually lived: as his secretary perceived, "When he walked out of the refuge of his study into the world and looked about him, he saw a place of torment, where creatures of prey perpetually thrust their claws into the quivering flesh of the doomed, defenceless children of light."[1] It was just such a perception of the world that Hawthorne alternately embraced and distrusted, and that alternation of feeling made it impossible for him to sustain the relation to experience which it implied. Yet he longed to be sure that experience really did reveal the operation of the spirit: and if he had been able to believe that unequivocally—as Emerson could—then he would not have had to turn away from present realities and address them only obliquely, as he found himself doing in *The Scarlet Letter*, but would have been able to make "the wiser effort" which (in his words) "would have been, to diffuse thought and imagination through the opaque substance of to-day, and thus to make it a bright transparency; to spiritualize the burden that began to weigh so heavily. . . ." And elsewhere in his writings he attributes the same failure to realize this "wiser effort" to one of his most reckless and obsessive characters, Aylmer in "The Birthmark": "had [he] reached a profounder wisdom," Hawthorne tells us, "he need not thus have flung away the happiness which would have woven his mortal life of the selfsame texture with the celestial. The momentary circumstance was too strong for him; he failed to look beyond the shadowy scope of time, and, living once for all in eternity, to find the perfect future in the present."

These last words might serve as a perfectly adequate description of the Emersonian relation to experience, but what is equally important in the present context is that they are clearly intended—and clearly serve—as a summary of the proper Christian relation to experience. Yet the logic of Hawthorne's well-known equivocations indicates that for all its appearance of quivering religiosity and piety at times, his work is the product of an essentially secular imagination—an imagination committed to (and perhaps ultimately limited by) the possibilities of self-definition and experience which derive from living in an actual society, in history. If Hawthorne seems fascinated by the Puritans, what captures his imagination most is Puritan society, the idea of a state which could, by fusing political and moral laws, make one's experience whole and not merely facilitate but actually compel a stable sense of identity.

It might be argued, then, that what made it possible for Emerson, in contrast to Hawthorne, to sweep aside the whole fabric of society so effortlessly, as though it were simply an insubstantial veil standing between him and the realm of the absolute, was a deep and undivided commitment to the imperatives of Christian thought. For when Emerson divested himself of his immediate social identity, he did not divest himself of identity entirely: he declared himself Christian Man, and claimed for himself an identity more glorious and absolute than any available in this world. If Emerson stands alone, he stands alone as a Christian secure in his moral obligation to scorn the judgments of this world. Hawthorne, on the other hand, though he too may (in Melville's words) say "No! in thunder" to the society in which he lives and cross "the frontiers into Eternity with nothing but a carpetbag,—that is to say, the Ego," pays dearly for the privilege in scattered imaginative energies and a nagging sense of guilt. When Hawthorne presumably abandons the reality of his surroundings and declares himself "a citizen of somewhere else," he is expressing a deep sense of frustration and dislocation; for Emerson, however, who might have used exactly the same words, such a declaration would have signified something entirely different: it would have served as an utterly blameless definition of the Christian—a potential saint, a transient in this world, a loyal citizen of none but the millennial society.

The sanction for Emerson's rejection of his historical identity, then, is the traditional Christian refusal to live wholly in this world and thus be subject to the melancholy fate of all mortals. Reborn as a child of light, the Christian is secure in the promise of eternal life. And such a rebirth requires an ultimate rejection of all those aspects of the self that locate one in time: it requires the denial of one's earthly father in favor of the eternal Father. This demand is made explicitly by Christ, whom Emerson, a Unitarian in this respect at least, regards as a man who had simply succeeded in grasping a possibility available to every man, that of realizing the divinity in himself. "Call no man your father upon the earth," Christ preached: "for one is your Father, which is in heaven." (Matt. 23:9)

To embrace this form of self-definition requires that one free oneself of the hold of worldly occupations, just as Matthew, called by Christ, rises up and deserts the place where he has been sitting in receipt of custom—that same place, as a Transcendentalist might say, from which Nathaniel Hawthorne was expelled some eighteen hundred years later by a change of national administrations. But Hawthorne, who was hardly unaware of the irony (indeed there were unfortunately few ironies of which he was unaware), could not finally come to believe himself a man on "an apostolic errand": his mission involved recognition of the painful inevitability of institutions, and it is worth remembering that he, a locofoco rather than a cosmic democrat, was the only major New England writer who attempted to live in the at least marginally worldly community at Brook Farm. Emerson, in contrast, at least the early Emerson, with whom we are most concerned, is insistent on the necessity for rejecting all available earthly occupations, including those which are usually identified as involving highly idealistic motives. Hence his decision to step down from the pulpit, in a sense in response to Christ's command in Matthew: "Be ye not called rabbi."

Consequently, invited to explain the "new views" abroad in New England to a Boston audience seeking enlightenment, "it is a sign of our times," Emerson observes, making his own relation to his audience clear by alluding to the reply made by Christ to the hypocrite Pharisees who came to him demanding that he show them a sign from heaven:

> It is a sign of our times, conspicuous to the coarsest observer, that many intelligent and religious persons withdraw themselves from the common labors and competitions of the market and the caucus, and betake themselves to a certain solitary and critical way of living, from which no solid fruit has yet appeared to justify their separation. They hold themselves aloof: they feel the disproportion between their faculties and the work offered them, and they prefer to ramble in the country and perish of ennui to the degradation of such charities and such ambitions as the city can propose to them. They are striking work, and crying out for somewhat worthy to do![2]

The unspoken question that Emerson is answering of course is "What do these people do for a living?" In fact, he had to admit, no earthly occupation could be found to correspond to the Transcendentalists' sense of their own finest possibilities. "Nay, they have made the experiment," Emerson says, "and found that from the liberal professions to the coarsest manual labor, and from the courtesies of the academy and the college to the conventions of the cotillion-room and the morning call, there is a spirit of cowardly compromise and seeming which intimates a frightful skepticism, a life without love, and an activity without aim." Even the noblest and most philanthropic callings are scorned as mere shrunken forms empty of spirit. "What you call your fundamental institutions, your great and lofty causes," Emerson declares, "seem to [the Transcendental-ist] great abuses, and, when nearly seen, paltry matters. . . .

Each 'cause' . . . becomes speedily a little shop . . . and the philanthropies and charities have a certain air of quackery."

But if the whole range of available employments is regarded as unworthy, then what, his audience might have continued to wonder, are these "exacting children" (in Emerson's phrase) to do?

The function of the Transcendentalist in the economy of Massachusetts is to stand in a self-sufficient antithetical relation to it. (Hence Thoreau's punning application of the terms of worldly commerce to the economy of the self, his insistence on being "self-employed," the editor of his own journal, etc.) The role of such persons is to deny the claims of society in the name of the perfected self, just as the role of Christ is to deny forever the claims of all earthly states in the name of the kingdom of heaven. And it is, as Emerson suggests, in the spirit of Christ, the most exacting of perfectionists, that the Transcendentalists deny the world as given, attempting to eradicate all traces of it in themselves. Accordingly, though "they are not good citizens, not good members of society," the value of such otherworldly creatures must be recognized:

> Society also has its duties in reference to this class, and must behold them with what charity it can. Possibly some benefit may yet accrue from them to the state. In our Mechanics' Fair, there must be not only bridges, ploughs, carpenters' planes, and baking troughs, but also some few finer instruments—rain-gauges, thermometers, and telescopes; and in society, besides farmers, sailors, and weavers, there must be a few persons of purer fire kept specially as gauges and meters of character; persons of a fine, detecting instinct, who note the smallest accumulations of wit and feeling in the bystander. Perhaps too there might be room for the exciters and monitors; collectors of the heavenly spark, with power to convey the electricity to others. Or, as the storm-tossed vessel at sea speaks the frigate or "line packet" to learn its longitude, so it may not be without its advantage that we should now and then encounter rare and gifted men, to compare the points of our spiritual compass, and verify our bearings from superior chronometers.

To my knowledge the connection has never been made, but this passage is very likely the basis for the remarkable "Chronometricals and Horologicals" passage (the pamphlet by "Plotinus Plinlimmon") in Melville's *Pierre*—and it might conceivably have served as the chief inspiration for the novel as a whole. I cannot here consider the implications of this connection,* except to say that the depiction of Emerson as Plinlimmon, brilliant author of a pamphlet which represents only the first of three hundred thirty-three projected lectures, the surviving fragment of which closes with the words "Moreover; if—" ("a most untidy termination," as Melville observes), reveals the rough outline of one of Melville's finest and most satisfying philosophical jokes.

These chronometrical souls, then, serve to give the lie to the ordinary logic of this world, and to suggest the possibility of at least an intermittent commerce with what Thoreau refers to in *Walden* as the "celestial empire" (though readers inclined to find such formulations suggestive may be surprised to discover that in the Norton edition this phrase is identified as simply "a common mid-nineteenth century name for China"). And even though those of whom Emerson speaks are, as he says, not "proficients" but "novices," for "of a purely spiritual life, history has afforded no example," yet they must be recognized as "prophets and heralds" of the Transcendental state, the state of unending miracle. Like saints, the Transcendentalists show us the way out of the world, "the road in which man should travel [in Emerson's words] when the soul has greater health and prowess."

But however much these novices strive to deny "everything around them," Emerson says, "it takes all their strength to deny, before they can begin to lead their own life." And in the early years he himself acknowledges his wavering faith in the assurance that the things of this world have no reality in

---

* I am, however, in the process of doing so elsewhere, in an essay concerned with Melville's critique of Transcendentalism in general and Emerson in particular.

themselves but merely hint darkly at the joys of eternity. "I believe the Christian religion to be profoundly true," he writes in his journal at the end of 1834: "true to an extent that they who are styled its most orthodox defenders have never, or but in rarest glimpses, once or twice in a lifetime, reached." And still, he confesses, "I . . . do yet catch myself continually in a practical unbelief of its deepest teachings":

> It taught, it teaches he continues the eternal opposition of the world to the truth, and introduced the absolute authority of the spiritual law. Milton apprehended its nature when he said [the quotation is from the *Reason of Church Government*], "For who is there almost who measures wisdom by simplicity, strength by suffering, dignity by lowliness?" That do I in my sane moments, and feel the ineffable peace, yea and the influx of God, that attend humility and love,—and before the cock crows, I deny him thrice.[3]

In those "sane moments" of "ineffable peace," Emerson is delivered out of his experience by a perception of that experience as nothing more than a shadowy evocation of the life to come: at such moments the future is experienced as vividly present, the present as vague and insubstantial. And witnessed as if in retrospect from the perspective afforded the faithful by the promise of salvation at the end of time, the sufferings of the present become instances of dramatic irony.

Hence what enabled Emerson to overcome the suffering associated with his actual experience was his ability to see that experience as essentially symbolic—and more precisely as Christian experience, which inevitably had a comic shape. The general principle governing this perception was that of compensation, which guaranteed that all earthly losses would be made up in heaven. "The whole of what we know is a system of compensations," he observed in his journal when he was twenty-two: "Every defect in one manner is made up in another. Every suffering is rewarded; every sacrifice is made up; every debt is paid."⁴ And five years later he reasserted his conviction that "I have nothing charactered in my brain that outlives this word Compensation."⁵

The principle is rooted in the structure of Christian paradox, which manifests itself in many of the utterances found in Matthew and John particularly, the two gospels to which Emerson devoted his most intense study when his failing eyesight made it difficult for him to pursue his formal studies with any great regularity. The Beatitudes enumerated by Christ in the Sermon on the Mount are clearly to the point here (*Matthew*, 5: "Blessed are the poor in spirit, for theirs is the kingdom of heaven"; "Blessed are they that mourn, for they shall be comforted"; "Blessed are the meek, for they shall inherit the earth," and so on), as well as such assertions as "the last shall be first and the first last" (*Matt.* 20:16) and "whosoever will save his life shall lose it: and whosoever will lose his life for my sake shall find it." (*Matt.* 10:39; *Luke* 17:13)

Similarly, in John, at just that point when Christ says, "Father, the hour is come; glorify thy Son" (*John* 17:1), he goes forth to be betrayed, humiliated, and finally crucified—indicating the central paradox that suffering and humiliation are the form which the glorification of the Son of God takes in this world. Precisely the same kind of paradox, in which the earthly and the heavenly condition are juxtaposed and contrasted, is affirmed in Matthew when Christ exhorts his followers to "rejoice, and be exceeding glad: for great is your reward in heaven: for so persecuted they the prophets which were before you." (5:12)

Needless to say, faith in such a principle of just compensation in the next world for all the losses one has suffered in this hardly implies a shallow denial of human suffering: on the contrary, its chief function is to make just such suffering endurable, and the more keenly felt the pain, the more intense will be the affirmation of its ultimate value as joy. Thus, despite the numerous complaints about Emerson's notorious neglect of the problem of evil and his presumably ill-advised cosmic optimism, no reader of the more private and unguarded writings (the journals and early sermons especially) can fail to recognize how much the energy of his affirmations is a function of his potential for despair.

"We are no longer naïve enough to believe that anybody is an optimist by choice," Quentin Anderson points out, "but we have somewhat played down what was apparently compelling for Emerson."[6] And Professor Anderson goes on to remind us of the mounting death toll into which Emerson's domestic life seemed to resolve itself relentlessly until he was almost forty, noting that the effect of such losses can hardly be discounted "by reference to the high mortality rates of the period."[7] The emotional basis for Emerson's faith in divine compensation emerges clearly enough in the sermon which he preached less than two weeks after the death of his first wife, Ellen, with whom he was very deeply in love. "In the wreck of earthly good," he told his congregation, "the goods of the soul show a lustre and permanence divine. Blessed be God that there are these consolations. . . . Blessed be his name, that he has provided every soul among us in the truth of the New Testament with the means of depriving death of its sting."[8]

But no one was more aware than Emerson of the painful disjunction between future joy and present grief. Two months after the death of his son Waldo, he wrote: "I am *Defeated* all the time; yet to Victory I am born."[9] But that his bereavement remained an enduring part of his emotional life can hardly be doubted: a day before his own death forty years later Emerson was heard to exclaim, "Oh that beautiful boy," apparently referring to his lost firstborn son.[10]

Nevertheless, by 1870 Carlyle could attack the author of *Society and Solitude* as a man who no longer seemed to take adequate account of the facts of experience, those innumerable obstacles which cast doubt on the ultimate triumph of the spirit. "How you go," he wrote, "as if altog^r on the 'Over-Soul,' the Ideal, the Perfect or Universal & Eternal in this Life of ours; and take so little heed of the frightful quantities of *friction* and perverse *impediment* there everywhere are; the reflections upon wh^h in my own poor life made me now & then very sad, as I read you."[11] But Carlyle was addressing himself to a man who had finally succeeded in losing his place in time, who was beginning to have difficulty keeping the elements of past, present, and future in his experience distinct. "Memory went first," his daughter noted in 1872.[12] And this condition seemed to worsen after a fire destroyed a substantial portion of his house in the same year. According to his biographer, when, awakened by the low sound of the flames, he called to Lidian in the night, "she was so much alarmed by his voice that she was relieved to find that it was only the house on fire."[13] In his journal entry Emerson required only three words to record the event: "Our house burned"; and one cannot help remembering the text which he had taken from II Corinthians for the sermon he had preached after the death of his first wife thirty years before: "For we know that if our earthly house of this tabernacle were dissolved, we have a building of God, an house not made with hands, eternal in the heavens." (II *Cor.* V:1)

In any case, after the fire, according to his daughter, he was really no longer capable of putting his manuscripts in order without help.[14] Words failed him; and as his biographer points out, it was only a matter of time before Emerson, attempting to describe the capitol in Washington, would only be able to say of it: "United States—survey of the beauty of eternal government."[15] Henceforth his mind was somewhere else.

I have been maintaining that the chief tendency of Emerson's thought is to translate all experience into Christian experience, and therefore to perceive it, whatever its immediate appearance, as a dark hint of the joys of eternity. At this point I should like to consider a few of the ways in which this tendency manifests itself in the working of his imagination, and to explore some of its stylistic implications.

In one of the early journals—which are remarkable for the degree of harsh self-criticism and the sense of desolation which they reveal—there is a passage in which the author observes of himself: "In my frequent humiliation, even before women and children, I am compelled to remember the poor boy who cried, 'I told you, Father, they would find me out.'"[16] This observation, which occurs in a long passage of self-scrutiny in which Emerson catalogues what he regards as his numerous deficiencies, reflects a feeling which has not yet been understood in Christian terms, generalized and seen as a sign of the condition of all men. ("To believe your own thought, to believe that what is true for you in your private heart is true for all men—that is genius," he declared in "Self-Reliance"; but he was apparently unable to achieve this state until he had come to perceive the extraordinary power of generalization afforded by the framework of Christian doctrine.) And the antithetical form which such a melancholy feeling as Emerson is describing would assume when located in the framework of Christian doctrine is suggested by the Transfiguration, that scene in which Jesus is clothed with glory by his heavenly Father, who speaks out of a cloud, saying, "This is my beloved Son, in whom I am well pleased; hear ye him." Hence it is hardly surprising that Emerson should have judged Raphael's depiction of that scene "the world's foremost picture."[17]

Orphaned at the age of eight, Emerson came to recognize that he had a father in heaven. Since in his view the example of Christ was literally applicable to all men, he could rest secure in the assurance that he was the son of God. And the son of God in this world is God Himself in the next: a God defined as that eternal reality of spirit in which all personal earthly identity is dissolved. Thus, there were moments when Emerson, reaching through the temporal particulars of his experience, was able to feel not simply that he had "become part or parcel of God"—as he did in a nature emptied of other people—but that he was actually on the verge of becoming God. Only time separated him from that ultimate identity, and all his instincts sought to deny the separation. "It is wrong to regard ourselves so much in a *historical* light as we do, putting Time between God & us," he wrote when he was twenty-three. And at times the possibility of divinity seemed so real he could feel as though it had been all but accomplished. "I grow in God. I am only a form of him. He is the soul of me," he reflected in his journal. "I can even with a mountainous aspiring say, *I am God. . . .*" But such feelings—which might have come to trouble those around him if they persisted—could not be sustained. "A believer in Unity, a seer of Unity," he confessed, "I yet behold two."[18]

Emerson's tendency to convert the particulars of his experience into Christian generalizations enables him to effect an emotional reversal in which the generalization takes on great immediacy, while the particular becomes more remote and dim, receding into the background of experience. This tendency dates from Emerson's early youth, and it helps to explain how he was able to overcome some of the feelings alluded to when (at twenty-two) he remarked: "'My recollections of early life are not very pleasant."[19] In his forties Emerson could still vividly recall episodes which had taken place when, at the age of six, he had been given salt baths as a cure for "some eruptive disease." And it was not simply the fear of deep water that returned to his consciousness when he remembered how his father had "twice or thrice put me in mortal terror by forcing me into the salt water off some wharf or bathing house," and "the fright with which, after some of this salt experience, I heard his voice one day, (as Adam that of the Lord God in the garden,) summoning us to a new bath, and I vainly endeavoring to hide myself."[20] The complexity of the psychic transformation of experience revealed here seems evident enough; but leaving aside the crosscurrents of feeling, what I wish to indicate is simply how what begins as an intensely particular experience emerges as an emblem of man's condition after the fall: how a specific act of disobedience becomes, in Emerson's imagination, "Man's first disobedience."

And what Emerson was able to do with his own experience, he was, to judge from his following, also able to do with that of his contemporaries. In his work, the world in which his audience lived, the very texture of their experience, fell away, and in its place stood its glorious celestial counterpart. In Quentin Anderson's compelling formulation, Emerson "became the divine child who eats up the world and then, godlike, restores it as the Word."[21] In this way the world was rendered sacred: all experience became religious experience—the religious experience of a Christian who was Puritan in his inclination to read the world like a text in which signs of the operation of God's providence could be detected, but Unitarian in his conviction that men were not simply innately good but as inherently divine as Christ himself.

It is this aspect of Emerson that Henry James had in mind when he noted that "there is even yet a sort of drollery in the spectacle of a body of people among whom the author of *The American Scholar* and of the Address of 1838 at the Harvard Divinity College passed for profane. . . . They were shocked at his ceasing to care for the prayer and the sermon. They might have perceived that he *was* the prayer and the sermon: not in the least a secularizer, but in his own subtle insinuating way a sanctifier."[22] Indeed, when he relinquished his pulpit, far from surrendering his pastoral role Emerson felt that he had come into more complete possession of it. Six months before the break he noted in his journal: "I have sometimes thought that, in order to be a good minister, it was necessary to leave the ministry"[23]—a fine instance of Christian paradox, which requires that a man give up his life in order to find it. Hence, following the example of Christ meant becoming a solitary wanderer—a spiritual leader who derived none of his authority from existing forms and institutions, and whose congregation was the world. (It is worth remembering, I think, that during his lifetime Emerson made at least fifteen hundred recorded appearances in the United States alone.)

And what Emerson provided for his audience was an experience of revelation: that is the effect toward which every element of his style strives. The utterance is discontinuous: it crystallizes suddenly in flashes of intuition. Statements are not arranged in the form of an orderly progression through time, but according to some other logic only intermittently revealed, in sequences of short duration. The reader is consequently left with the sense of a world of meaning communicated only in fragments: he is haunted by a vision of wholeness which seems to be withdrawn almost as soon as it is offered.

These formal aspects of Emerson's writing correspond to its theological preoccupations: they are the stylistic embodiment of religious ideas. The fragmentary utterance, for instance, may be seen as a reflection of Emerson's conviction that no complete experience is possible in this world, since the ultimate meaning of Christian experience is revealed only at the end of time. Hence the style must woo the listener away from the false sense of coherence and sufficiency which characterizes his everyday reflections on his experience, enticing him with glimpses of a more mysterious and splendid possibility. But they must remain only glimpses: the completed form of human divinity must remain unspecified and undisclosed, dimly present but still unattainable. For if it were to emerge wholly, this would signify the destruction of time: in Melville's terms, chronometricals and horologicals would correspond, and that could only mean either that the celestial watch was wrong, or that the millennium had arrived.

The apparent awkwardness and inconsistency of Emerson's diction has, I think, a similar theological basis, this one related to the traditional Christian reversal of the levels of classical rhetoric. As Erich Auerbach has explained, the example of Christ's humility made it necessary for early Christian writers (Augustine in particular) to reinterpret such demands as that made by Cicero in the *Orator*: "He therefore will be eloquent who can speak of small things in a simple manner, of middling things in the intermediate style, and of great things in the grand manner."[24] A problem arose for the Christian attempting to abide by such rhetorical rules, because what was for him the greatest and most sublime of subjects—God Himself—had chosen to enter history in the humblest of human forms. And as Auerbach points out, "the humility of the Incarnation derives its full force from the contrast with Christ's divine nature: man and god, lowly and sublime. . . ."[25] Just this sort of Christian irony is at the heart of Emerson's style, which seeks to suggest how divinity is veiled in the homeliest appearances by combining regional wisecracks with the most abstruse formulations, the most commonplace with the most exalted rhetoric. (What he most admired about Raphael's "Transfiguration," after all, was the depiction of the face of Christ, "this familiar, simple, home-speaking countenance.") Francis Bowen, for many years one of Emerson's most exacting Unitarian critics, reveals himself to be out of touch with the spirit of such irony when he complains (in his review of *Nature*) that "the writer aims at simplicity and directness, as the ancient philosopher aimed at humility, and showed his pride through the tatters of his cloak."[26]

I have been arguing that the central impulse governing Emerson's work is the impulse to convert actual particulars into Christian generalizations—to treat immediate concerns as though they were ultimate concerns. That a similar impulse manifests itself on a national scale in the decades preceding the Civil War has been suggested with increasing force by the work of numerous American historians in our own time. Indeed, as the very important work done in the past ten or fifteen years by Stanley Elkins, John L. Thomas, David Brion Davis, and George Frederickson has shown,[27] the history of the slavery issue, the most burning issue of the first two-thirds of the nineteenth century in America, presents a vivid demonstration of how a troubling political problem could be transformed into a question of sin. As a consequence of this imaginative transformation, the question of how to dismantle a peculiar institution became a question of what form of atonement would be adequate for such a monstrous affront against God.

How this state of affairs came about has been well documented by the scholars I have named, and there is no need to rehearse the details here. But the general pattern is very much a part of our subject. Exploring the cultural origins of the question, David Brion Davis has argued that inasmuch "as early Christians repeatedly conceived of sin and salvation in terms of slavery and freedom, the words acquired complex layers of meaning that necessarily affected men's response to the institution of slavery."[28] Consequently, he concludes, in the nineteenth century in America "the significant point . . . is that attitudes toward slavery were interwoven with central religious concepts."[29] As anyone familiar with the rhetoric of abolitionism knows, Davis is putting things mildly.

And John L. Thomas, tracing the peculiar logic of American reform in the nineteenth century, has shown how what began as an essentially conservative response on the part of American churchmen to maintain control over those forces which eventually produced the election of Andrew Jackson, itself became caught up in those forces and ultimately issued in the perfectionism associated with John Humphrey Noyes and others who took as their text Christ's exhortation in Matthew: "Be ye therefore perfect, even as your Father in heaven is perfect." (5:48) This drive came to dominate all aspects of reform thought, and it eventually forced the abolition issue to the center of the nation's consciousness. The "abolitionist pioneers," as Professor Thomas reminds us, "were former colonizationists who took sin and redemption seriously and insisted that slavery constituted a flat denial of perfectibility to both Negroes and whites." For them, "destroying slavery . . . depended first of all on recognizing it as sin; and to this recognition they bent their efforts."[30]

In this way the Union as it stood came to be regarded as all but the construction of the devil: the Union had to be destroyed in order to be saved, had to be lost so that a more perfect Union could be found. As Samuel Gridley Howe observed in 1860—and his language is significant—". . . there is the prospect that with so many sparks flying about in the powder magazine there may be a blow up. Well—the Lord will save the pieces, and we'll have a Northern Union worth saving."[31] And Emerson expressed a similar sentiment, though with much greater theological cunning, when he blandly observed of the fanatical John Brown that "he believes in the Union of the States, and he conceives that the only obstruction to the Union is Slavery, and for that reason, as a patriot, he works for its abolition."

Both Emerson and Thoreau regarded Brown as a kind of martyred Puritan saint; indeed, after Brown's capture Emerson is reported to have referred to him in a lecture as "the Saint, whose fate yet hangs in suspense, but whose martyrdom, if it shall be perfected, will make the gallows as glorious as the cross" (to which Hawthorne predictably responded, "Nobody was ever more justly hanged").[32] And indeed, Brown's actions might have seemed to Emerson the very embodiment of a principle he had set down less than twenty years before when he observed of "The Transcendentalist": "From this transfer of the world into the consciousness, this beholding of all things in the mind, follow easily his whole ethics. It is simpler to be self-dependent."

Equally to the point is a statement made by Emerson in an address on behalf of Brown before his execution. "He believes in two articles—two instruments, shall I say?—the Golden

Rule and the Declaration of Independence; and he used this expression in conversation here concerning them, 'Better that a whole generation of men, women and children should pass away by a violent death than that one word of either should be violated in this country.' There is a Unionist," Emerson concludes, "there is a strict constructionist for you."[33]

Emerson's endorsement of Brown's astonishing and conceivably insane pronouncement would seem to corroborate Joel Porte's observation, made in response to the gnashing of Yvor Winters's teeth, that notwithstanding "Winters's denunciation of Emerson as a 'moral relativist' . . . the careful student of Emerson's writings finds that the opposite is true: Emerson is much closer to being an absolutist in morals."[34] Moreover, as his biographer points out, Emerson reasserted the view expressed by Brown even after the years of bloodletting: claiming that war was "a marked benefactor in the hands of providence," he expressed his gratitude in a commemorative address to all those who had fought for "a new era, worth to mankind all the treasure and all the lives it has cost; yes, worth to the world the lives of all this generation of American men, if they had been demanded."[35]

Though Emerson leaves the women and children out of his formulation, the apparent callousness of his remarks remains incomprehensible, until one realizes that the lives Emerson is speaking of were, to him, essentially symbolic expenditures required to advance the progress of the spirit and fulfill God's providence: in short, these lost legions were to be conceived in roughly the same terms as the nameless inhabitants of the earth in the time of the flood, who perished when the whole earth was uncreated and restored in the image of justice.

To the extent that the slavery issue was a symbolic issue, it revealed a demand to be free not only of the limitations of a particular society regarded as unjust, but of the condition of sin itself, of all human imperfection. The merged political and religious rhetoric of the period offered the assurance that each individual, acting on his own, could achieve such a state of perfection. And the ultimate character of such expectations was revealed unequivocally by Whitman when, in lecture notes he made during the 1850s, he asserted that his "final aim" was "to concentrate around me the leaders of all reforms—transcendentalists, spiritualists, free soilers—We want no *reforms*, no *institutions*, no *parties*—We want a living principle as nature has, under which nothing can go wrong."[36] Society, in short, would vanish: the dead forms and institutions of this world would fall away, and each man would find himself standing perfectly alone in nature.

This brings us back at last to Henry James's account of the emptiness of America, a country in which, at least in the imagination, contact could be made with the state of perfection beyond society, beyond the conditions of history, beyond time. For if Americans were asked to become a nation of saints —persons, in William James's revealing definition, "entirely adapted" to a "millennial society"—then how could their imaginative allegiance be given to any state but that of perfection? "Where your treasure is, there will your heart be also," Christ says in Matthew: "No man can serve two masters. . . ."

Thus, James's catalogue of absences assumes another aspect in the light of such observations as that made by Melville on a trip to the Holy Land in 1856. Overwhelmed by the barrenness of the place, he asked himself: "Is the desolation of the land the result of the fatal embrace of the Deity? Hapless are the favorites of heaven."[37] The promise of the celestial kingdom, in other words, renders desolate the kingdoms of this earth.

"Moreover; if—" as Emerson suggests, men can at times reach beyond their temporal condition and achieve a sense of the celestial kingdom by standing alone in nature—a nature conceived as the antithesis of society—it is significant that this experience of perfection itself involves (as it does in Whitman as well) a form of self-extinction, the final obliteration of personal identity. For the injunction to be perfect requires the destruction and recreation of the self in the image of perfection itself—that is, God's will. At its most absolute, the Christian imperative demands a process of self-conquest in which the actual is ceaselessly transformed into the ideal, and humanity continually strives to attain the condition of divinity, pure disembodied spirit. The grim logic of this drive is, I think, best described by Nietzsche, who was as much its victim as its judge, when he remarks in *Zarathustra*; "The lust to rule: the terrible teacher of the great contempt, who preaches 'away with you' to the very faces of cities and empires, until it finally cries out of them themselves, 'Away with *me!*' "[38]

NOTES

1. Theodora Bosanquet, *Henry James at Work*, The Hogarth Essays, London, 1924 [?], p. 275.
2. This quotation and those that follow are from the lecture entitled "The Transcendentalist," which Emerson first delivered in Boston in the winter of 1841–42.
3. Journal entry for December 27, 1834, *The Journals of Ralph Waldo Emerson*, 10 vols., ed. E. W. Emerson and W. E. Forbes, Boston and New York, 1909–1914 (hereafter cited as "Journals"), III, pp. 415–416.
4. Journal entry (undated) for 1826, *Journals*, II, p. 72.
5. Journal entry for June 29, *Journals*, II, p. 389.
6. Quentin Anderson, *The Imperial Self: An Essay in American Literary and Cultural History*, New York, 1971, p. 51.
7. Ibid., pp. 51–52.
8. "Consolation for the Mourner," in Arthur C. McGiffert, ed., *Young Emerson Speaks*, Port Washington, N.Y., 1968 [1938], p. 144.
9. Journal entry for April 6, 1842, Bliss Perry, ed., *The Heart of Emerson's Journals*, Boston and New York, 1926, p. 178.
10. Quoted in Ralph L. Rusk, *The Life of Ralph Waldo Emerson*, New York, 1949, p. 508.
11. Letter from Carlyle to Emerson, April 6, 1870, in Joseph Slater,

ed., *The Correspondence of Emerson and Carlyle*, New York and London, 1964, p. 567.

12. Quoted in Rusk, *op. cit.*, p. 455.

13. Ibid., p. 453.

14. Ibid., p. 456.

15. Ibid., p. 491.

16. Journal entry for April 18, 1824, *Journals*, I, p. 365.

17. Rusk, *op. cit.*, p. 178.

18. Quoted in Rusk, *op. cit.*, pp. 118 and 261.

19. Journal entry for March 27, 1826, *Journals*, II, p. 86.

20. Rusk, *op. cit.*, p. 23.

21. Quentin Anderson, *op. cit.*, p. 14. Consider, in relation to this account, Emerson's observation that "The sky is the daily bread of the eyes" (*The Journals of Ralph Waldo Emerson*, Boston, 1909–1914, VI, p. 410, quoted in Alfred Kazin and Daniel Aaron, eds., *Emerson: A Modern Anthology*, New York, 1958, p. 39), and another passage from the *Journals*: "I dreamed that I floated at will in the great Ether, and I saw this world floating also not far off, but diminished to the size of an apple. Then an angel took it in his hand and brought it to me and said, 'This must thou eat.' And I ate the world." (*Journals*, V, p. 485, quoted in Kazin and Aaron, *op. cit.*, p. 21.)

22. James's essay was first published in *Macmillan's Magazine* at the end of 1887, and was included in *Partial Portraits*, which appeared the following year.

23. Journal entry for June 2, 1832, *Journals*, II, p. 491.

24. Erich Auerbach, *Literary language and its public in late Latin antiquity and in the Middle Ages*, New York, 1965, p. 35.

25. Ibid., p. 4.

26. Francis Bowen's review of *Nature* (which first appeared in two parts, in the January and November issues of *The Christian Examiner* for 1837), in Milton R. Konvitz, ed., *The Recognition of Ralph Waldo Emerson*, Ann Arbor, Mich., 1972, p. 3.

27. See, for instance, Stanley M. Elkins, *Slavery, A Problem in American Institutional and Intellectual Life*, Chicago, 1959; John L. Thomas, *The Liberator: William Lloyd Garrison*, Boston, 1963, and "Romantic Reform in America, 1815–1865," *American Quarterly*, XVII (1965), 656–681; David Brion Davis, *The Problem of Slavery in Western Culture*, Ithaca, New York, 1966, and "Slavery and Sin: The Cultural Background," in Martin Duberman, ed., *The Antislavery Vanguard: New Essays on the Abolitionists*, Princeton, New Jersey, 1965, pp. 3–31; George M. Fredrickson, *The Inner Civil War: Northern Intellectuals and the Crisis of the Union*, New York, 1965.

28. David Brion Davis, "Slavery and Sin: The Cultural Background," in Martin Duberman, ed., *op. cit.*, p. 25.

29. Ibid., p. 30.

30. John L. Thomas, "Romantic Reform in America, 1815–1865," *American Quarterly*, XVII (1965), p. 661.

31. Quoted in George M. Fredrickson, *op. cit.*, pp. 48–49.

32. Both remarks are from a *New-York Daily Tribune* account in Rusk, *op. cit.*, p. 402.

33. These remarks appear in the published text of the speech Emerson gave on behalf of Brown in Boston on November 18, 1859.

34. Joel Porte, *Emerson and Thoreau: Transcendentalists in Conflict*, Middletown, Connecticut, p. 77.

35. Quoted in Rusk, *op. cit.*, p. 429.

36. Quoted in Fredrickson, *op. cit.*, p. 21.

37. Herman Melville, *Journal of a visit to Europe and the Levant, October 11, 1856–May 6, 1857*, ed., Howard C. Horsford, Princeton, N.J., 1955, p. 154.

38. *Thus Spoke Zarathustra*, Part III, in Walter Kaufmann, ed. and trans., *The Viking Portable Nietzsche*, New York, 1968, p. 301.

THE BURDEN OF SUCCESS:
REFLECTIONS ON GERMAN JEWRY

F R I T Z   S T E R N

Memories fade—and the health of nations as of individuals depends on some measure of release from the wounds of the past. But memories not only fade; they are rearranged as well, in accordance with some perceived need of the present. Historians abet—and sometimes correct—this rearrangement of the past so that a society can find a tolerable or livable past for itself, for "try as we may, we cannot, as we write history, escape our purposiveness."[1]

Our recollection of the holocaust is an example of this double process: for many, the memory has become a dim one and reminders are likely to stir embarrassment or resentment. The memory of the holocaust has also become assimilated to our present needs and predicaments. For a shrinking number who witnessed the first moment of horror helplessly from afar, the extermination of a people will remain engraven in their minds. But even their immediate response was designed to salvage something of the collective self-respect of humanity, and many Westerners, face to face with the horror of the holocaust, believed at first that somehow the perpetrators of this most calculated and perhaps most heinous of all crimes in Europe's history, the Germans, were uniquely evil—with the implicit belief that our civilization was largely exculpated and that such terror, foreign to our collective nature or experience, would not be visited upon the world again. This—here rendered most inadequately—was a not uncommon moral response of the late 1940s; it was also a professional response. Historians re-interpreted German history, often very fruitfully, in the light of the intervening disaster. The perspective of 1945 became a valuable hermeneutical instrument.

The judgment of the holocaust as a uniquely German crime has begun to fade from our consciousness and our professional concerns. In the rearrangement of our collective memory, the gap between perpetrators, bystanders, and victims has been allowed to narrow. We have had to distance ourselves from the once comforting view that only Germans or National Socialists could have committed so terrible a crime in so meticulous a fashion; we have come to understand the many acts of com-pliance, collusion, or willful passivity on the part of so many others, inside Europe and even outside, that had made the "final solution" feasible. But there is more to our rearranging of the past than that, more too than the realization that Soviet terror had claimed even more lives than had the Nazis. In our present mood of willful self-denigration, we have come to assimilate the crimes of the past still further by linking them to our own; the gas chambers and the massacre of My Lai are somehow deemed comparable, and the very term holocaust is often heedlessly invoked. All of this is morally problematical; to exaggerate guilt is no better than to repress or deny it. To understand the process of fashioning memories of the holocaust is more than an historical exercise; it might well reveal that the historical fact of the extermination of six million Jews, how-ever interpreted in the intervening thirty years, may have wrought more of an injury to our self-confidence, so often and in so many ways assaulted in the last century, than is realized.

In this rearranging of our collective memory, there has also been a reappraisal of German Jewry, of the earliest victims of National Socialist persecution. Gradually a negative judgment has sprung up, based on some ill-considered generalities and useful perhaps to present political or psychological interests, but neither reflective of the complexity of the issue nor without its own polemical design. I refer here to what an eminent scholar has recently called the " 'bad press' that German Jewry has had in recent literature."[2] It has become a common view to hold that German Jewry somehow represents the epitome of craven assimilation and submission; implicit in this view is that the fate of German Jewry and its character were somehow linked, and that character was therefore historically culpable.

Historians are only now beginning to study the German-Jewish community in depth and with some perspective.[3] I mean to limit myself to the setting out of what I consider to be the principal themes. If this essay suggests something of the complexity of the subject and thus cautions against facile generalities or dangerous analogies, it will serve some purpose. German Jewry has become a category of disapprobation; as such, it may neither do justice to the past nor serve as a correct guide to the future.

This essay is based on two assumptions: that the whole course of German history should no longer be seen principally from the perspective of 1945, that is to say, not from the disaster backward, with the inevitable consequence that the strands preparing the disaster are given particular attention and the others slighted, but from a particular past, with all its un-certainties, aspirations, and illusions, forward. The second as-sumption is that in such a new perspective on German history, the role of the Jewish community within Germany should be analyzed, freed from the many taboos that have always clung to the subject, because that role was a signal element in the history of modern Germany.

We must see the history of the German Jews as a special current, itself made up of many rivulets, within the broader German stream. It is a difficult subject for study because the formal integration of Jews into German life was something that German Jews desired; hence so much of what would be considered the essence of German-Jewish life remained unspoken, unacknowledged, and the study of it now is overladen with feelings of guilt and unease. And still one must try to recover something of the cast of mind and feelings of this community, for it illuminates the social history of modern consciousness.

For decades, most studies of German Jewry circled around the themes of "Jewish contributions" and of the unrequited love that Jews had for Germans. It was easy to fit the German experience into what has been called the lachrymose tradition in Jewish historiography, dwelling as it did on the sufferings of the Jews. (Sir Isaiah Berlin recalls an incident that epitomizes this tradition. He relates that "the late Sir Lewis Namier once reported that, upon being asked by a splendid British peer why he, a Jew, devoted himself to writing English history, and not Jewish history, he replied: 'Derby! There *is* no modern Jewish history, there is only Jewish martyrology, and that is not amusing enough for me.' ") But the history of German Jewry which ends in martyrology began in greatness. It is a momentous story in the history of Jewry and of Germany, and it exemplifies and illuminates the vast complexity of the transformation of Europe. It is a process to ponder and acknowledge, not so much because of its achievements or its sufferings, but because it may be one of the most dramatic instances of Europe's encounter with what we commonly call modernity, the uprooting of society in a spiritual, social and economic sense. In that climate of nineteenth-century modernity, German Jews throve visibly—and suffered invisibly. As a group, they compressed the experience of European man becoming an individual; the process had begun earlier and has been defined by Lionel Trilling as leading a man to "have an awareness of what one historian, Georges Gusdorf, calls internal space. . . . It is when he becomes an individual that a man lives more and more in private rooms; whether the privacy makes the individuality or the individuality requires the privacy the historians do not say."[4] I would suppose that German Jewry—if we could ever recapture the welter of its innermost feelings—would be seen to have had a highly developed sense of individualism, with all the freedom and the loneliness and the self-doubt that the new condition entailed.

To understand what I have called the great leap forward it is necessary to recall the preemancipation condition of debasement and debarment, of legally defined and enforced marginality. Jews were tolerated because they were useful; they performed services that the society around them neither condoned nor could do without.

For centuries, the Germans had lived a divided existence, divided by confession, region, status, and divided also by their attachment to particularist rulers or separate communities. That ordered life has been sympathetically and brilliantly evoked in Mack Walker's recent *German Home Towns*: a world of established order, of community, a world limited in some ways by the nearest church-steeple. It was a life of known obligations and expectations, with appropriate values and continued religious sanctions. Jews lived on the margin of that society; they lived on the whole an uncertain, debased existence, as befit a people that was still thought to be separate and inferior, to be in some essential ways depraved.* In German eyes, Jews were inferior because of their seeming aptitude for peddling and money changing and because of their religious customs, their strange, clannish orthodoxy, by their continued attachment to a primitive divine dispensation that had been fulfilled only in Christianity. It was a time when Jews and

* The marginality of Jewish existence is illustrated by Mack Walker's definition of outsiders who "were excluded for some other reason denoting inferiority: the illegitimately born for example, or Jews, or indigent aunts, or menial servants, or immigrants from the country who settled in the suburbs. . . . Other laws on beggars, wandering tinkers and sharpeners, players, musicians, peddlers, Jews—the old dishonorable wanderers—reiterated the need to protect the community against such people." Mack Walker, *German Home Towns. Community, State, and General Estate 1648–1871* (Ithaca and London 1971), pp. 29, 271.

Christians were still divided by a common God, when to both the struggle over the religious patrimony assumed central importance. The separateness of Jews and Germans, then, was an acknowledged fact on both sides, and the ghetto nurtured a strong sense of Jewish identity and community.

Into this slowly changing world of the Germanies, where everything still had its ordered place and Jews were in a sense shielded from outside life and even violence by the walls and laws surrounding them, came the recognition, spurred on by precept and example from across the Rhine, that subjects should become citizens, that rights granted would lead to a more ready acceptance of duties demanded, and into that period of the late eighteenth and early nineteenth century fell the concern with the emancipation of Jews. Some Jews had thirsted for that liberation while still cut off from the public and cultural life of the Germans; the desire for emancipation and the discussion of it arose during a momentous flowering of German thought, often called the great Idealist Age, and some Jews yearned to embrace the new faith of the Enlightenment and European romanticism. Within the various German states, the argument for emancipation was made: Jews were to be released from their special disabilities, gradually or all at once, and allowed to enjoy some of the attributes of recently promulgated citizenship. But emancipation, as recent studies have shown, was a gradual and grudging process; it was justified by the expectation that emancipation would lead to the moral improvement of the Jews, to their "civic betterment" ("*bürgerliche Verbesserung*," in the classic words of Christian Wilhelm Dohm's essay of 1783), to their assimilation to Christian life, though the exact nature of that assimilation was rarely specified. The Jews in Germany were released from their disabilities gradually and on what might be called a moral installment plan: they were to remain indebted for the goods received for a long time, and until they had paid for them in full, the goods were not considered fully theirs. Some scholars have recently argued that from the beginning emancipation included the presumption of the final measure of assimilation, i.e., conversion to Christianity. Not all the emancipators may have had this goal in mind, but the unanimous expectation of the moral improvement of Jews implied at the very least a blending into the German scene, an end to any kind of uniqueness or separateness in any realm. The debate over emancipation reflected the distinctive nature of German liberalism; neither the vision of a pluralist society nor a commitment to the natural rights of man inspired the emancipators.

"The march out of the ghetto" was painful and precarious, and it coincided—as none of the emancipators could have foreseen—with a general upheaval in German society, indeed, with one of the greatest upheavals of European history.[5] I refer, of course, to the upheaval which we invariably label as the emergence of a capitalistic-industrial society, gradually secularized and democratized. It was a world characterized by a sudden, ceaseless mobility across boundaries of thought, traditions, classes, received customs. Put much too simply, in that new society of the nineteenth century, the possibilities of the market replaced the constraints of birth, and wealth became the new criterion of success. It is a world that the great novelists of the last century depicted and that Karl Marx described in his own poetic-revolutionary manner in the *Communist Manifesto*. To a greater extent than ever before, if still much less than proclaimed in the mythologies of Samuel Smiles, and by the apostles of laissez-faire, the new economic order made possible an open society, a society based in part on Napoleon's revolutionary principle of careers open to talent. (Napoleon's call for such a society was a striking instance of a man raising his personal experience to the level of a universal principle. And Napoleon's entire career and most especially the dramatic act of his placing the crown on his own head were paradigmatic acts for the nineteenth century, with special relevance for Jews, a relevance duly felt by Jews. By the end of the century, it was widely thought that careers were open to wealth, not talent, and that the rich, often thought unworthy, were, in fact, throttling the very freedom that had created them.)

It is enough to recall that the economic upheaval coincided with a moral upheaval as well; just as the traditional social order was breached, so was the traditional moral-religious authority; the falling away from God, disguised, uncertain and uneven though it was, was nevertheless a social fact, as was the emergence of the new faith in progress, rationality and science, with its own prophets and practitioners. Secularization affected Jews as it did Christians; in some ways, it affected them more profoundly because their faith had ensured their survival as a distinct group; other groups had for a long time been able to define their identities in a religious and a national sense. For Jews, as the religious bonds were loosened and as the new secular faith of nationalism beckoned, the danger of ever greater alienation from their own traditional identity became considerable.

In this new world of the mid-nineteenth century, the symbols of success changed as well. The palaces and temples of the time were railroad stations and banks; the self-made men built themselves mansions of pomp, and the European plutocracy thought to dazzle the world by their visible presence, by the old manor houses they could buy or the new pomposities they could construct. The new presumption was cast in stone and marble and everywhere visible; the old prejudices against the new wealth, against money grubbing and against the new commercial dispensation was less visible, but nonetheless real and powerful. Historians—and political dogmatists—have often spoken of the triumph of capitalism as the chief characteristic of the last century. The triumph, in retrospect, may have been more apparent than real; at the very least, the prejudices against capitalism grew rather than diminished with time and received a new sanction from the various strands of socialism. Marx was one of the first to understand the dynamic and exploitative character of capitalism, but precisely because he denied or denigrated the autonomy of sentiments and misunderstood the force of nationalism, he did not envision the possibility of a strong nonsocialist anticapitalist movement arising; in Germany it played a decisive role.

In this uneasily capitalistic, secularizing age, German Jews did superbly well. Nimble and rootless, they seized every possible chance; economic opportunity beckoned for all, often at the price of moving to new and unknown quarters; Jews had little to lose and hence responded to the lure of the new city with untroubled eagerness. Once there, they excelled in certain traditional functions, quickly adapted to modern needs. The experience of Jewish success must yet be fully explored in all its ambiguous glory; I came upon it by reconstructing the life of Bismarck's banker, Gerson von Bleichröder. The Rothschilds, of course, were the visible pinnacle of power, and already in the 1820s they were referred to as the uncrowned kings of Europe. Perhaps it will suffice if I suggest some dimensions of that success: Jews attained a unique prominence in the new German society. Proportionately they were richer, better educated and—at least in some areas—held better positions than their Christian colleagues and competitors. In some fields, such as banking and journalism, for example, Jews gained such prominence as to come close to dominance. They were disproportionately concentrated in a few large cities. These are the landmarks of their success, won in the face of barely suspended hostility. This success is attested by figures and by the reports of foreign observers.*

There was something asymmetrical in almost every aspect of

° One English observer noted that in 1870, "whilst the Christians of Berlin have, as a rule, to bear the burden and heat of the day, a disproportionate share of the material loaves and fishes falls to the lot of the more fortunate Jew. . . . [The Jews] inhabit the best houses in the best quarters of the town, drive about the parks in the most elegant equipages, figure constantly in the dress circle at the opera and theatres, and in this and other ways excite a good deal of envy in the minds of their less fortunate Christian fellow-citizens." Taylor continued that in England there would be far greater animus against Jews if they held a similar position;

the German-Jewish coexistence. The Jews were far more urbanized than the rest of the population; Jews had traditionally been banished from agriculture, and they were not about to return to the soil where they would have met with considerable hostility from the existing population. (Wealthy Jews did buy themselves large, formerly noble estates and returned to the soil by becoming landowners and *Gutsherren* on a grand scale. The Junkers, obsessed with what they took to be their catastrophic economic decline, so injurious to themselves and to the traditional order of the state, always assumed that when penury would finally lead them to have to sell their ancestral home, a rich commoner, and usually the worst kind of commoner, a Jew, would replace them.) They shunned the industrial sector, where either as worker or entrepreneur they would have to deal with a large number of non-Jews. They flocked to occupations where they could operate alone or with one another—and this, too, fed the notion of the invisible Jewish power. Jews also made disproportionate strides in higher education and thus gave sustenance to the notion that Jews were somehow more cunning, more clever, more scheming, more—aridly—intelligent, and more given to "soulless" learning than others.

The story of German Jewry may well constitute one of the most spectacular social leaps in European history. Fifty years after emancipation, the Jews *had* bettered themselves, but in ways almost always antithetical to the wishes and expectations of the emancipators. They had bettered themselves in ways that the emancipators had hoped they would leave to Christians; it must have seemed as if they had transmuted their pauperish peddling into plutocratic grandeur.

Under the best of circumstances, this kind of sudden rise

---

the whole problem, he thought, would disappear because "it would almost seem as if the end of Judaism were near at hand in Berlin." By this he meant that the traits of Jewishness were on the decline. Shepherd Thomas Taylor, *Reminiscences of Berlin During the Franco-German War of 1870–71* (London 1885), pp. 236, 237, 241.

would have caused consternation; it is not surprising that many Germans (and some Jews) viewed the new prosperity and prominence with misgivings and resentment. In the 1850s and 1860s, there was relative silence, in part perhaps because the society was far less aware of change than it was to become later; also among the literate groups there was a general presumption in favor of economic progress and laissez-faire, of which the Jews were at once exemplars and promoters. By the 1870s, a radical shift occurred: after a few years of frantic speculation, in part triggered by the German exultation over unification and the defeat of the French as well as by the sudden inflow of five billion francs as French indemnity, the Berlin stock market crashed, many of the newly and often fraudulently spawned corporations went bankrupt, and a serious and protracted depression ensued. Amidst this crisis, a storm against Jewish power and corruption erupted; pamphleteers began it, but by 1875, the most respectable papers of the old Protestant orthodoxy and of the embattled Catholic party charged that Jews had suddenly come to dominate German life, and that they were using their new position to corrupt, exploit and destroy the German people and its traditions. The variations on these charges were endless, but common to all of them was the fear that somehow the Jews had achieved a kind of secret domination—and as evidence was offered the position of Jews in the economy, in journalism, in banking. The more scurrilous the paper, the more lurid the picture of this spider which caught ever new victims in its web; in the more respectable papers, the charges were often made more in sorrow than in anger, and everywhere Bleichröder was held up as the principal exhibit of mysterious Jewish power, consisting of political connection, vast wealth and boundless ambition. As I have pointed out elsewhere, Bleichröder was a Jew such as the most imaginative and enterprising anti-Semites could hardly have invented. He was the hostage of this first generation of new anti-Semites (the very term, anti-Semitism, was coined in

Germany in the 1870s). If he had not existed, they would not have been able to invent him. As Richard Hofstadter has pointed out, political cranks need this "quality of pedantry"; they need some basis in fact, some evidence to bolster their extravagant charges.* In the 1870s, this demonology was broadened by the emergence of racial anti-Semitism, the "scientific" assertion that racial characteristics were hereditary and that the evil essence of Jews was thus ineradicable.

After the 1870s, the ideological attacks on the Jews were not born of economic distress nor products of vague economic forces. But they seemed plausible because of the economic and psychic dislocations of the day. The subsequent history of anti-Semitism had very little to do with social actuality or the real position of Jews, which in any case gradually weakened.

Nothing so enraged the anti-Semites as the notion of a secret Jewish conspiracy ruling the new Germany. Their warnings had resonance, in large part because in an economically minded century, Germans and others mistook wealth as power, but in fact the position of German Jewry demonstrated that wealth begets the power to amass more wealth, that it commands special considerations and privileges, but that in the Germany of Bismarck (and subsequently) it did not command political power. Despite the suspicion, so carefully nurtured by many critics of the time, that wealth and power were synonymous and that hence Jews were to be thought as holding both, the structure and substance of German politics were remarkably sealed off from any possible Jewish penetration.

The role of Jewry was asymmetrical, as I suggested earlier. In Germany, Jews were tacitly banned from all positions of

---

* "One of the impressive things about paranoid literature is precisely the elaborate concern with demonstration it almost invariably shows. One should not be misled by the fantastic conclusions that are so characteristic of this political style into imagining that it is not, so to speak, argued out along factual lines. The very fantastic character of its conclusions leads to heroic strivings for 'evidence' to prove that the unbelievable is the only thing that can be believed. . . . But respectable paranoid literature not only starts from certain moral commitments that can be justified to many nonparanoids but also carefully and all but obsessively accumulates 'evidence'." Richard Hofstadter, *The Paranoid Style in American Politics and Other Essays* (New York 1965), pp. 35–36.

political power, indeed from all visible identification with *dignified* power. They could become *Kommerzienräthe* and, in rare instances and in some fields, university professors; a few of them, beginning with Bleichröder in 1872, were even ennobled. But the upper reaches of the state service and the sanctum sanctorum, the officer corps, were closed to them; in the Prussian army, they were unable to become regular officers and the prize that all bourgeois elements strove after—the coveted title of reserve officer—was beyond the reach of Jews after 1878 or so. Perhaps in no other country in which Jews enjoyed civic equality was the officer corps as important as it was in Germany, and in none, I believe, were Jews so resolutely excluded. In Germany, there was no Dreyfus Affair because there was no Dreyfus. One has to remember what the army meant in the hierarchy of power and values; it embodied, certainly by consensus of the governing classes, the noblest traditions of valor, honor, service, manliness. The symbolic and psychological importance of that exclusion was incalculable, and Jewish acceptance of it—with only occasional protests—suggests not only that they had to some extent taken over the stereotypes of their excluders, but that they had it too good to cope psychologically or politically with remaining indignities, just as the German bourgeoisie was too prosperous and too fearful ever to mount the barricades.

Self-perception is never easy, and German Jews found it excruciatingly hard to assess their place in German society. Nor were their views uniform—far from it; the Jewish community was split into recognizable divisions, varying with economic and social status, and marked by different views on political and religious issues, and especially on the problems of Jewish destiny itself. The countercurrents were violent: the drive to ever greater assimilation seemed consonant with rational self-interest and sentimental identification with the German nation and its culture; but if assimilation was the goal, how far should it go, how much religious heritage was one to surrender, how many discriminations and indignities to accept in order not to call attention to separateness of one's group? Should one accept the remaining barriers, perhaps expecting, as did the rest of the German bourgeoisie, that in time these lingering survivals of a feudal age would disappear? Should one not be grateful for the safety won—after all, was not the fate of Eastern European Jewry, steadily deteriorating after Russia adopted a new repressive anti-Semitism after 1881, a constant reminder of how immeasurably far German Jewry had traveled?

Wealthy Jews, of course, tended to be the most conservative and hence were least likely to want to criticize existing German conditions. How were such Jews to adapt to the successes they had scored? Meekly, modestly, unobtrusively, as if Stendhal and Dickens had never portrayed the bourgeoisie's irrepressible drive to dazzling heights of opulence and vulgarity, to the reification of tastelessness? Were they to be better than the "brannew" Veneerings, the Podsnaps, and the Merdles? The temptation to snobbery was irresistible, and the costs were great as well, for as Lionel Trilling noted, "The dominant emotions of snobbery are uneasiness, self-consciousness, self-defensiveness, the sense that one is not quite real but can in some way acquire reality."[6] The record suggests that Jewish plutocrats in Germany were just as garish in their grasp for social prominence as any bourgeois anywhere; the life of Bleichröder showed how important this social ascent was to the most prominent of economic Jews of the German Empire. Their efforts earned them the disdain of the very group they most sought to emulate, the older classes. And in the process of ever reaching out and ever being rebuffed, some of the Jews earned the reputation of being especially pushy, vulgar, loud, brazen and money-conscious.

In the 1880s, various leaders of German Jewry admonished their coreligionists to be more "modest," an injunction that a great many critics, Nietzsche and Burckhardt included, also preached. The German Jews, it has often been noted, were especially censorious of the so-called *Ostjuden,* with their less cultured ways and peculiar speech and garb—reminders perhaps of what once upon a time German Jews themselves looked like. But self-critical admonitions went out to German Jewry as well, and especially to the most affluent who were also often less cultured and more visible than the rest of the community.

In the 1870s and 1880s, that is, in the beginning of the new anti-Semitism, the principal target was Jewish economic power. By the end of the century, Jews had also become remarkably prominent in the academic-scientific field. For whatever combination of reasons, German Jews achieved an unprecedented preeminence in the natural sciences, in the birth of what has come to be called the new physics, in chemistry and in medicine. In these fields, Germans and Jews complemented each other and collaborated in what may well have been a singular crucible of genius. And yet even in that field, there must have been bred resentments and unease; for every Jewish discovery made, for every Nobel Prize won, there were ten Germans who felt aggrieved. Nor can it be forgotten that both Germans and Jews occasionally thought that there was a distinct Jewish component to Jewish success. In part, it was the spur to greater effort; the need to excel was instilled by tradition and nurtured by hostility. Not safety or security, though those too were present in the domesticity of German-Jewish life, but hidden wounds inspired visible achievement.

It was Freud who in 1926 suggested something of what might be called the Jewish source of his work. In his address to the B'nai B'rith, in which he averred that he was an unbeliever and even an opponent of all national, including Jewish, enthusiasms, he added, "But plenty of other things remained ever to make the attraction of Jewry and Jews irresistible—many obscure emotional forces, which were the more powerful the less they could be expressed in words, as well as a clear consciousness of inner identity, the safe privacy of a common mental construction. And beyond this there was a perception that it was to my Jewish nature alone that I owed two characteristics that had become indispensable to me in the difficult course of my life. Because I was a Jew I found myself free from many prejudices which restricted others in the use of their intellect; and as a Jew I was prepared to join the Opposition and to do without agreement with the 'compact majority'."[7] It is a paradoxical fact that it was German Jews, so many of whom were thought to be in craven submission to the dominant group among whom they lived, who in the century between emancipation and extinction produced some of the most fiercely independent minds, willing to break not only with the majority but to expose the taboos that characterized German society. The Germans cherished a certain type of sentimental domesticity or, put differently, transmuted the aggressive strains of human nature to fairy tales; it was Heine who could in unmatched lyrics express these yearnings for love and beauty and with searing irony expose the taboos as well. The Germans were also always peculiarly reticent about matters of money and sex, both considered "dirty" and unmentionable; Marx and Freud dedicated their lives to analyzing the material and sexual origins of collective and individual behavior.*

The Jews had made an unprecedented leap, but their success, partial in any case, had brought them grave costs as well. So many of them had willingly tossed most of their own traditions aside, content to merge with the dominant, secular, nationalist culture of the Germans. The varying degrees of hostility they encountered puzzled and divided them; the

---

* Freud cited one splendid instance of Heine's satirical exposure of German sentimentality: "A great imaginative writer may permit himself to give expression—jokingly, at all events—to psychological truths that are severely proscribed. Thus Heine confesses: 'Mine is a most peaceable disposition. My wishes are: a humble cottage with a thatched roof, but a good bed, good food, the freshest milk and butter, flowers before my window, and a few fine trees before my door; and if God wants to make my happiness complete, he will grant me the joy of seeing some six or seven of my enemies hanging from those trees. Before their death I shall, moved in my heart, forgive them all the wrong they did me in their lifetime. One must, it is true, forgive one's enemies—but not before they have been hanged'." Sigmund Freud, *Civilization and its Discontents* (London, 1949), p. 84.

Jewish response to lingering resentment and burgeoning anti-Semitism, which by the end of the century included a new form of racism, was a composite of design and passivity. Different groups were predisposed toward different responses, and German Jewry embraced simultaneously a set of conflicting strategies.* Some counseled still greater efforts at assimilation, even conversion; others wished for a more assertive policy, that would demand the implementation of civil rights which had been formally granted in the various emancipation decrees; others still embraced a new Jewish nationalism which in its own way echoed the charge of anti-Semites that Jews were an alien people that should be extruded from the German body politic. For all the conflict and unease within the Jewish community, there was a kind of unarticulated cohesion as well; religious and secular, conservative and radical Jews, however much they warred among themselves, understood that they shared certain traditions and certain talents, and they were at once proud and ashamed of these traditions. There remained a measure of cohesion that mingled pride with shame, that by being largely covert gave less psychic reassurance than it might have done. The spiritual stance of German Jewry can perhaps best be described by the word ambivalence: ambivalence about themselves, ambivalence about the Germans, ambivalence about their role in German life. The history of German Jewry in its

---

* It is worth recalling that Tocqueville, reflecting on the democratic inclination to elect mediocre leaders, observed that "when serious dangers threaten the state, the people frequently succeed in selecting the citizens who are the most able to save it. [But] extreme perils sometimes quench the energy of a people instead of stimulating it; they excite without directing its passions; and instead of clearing they confuse its powers of perception. The Jews fought and killed one another amid the smoking ruins of their temple." *Democracy in America* (New York, 1945), 1:210. How could it be otherwise, given the myriad reactions of individuals at the time? Consider two statements from the early 1890s: the nineteen-year-old Chaim Weizmann, apprenticed in a German-Jewish school and in full rebellion against the assimilated principal who lectured Weizmann that the Germans would overcome their anti-Semitism as soon as they fully realized the magnitude of Jewish contributions, cried out: "Herr Doktor, when someone has something in his eye, he doesn't care whether it is a piece of gold or a piece of mud—he wants it out." In 1890 the great German novelist, Theodor Fontane, wrote: *"At least here in Berlin,* all freedom and higher culture has been mediated for us primarily by rich Jewry. It is a fact one has to accept finally, and as an artist or a literary person, one has to accept it with pleasure (because without it, we could not exist at all)." Weizmann, *Trial and Error* (New York, 1949), p. 32; Theodor Fontane, *Briefe,* II (Berlin, 1909), p. 245.

century of seeming freedom described in a particularly intense and elusive manner what we commonly call the problem of identity.

In seeking to understand this buffeting, one must remember that Jews were nurtured in the political culture of modern Germany, and one must remember the degree to which the Germans themselves experienced the same fate, both internally and in their relations to the outside world, as did the Jews. Did the Germans of the new Empire not astound the world by their material triumphs, by their great power, by what appeared to all as their disciplined genius? And yet their appearance aroused not only resentment but contempt, for they, too, were thought to appear simultaneously as craven and commanding. And the Germans faced this world in jackboots and with bombast, wishing to be loved and feared at the same time. They mixed arrogance and *angst*, and they too had deep misgivings about their identity and national destiny, and nostalgia for traditions lost. And did not Germans—at least those that were not titled or powerful—suffer the same kind of lingering nonage that the Jews experienced? For the Germans, in their erratic thrust for world power, their relationship to the great declining Imperium of Britain was the central political problem; the antagonism that developed between Britons and Germans was perhaps the single most important element in the later self-destruction of Europe. And the Anglo-German antagonism, while rooted no doubt in substantive conflicts and rivalries, was also nurtured by the multiple misunderstandings and misperceptions that the British formed of the Germans— misperceptions and suspicions that often paralleled the Germans' view of their Jews.

In their own great triumph, the German Jews anticipated and approximated the triumphs of their country. They contributed to that larger national triumph, and they too exulted in it. As we have seen, they were also the victims of their own success and that of the Germans, but their real tragedy began when the Germans suffered the defeat of 1918, embittered by the sense that the world had denied them their rightful place as Europe's imperial power, for which their military, industrial, and scientific might had predestined them. After 1918, the Germans experienced a succession of reverses, none of which they understood, all of which were made more galling by the fact that they felt as if they were treated as the moral pariahs of the world. It was in those years of inflation and depression, of outraged nationalism and a sense of aggrievement at being treated as outcasts, that the accumulated anti-Semitism in Germany became concentrated into a frenzied political gospel and directed against a Jewish minority that had long since lost the strength or power it had once possessed.

But even then there was no single road that led to Auschwitz. What the National Socialists aimed at was the total repudiation of emancipation and the extrusion of Jews from German life. They proceeded slowly, by design and improvisation; what emboldened them was the passivity with which the German elites, long nurtured on a kind of presumption against Jewry, watched the elimination of Jewish colleagues and competitors from almost every sphere of activity. The outside world, which until the outbreak of the Second World War the Nazis watched with some concern, expressed but mild reproval and intermittent opposition. In the end, the Nazis, nurtured on a hatred of German Jews, unleashed their full wrath on European Jewry, made defenseless by Nazi conquest. For a generation, the memory of the holocaust smothered the ancient prejudice against the victims; under the impact of new events and a new generation, the world may forget the fate of these millions, and their memory may be violated by polemical invocation on the one hand and increasing resentment or impatience on the other: the living wish to be freed from the incubus; the victims embarrass.

The term German Jew, long since emptied of much specific historic meaning, has become synonymous with meek surrender, self-immolation, cravenness, with victims digging their own graves. This memory as the indictment of victims is a terrible simplification, unfaithful to the past and portentous for the future; for it could encourage truculence and moral defeatism. But the cultivation of this memory is nurtured by many sources; time was when the liberal mind essentially affirmed the rational, the secular, the democratic ethos. It is a terrible irony of our time that after having encountered and finally, at hideous cost, vanquished the embodiment of political irrationality, our culture is full of voices extolling the irrational. In the haunting, final words of *Sincerity and Authenticity*, Lionel Trilling evoked that new facile inclination toward irrationality, toward "an upward psychopathic mobility," that mocks the dead and threatens the living.

At such times, German Jewry will hardly be assessed with sympathetic understanding. For the German-Jewish community epitomized too many of the things now held in disrepute: they lived by what were once regarded as the proper modern habits of rationality, discipline, repression, and with these came both self-denial and alienation. The record moreover bespeaks submission and servility; it also describes a great flowering of the human spirit and imagination. If, in the end, the hope for an untroubled German-Jewish partnership or collaboration is to be judged an illusion, it must be said that for a brief moment it was an enticing illusion, an illusion productive of greatness. For the rest it remains a subject that we must treat with a new candor and with the greatest degree of empathy as well as factuality. It is a subject that speaks to all those who are concerned with the questions of integration and pluralism. Would it be permissible to go even further—to say that such knowledge would illuminate the human experience in a modern, often hostile, society generally? It is a subject touched by the tragedy of our civilization and a wiser understanding may enlighten our present predicaments and diminish the danger that the pain of the past by twisted memory confounds the present.

NOTES

1. Lionel Trilling, *The Liberal Imagination: Essays on Literature and Society* (London, 1951), p. 188.

2. Gerson D. Cohen, "German Jewry as Mirror of Modernity. Introduction to the Twentieth Volume," *Leo Baeck Institute Yearbook*, XX (London 1975), p. xi.

3. An outstanding example of this new approach is Ismar Schorsch, *Jewish Reactions to German Anti-Semitism 1870–1914* (New York, 1972); this present essay does not mean to deal with the new literature, and I would refer the reader to the more general discussion and comprehensive bibliographical references in my *Gold and Iron: Bismarck, Bleichröder, and the Building of the German Empire* (New York, 1977).

4. Lionel Trilling, *Sincerity and Authenticity* (Cambridge, Mass., 1972), pp. 24–5.

5. See Jacob Katz's important work, *Out of the Ghetto. The Social Background of Jewish Emancipation, 1770–1870* (Cambridge, Mass., 1973).

6. Lionel Trilling, *The Liberal Imagination*, pp. 209–210.

7. Sigmund Freud, *The Standard Edition of the Complete Psychological Works*, XIX (London, 1959), pp. 273–4. (I owe this reference to my friend Peter Loewenberg.)

THE PLEASURES OF *KIM*

IRVING HOWE

For the past several years, whenever I would meet Lionel Trilling, we would move into a bit of amiable badinage about *Kim*. We had discovered that we both admired this book passionately, and that we shared a disdain for those advanced critics who failed to see it as one of the great fictions of the modern era. Both of us kept saying we were going to write an esay in praise of *Kim*, and a sort of rivalry—friendly but real—grew up as to which would do it first. When the editors of this volume invited me to contribute, I thought it might amuse Lionel if I wrote briefly about *Kim*—and wrote, as he would have been quick to notice, by using some of his own favored terms and phrases. Now that he is no longer here to read what I have written and then make one of his characteristic jokes, I can only hope his friends will share my feeling that to speak in praise of Kipling's book is a way of recalling Lionel's presence, the love he felt for this book, indeed, the love he felt for good and beautiful books.

That sense of evil which for cultivated people has become a mark of wisdom and source of pride, indeed, the very sun of their sunless world, is not a frequent presence in the pages of *Kim*, and when it does appear it can rarely trouble us with either its violence or grasp. We are inclined these days to exalt the awareness of evil into a kind of appreciation. We find it hard to suppose that a serious writer could turn his back upon the malignity at the heart of things; we urge it as a criticism of writers like Emerson and Whitman that they are weak in the awareness of evil, as if nature had denied them a necessary faculty. But *Kim* is unsubdued by the malignity at the heart of things. Whatever evil it does encompass tends to be passed off onto a troop of bumbling Russian spies who muddle along on the northern borders of India, stage-comic Russians about as alarming as Laurel and Hardy. *Kim* is at ease with the world, that unregenerate place which is the only one most of us know, and because at ease, it can allow itself to slide toward another possible world, one that some of us may yet come to know. For readers trained in the severities of Kafka and Sartre, all this may constitute a literary scandal, especially if one goes so far as to make a claim for the seriousness and greatness of the book; and precisely this scandal is what I propose here to cultivate.

There is greater scandal. *Kim* evokes and keeps returning to sensations of pleasure, a pleasure regarded as easy, natural, and merited. Our sophistication teaches us that all the literary works we esteem can be expected to yield pleasure; that the torments, dryness, and even boredom of certain exemplary twentieth-century texts can also be made to yield pleasure. Our sophistication muddies the issue. For the pleasure of *Kim* is of a more traditional and unproblematic sort, a pleasure in the apprehension of things as they are, in embracing a world as enchanting as it is flawed. Kipling's book accepts the world's body, undeterred by odors, bulges, wrinkles, scars. Life, in its final bearing, may prove to be absurd, but *Kim*, though far from an innocent book, has little commerce with this view, since it is a book that takes delight in each step of the journey bringing us closer to the absurd: delight in our clamor, our foolishness, our vanity, our senses, and—through the lumbering radiance of the lama who comes from and goes back to the hills of Tibet—delight in an ultimate joy of being which beckons from the other side of sensuous pleasure but which, implies Kipling, those of us not lamas would be advised to seek through pleasure.

Part of the pleasure that *Kim* engages is that of accepting, even venerating sainthood, without at all proposing to surrender the world, or even worldliness, to saints. *Kim* embraces both worlds, that of the boy and the lama, the senses and beyond, recognizing that anyone who would keep a foot, or even a finger, in both of these worlds must have some discipline in adjustment and poise—otherwise, what need would there be for the lama's or any other serious education? But never for a moment does the book propose to smudge the difference between the senses and beyond, or worse still, to contrive some facile synthesis. The "Wheel of Things," to which we are all bound in this world, and the "Search," by which we may penetrate another, have each their claim and dignity. The two speed along in parallel, but what they signify cannot readily be merged. There is earth, there is spirit, both are real. In any case, a writer open to the allurements of pleasure is more likely to explore the Many than strain toward the One.

And greater scandal still: *Kim* is the work of a man quite unable to evoke the admiration we give to culture heroes. He is a jingo and a bully, or defender of bullies; he swaggers in the style of an overgrown schoolboy; he is usually more talented than wise. That there was a "wound behind his bow" hardly excuses all that we find unattractive in Kipling: there is a wound behind every bow. He is not a writer we take to heart, as one takes Hardy, or respects unreservedly, as one respects Chekhov. Yet this often small-spirited writer composed, once in his life, a book of the most exquisite radiance of spirit, breathing a love of creation such as few of his greater contemporaries could match. There is a puzzle here, and I propose to let it remain.

The story starts with noises of sociality. Kim is a thirteen-year-old darling of the streets, a fast-talking urchin, white by birth and dark from the sun, who awaits each day as an encounter with possibility. Trading amiable epithets with the bazaar merchants who call him "Little Friend of all the World," Kim is neither innocent nor naive. He has "known all evil since he could speak," but he does not let it determine or overwhelm him; he absorbs and then puts aside that knowledge, as if breaking a skin, for there is always something to see and experience in the streets of Lahore, that "wonderful walled city." In these streets he is as shrewd as his distant cousin Huck Finn is shrewd along the shore; like that cousin, he has learned "to avoid missionaries and white men of serious aspect," and also has learned the fine art of doing "nothing with an immense success." Whenever he sidles up to a booth, the men of the city smile, knowing they will hear something clever or mischievous and will enjoy his command of the Indian art of cursing. He is a young entrepreneur and apprentice con man, a quick-change artist who does not care for any fixed or even steadily emergent self because life offers so many selves to discover and try out. "Who is Kim?" he will ask himself later in the book, and each chapter will yield the happy answer that there are many answers. He loves "the game for its own sake" —the "game" standing here for both the British secret service, with which he will become enmeshed through his worldly self, and the entirety of the business of life. "The game" is not an adequate term, or concept, at all; it reflects the all-too-familiar side of Kipling's sensibility which is adolescent and stunted.

When Kim meets the lama, an ungainly rhapsodist who makes transcendence seem a familiar option, the two of them quickly find common ground. They share a meal, they bound their territory, they match prospects for the future. To the boy, the old man represents a new experience, a guru such as the mainland does not yield; for the old man, the boy is a guide through the bewilderments of India and a friend ripening into a *chela* or disciple. Kim is possessed by the evidence of his senses, the lama with a vision beyond, and the book will make as its central matter an unfolding of the love between the two, that thrill of friendship which in nineteenth-century literature comes to replace the grace of God.

At first Kim literally takes the old man in hand. He goes to beg food for him, charmingly vain in the confidence with which he can tap the city. "They ate together in great content" —so begin and end half the great stories of mankind. Awakened after a sleep brought on by the meal, the old man looks for the boy and is bewildered to find Kim in one of his transmutations, "a Hindu urchin in a dirty turban." One thinks to compare this moment with the trick Huck plays on Jim, but only to reject the comparison, since everything is far gentler in Kipling's India than in Twain's America, and Kim need not go through torments of conscience in order to declare himself "thy chela," certainly need not declare himself ready, like Huck, for perdition. Because he is utterly fortified in his sense of being at home in the world and feels some mild superiority to the unworldliness of the old man, Kim can also begin to see, in an incipient way, that the lama represents other possibilities for him: " 'I have never seen anyone like to thee in all this my life. I go with thee. . . .' " It is not yet a spiritual discipleship; it is simply a companionship of the road. "Boy-like, if an acquaintance had a scheme, Kim was quite ready with one of his own." Perhaps, he smiles to himself, "they will make me a king" during the journey. To which the lama replies: " 'I will teach thee other and better desires upon the road.' "

But not yet, not at the beginning. The first five chapters of the book form a picaresque entry into "the great good-tempered world," first on the "te-rain" and then along the Great Trunk Road (India's Mississippi). It is an India refracted through Kipling's adoring memory and in its relation to the "real" India complex beyond hope of disentangling. It is an India Kipling loves for its rough vivacity, its easy mixture of manners, its encompassing of gutter and cloud; and it is praised by him (as if to unsettle all those who declare settled views of his work) as the "only democratic land in the world" —by which he means, I gather, not the absence of rank or distinction but a readiness to live with and intermingle all ranks and distinctions. (At this point historical fact and imaginative vision may find themselves at considerable odds: a problem by no means confined to Kipling, indeed, common to all serious novelists.) In Kipling's India—Kim's playground—the boy is a trickster delighting in his tricks and expecting that his audiences will delight with him in seeing, and seeing through, them. A people raised with a sense of hazard appreciates the boy's virtuosity; shrewdly eyes his performance, an utterly this-worldly performance; yet looks tolerantly upon "holy men stammering gospels in strange tongues." The multiplicity of visions and ways that Kipling attributes to India becomes the ground of his delight.

Kim and the lama now move through a world that is like a vast, disorderly bazaar. People are quick to embrace and to anger. They speak suddenly from the heart, as if any traveler may be a friend. They curse with the expertness of centuries. ("Father of all the daughters of shame and husband of ten thousand virtueless ones, thy mother was devoted to a devil, being led thereto by her mother. . . .") Their ripeness shows itself in a linked incapacity to be surprised and readiness to enjoy the familiar. Running errands for Mahbub Ali, the free-thinking Afghan horse trader who initiates him into the British secret service, Kim charms a fierce-tongued old Indian lady (straight in the line of Chaucer, from one pilgrimage to another) into helping him and the lama. He trades stories with retired soldiers, jests with travelers, even pokes a little tender fun at his lama—for this is Kim's world, a stage for his multiple roles as urchin, beggar, raconteur, flirt, apprentice spy, and apprentice *chela*, who is always eager, as Kipling shrewdly notes, for "the visible effect of action." Picked up by some British soldiers who propose to educate him ("sivilize," says Huck), Kim tells the lama: "Remember, I can change swiftly."

It is the motto of every youth trying to evade the clamp of civilization.

And the world's evil? The poverty, injustice, caste rigidities which must have been so grinding in the India of eighty years ago? If it would be morally shameful to suppress these questions entirely, it would also be foolish to let them deprive us of the pleasures of *Kim*.

There is a "literary" way of coping with these questions, but like all merely "literary" ways, it seems to me finally unsatisfying. Kipling's book releases a distinct, which is necessarily to say, a limited vision. It seeks to give life a desirable look; it brushes past social misery as more recent novels brush past personal happiness; it neglects the shadows as others neglect the lights; it sees the world as fresh, alluring, and young—young, in India! But *Kim* is not an idyll, not a retreat from the world; it is a celebration of, a plunge into the world.

Let us try another tack. The book has no assured answers to the questions of Indian poverty, injustice, and caste rigidity, partly because it does not choose to give them priority, though we surely know that it is not an evasive or willfully "positive" book. All the wrongs and evils of India are there, steeped in the life of the people, yet these do not keep them from grasping the sensations of their moment, or from experiencing the appetites and ceremonies they rightly take to be their due. What so wonderfully distinguishes Kipling's characters is their capacity for shifting from treble to bass, from pure spirit to gross earth, from "the Search" to "the Game." It is as if their culture actually enables them to hold two ideas in their heads at once. The India of Kipling is a place in which people live by custom and caprice, fixed in ways given them yet ready to move past those ways when they feel a need to. They make life for themselves, and it has its substance.

One great flaw in the reforming passion, as Ralph Ellison reminded me during a polemic about black fiction a decade ago, is that in its eagerness to remedy social wrongs it tends to neglect the experience, certainly to undervalue the experience, of those whose lives it wishes to improve. It does not weigh or honor fully enough the life-hungers, the life-capacities of the oppressed. Now Kipling, it is true, did not see India as particularly oppressed, and I am as ready as the next liberal or radical to deplore this failure; but he did see the people of India as vigorous, full of humor and energy, deeply worthy. How are we to explain that in the pages of this apologist for imperialism, the masses of India seem more alive, more autonomous than in the pages of writers claiming political correctness?

Regarding Kipling's apparent indifference to the social evils of India there remains another and more radical "answer." Though in much of his work he shows a quite sufficient awareness of evil, even at some points an obsessive concern, he seems really to want to persuade us through *Kim*, his most serious book, that in the freshness of a boy's discoveries and the penetration of an old man's vision, evil can become ultimately insignificant, almost as nothing before the unsubdued elation of existence, almost as nothing before the idea of moral beauty. Others in the West and the East, long before Kipling, have said as much, though few have embodied it with the plastic vividness that Kipling has. I will confess here to not entirely grasping the import of this vision of ultimate goodness or harmony; I find it a kind of moral slope, very slippery, very attractive. Yet in reading *Kim* one may yield to this vision, just as one might for a moment come to accept beatitude upon meeting a saint. Nor should we try to get round the problem by remarking that *Kim* is a children's book. For it seems intolerable that the best things in life should be supposed available only to children. Old bones have their rights too.

The middle portion of *Kim*, another five chapters, brings to an end the rapturous picaresque of boy and old man: it must come to an end. Kim is sent to the white man's school, to be trained as the son of a *sahib* that he is; he will be prepared for the "Great Game," the world of power, rationality, governance. Who is Kim, he now asks himself with an anxiety that is new to him. "He considered his own identity, a thing he had never done before, till his head swam." He submits to the disadvantages of the whites, though he is still persuaded in his heart that he is one of the blacks—" 'when the *madrissah* [school] is shut, then I must be free and go among my people.' " On vacations he "changes swiftly," drops his European being, dresses as an Indian, returns to "my people." The lama fades out of the picture, while still, in the style of a Dickens's benefactor, supporting Kim in the white man's school. "Come to me! Come to me! Come to me!" the boy writes to him in an outburst of longing, and when they meet for a short while it is now in open love. " 'If I eat thy bread,' cried Kim passionately, 'how shall I ever forget thee?' " The old man consoles him: " 'Do not weep; for look you, all Desire is illusion, and a new binding upon the Wheel. Go up to the Gates of Learning. Let me see thee go. . . . Doest thou love me? Then go, or my heart cracks. . . .' " The boy goes, to learn his trade, to be tested by other agents, British and Indian, to become part of the Game, a man who can govern.

These chapters are beautifully done, with delicacy in shifting from milieu to milieu, but they are minor Kipling rather than major: the adventures here are more like those of Tom Sawyer than those of Huck Finn. And they leave us somewhat uneasy. Edmund Wilson, who thought *Kim* "almost a first-rate book," put his finger on the source of this uneasiness: "What the reader tends to expect is that Kim will come eventually to realize that he is delivering into bondage to the British invaders those whom he has always considered his own people, and that a struggle between allegiances will result. . . . We have been shown two entirely different worlds existing side by side, with neither really understanding the other, and we have watched the oscillations of Kim, as he passes to and fro between them. But the parallel lines never meet; the alternating attractions felt by Kim never give rise to a genuine struggle."

About Wilson's criticism Noel Annan remarks:

> No doubt this is what a courageous liberal writing at a time when Gandhi and Congress were struggling for Indian independence did expect, but such a conflict is imposed by the critic on the novel. No doubt the future life of a young agent would have entailed confounding Indian resistance to the British, but this is an *ex post facto* judgment, and in the novel such a career is depicted as the maintenance of that minimum of order such as is necessary to prevent foreign intrigue, frontier invasions, and injustices by native princes and to permit the joyous, noisy, pullulating mess of Indian life on the Great Trunk Road to continue. . . .

Annan's reply is adequate as far as it goes, but we might try to go a little farther. And oddly, it is Wilson who, in the very course of his complaint, provides our answer. "The parallel lines [between what the lama signifies and what the English require] never meet; the alternating attractions felt by Kim never give rise to a genuine struggle." Precisely so; indeed, that is Kipling's major theme—the parallel lines *cannot* meet. For what impinges upon Kim's consciousness are not two systems of political beliefs, or social orders, but two ways of apprehending human existence, each of which is shown to have its own irreducible claims. The dualism that Wilson deplores yet keenly notices lies at the very heart of the book.

Would it, in any case, make much difference if Kim were to join an incipient Indian nationalist movement instead of the British secret service? Would he still not have to undergo a similar training in the ways of the world, a similar apprenticeship in stratagems and devices? Would he still not be torn between the irreconcilable claims of this world and another? Would not the lama still remain before him as a loving apparition of a "Way" never to be accepted wholly but never to be abandoned wholly?

Most of us, I suppose, would be happier if Kim worked for a Gandhi or some forerunner of Gandhi rather than Colonel Creighton, the head of the British secret service, since that would ease our discomfort with the part of Kipling which, intellectually, we find insupportable. But for the dynamic of the novel itself, for the inner development of Kim, it would not matter decisively. The secret service, rather than a secret underground, is what Kipling's experience made available to him at a fairly superficial plane of consciousness; it is a given of the world in which he grew up, the India of his youth, and it is not, one notes with gratitude, subjected to any quick "purification" by virtue of Kim's service to the lama. All that the Game—the secret service and its prep-school hijinks—need really do is to embody the Wheel of Things, that terrestrial "illusion" which the first portion of the book has shown to be the substance of delight.

The parallel lines of the two main actions draw closer and closer in the concluding chapters, a soaring movement of ecstacy, one of the most beautiful set-pieces in the English language. It is Kipling's skill, but behind that skill, his easiness and poise as a juggler of worlds, which leads him to see that the two lines of action can indeed be brought very close together but that their meanings, their "ways" must remain beyond conciliation.

Kim's mission for the British service leads him toward Tibet, in a pleasantly exciting rigmarole about chasing off Russian spies; his mission as the lama's *chela* leads him toward Tibet, where the old man, as a mighty walker of the hills, takes on a new energy, but also sins through his lapse into anger when he is struck by one of the Russians. Everything comes finally into place, even that coarse-grained love for the world which the lama, here if nowhere else, finds himself sharing:

> "These are the hills of my delight! Shadows blessed above all other shadows! There my eyes opened on this world; there my eyes were opened to this world; there I found Enlightenment; and there I girt my loins for my Search. Out of the Hills I came—the high Hills and the strong winds. Oh, just is the Wheel!" He blessed them in detail—the great glaciers, the naked rocks, the piled moraines and tumbled shale; dry, upland, hidden salt-lake, age-old timber and fruitful water-shot valley one after the other, as a dying man blesses his folk, and Kim marvelled at his passion.

Both Kim and the lama suffer brief, sharp moments of crisis: the boy, his mission successful, is diverted into helping the old man and succumbs to a kind of breakdown of uncertainty, while the old man, though believing himself at the verge of nirvana, forces himself to return to this world out of his love for the boy:

> Then a voice cried: "What shall come to the boy if thou art dead?" and I was shaken back and forth in myself with pity for thee; and I said: "I will return to my *chela* lest he miss the Way." Upon this my Soul . . . withdrew itself from the Great Soul with strivings and yearnings and retchings and agonies not to be told. . . . I pushed aside world upon world for thy sake.

It is a climax of rhapsodic union, but only of the boy and the old man, not of the two Ways. One of Kipling's best critics, J. M. S. Tompkins, notices that "the beauty of *Kim* lies largely in the figure of the lama. . . . Benign, courteous, humble and clean of heart, but a man of authority in his place and time, he draws Kim not to any mystical height—the boy remains firmly terrestrial and takes a very practical view of the lama's immersion in the River of the Arrow—but to a perception of these qualities in his master. . . ."

All through the last third of the book there run a series of anticipatory communions, moments of meeting between the two, in which all seems at peace in, and out of, the world. As they eat together, Kim recognizes: " 'And we are beyond all castes.' " The old man speaks "as a Seeker walking in humility, as an old man, wise and temperate, illumining knowledge . . . till Kim, who had loved him without reason, now loved him for fifty good reasons." And "each long, perfect day rose behind Kim for a barrier to cut him off from his race and his mother-tongue."

There are moments of pure charm: " 'These,' " says the lama, " 'are indeed my Hills. Thus should a man abide, perched above the world, separated from delights, considering vast matters.' " And Kim answers: " 'Yes, if he has a *chela* to prepare tea for him, and to fold a blanket for his head, and to chase out calving cows.' " There are moments of pure yielding, when they wearily make their way down from the hills, the lama weakens, and Kim "held the weary head on his lap through the noonday heats." The lama cannot help remarking how strange it is that a young sahib should serve him so, and Kim replies: " 'Thou hast said there is neither black nor white. Why plague me with this talk, Holy One? Let me rub the other foot. It vexes me. I am not a Sahib, I am thy *chela*, and my head is heavy on my shoulders.' "

For all that *Kim* can be seen (not very profitably, I think) to strike a contrast between East and West, Buddhism and Christianity, it is far more harmonious and accepting, far more "organic," than *Huckleberry Finn*, the book to which it bears so many surface similarities. In Twain's story there is hardly a profitable, let alone pleasurable entry into the world; there can only be an escape from it, for a moment or two, on a floating raft. Nothing along the shores of the Mississippi seems as rich or refreshing as the mundane world into which Kim and the lama plunge at the outset of their journey, and finally Twain's book comes to be a much more otherworldly, much more despairing book than *Kim*, even though, or perhaps because, it has no lama, no religious atmosphere, no invocation of the Great Soul. For Kim, while yielding himself to the lama, also feels "with an almost audible click . . . the wheels of his being lock up anew on the world without. Things that rode meaningless on the eyeball of an instant before slid into proper proportion. Roads were meant to be walked upon, houses to be lived in, cattle to be driven, fields to be tilled, and men and women to be talked to."

The parallel lines, then, move endlessly into the future, without joining or reconcilement. Yet a mark of transfiguration has been stamped upon the book; whatever he may do, Kim will forever and beyond forgetting be the old man's *chela*. That mark of transfiguration is of course the print of love, and one can only wonder, in putting down this incomparable book, how strongly Kipling was aware that in guiding his two friends through pleasure and into the joy of being, he may also have been leaving pleasure behind.

CAN WE SAY ABSOLUTELY
ANYTHING WE LIKE?

FRANK KERMODE

"There was a student once who wrote a paper saying that a couplet by Alexander Pope, 'no Prelate's Lawn with Hair-shirt lined, / Is half so incoherent as my mind' (*Epistle*. I.i. 165–6) ought to be read in the light of a couplet in another poem by Pope: 'Whose ample Lawns are not asham'd to feed/ The milky heifer and deserving steed' (*Moral Essays* IV. 185–6). Since I believe in the force of puns and all sorts of other resemblances in poetry, I do not know quite how to formulate the rule of context by which I confidently reject that connection."[1] So writes W. K. Wimsatt; he adds a note in which he tentatively proposes the kind of explanation a structural linguist might offer but, instead of endorsing or developing it, quotes I. A. Richards on the way in which "the semantic texture" of a poem might be held to forbid certain interpretations; Richards goes on to lament the state of affairs in which a prospective teacher of literature, such as the one whose reading of Marvell he is rejecting, should show so little sense "of what is and is not admissible in interpretation," and display "a reckless disregard of all the means by which language defends itself."

But when it comes to defining the means by which language and poems and plays defend themselves, most of us are in trouble. How, then, does it come about that in the absence of known and certain rules we are, like Mr. Wimsatt, confident in our rejections? Here is my subject. That we do reject confidently is not to be disputed. Even the nomoclastic Roland Barthes allows it, for he remarks, in the course of defending himself against the *ancien régime* and M. Picard, that "*le critique ne peut se dire n'importe quoi*," and speaks of constraints, "*less contraintes formelles du sens: on ne fait pas du sens n'importe comment (si vous en doutez, essayez)*." He does add that "*la sanction du critique, ce n'est pas le sens de l'oeuvre, c'est le sens de ce qu'il en dit*," which moves the problem away from the site upon which Wimsatt and Richards thought to examine it.[2] But it does nothing at all toward the solution of the problem as to how *we* know constraints are being violated, whether these constraints are in the "semantic texture" of the text or in the semantic texture of what we say about the text. It is assumed that *we know* what they are. And the matter that needs considering is therefore expressible as two questions: who are *we*? And how do we *know* what can be said of a poem and what cannot? We must find some tentative answer to these general questions before turning to the special case of Shakespeare. We shall then have to ask in what sense that case *is* special, and whether whatever speciality it has makes a difference to the way in which we know, whoever *we* may be, and whatever *know* can here mean.

First, the more general issue. Let me first put a view which is on the whole reassuring rather than dismaying; it is an application to our questions of the thought of Michael Polanyi. Simply as persons we each exercise considerable cognitive power without being aware of doing so, as for example when we recognize a face. Such tacit knowing works in combination with more readily identifiable operations of intellect. We combine knowing-what with knowing-how. Polanyi might agree with Barthes that in textual as in other matters we create by our ways of knowing an anamorphosis of the object attended to; he expressly states that meticulous attention to a text ought to provide material for the fuller understanding of it that comes only when we switch from "proximal" to "distal," that is, from a concentration on the detail to a remoter survey of the whole. In fact he argues that excessive concentration on the first stage can destroy the object for us. We have to move it into the phase in which our more subliminal intellectual powers can work on it; into what he calls the "tacit dimension."

Here, of course, it is not a matter of accepting or not accepting the whole Polanyi theory, which in any case I've hardly begun to expound. The point is simply that he is clearly talking about a state of affairs of which we each have personal experience. And I think we are even less likely to accuse him of talking about a situation unfamiliar to us when he turns to the question of how a professional body *knows*. Take for example the case of the paper published in *Nature*, in which the author observed that "the average gestation period of different animals ranging from rabbits to cows was an integer multiple of the number π." "The evidence he produced was ample," says Polanyi, "the agreement good. Yet the acceptance of this contribution by the journal was meant only as a joke. *No amount of evidence could convince a modern biologist that gestation periods are equal to integer multiples of the number π*" (my emphasis). Polanyi then gives instances from physics; revolutionary claims ostensibly of the most exciting order are simply ignored, not because anybody at the time of their announcement can disprove them, but because they are tacitly and instantaneously known to be wrong. Nobody would bother to disprove them even if he could, and there is even an implication that if their authors had been real physicists they would have known better than to propose them, "correct" though they be.[3]

One might here insert a caution: the process can go wrong. Mendel was ignored, but it turned out that his hypotheses were tacitly unacceptable only in the existing conditions of science; and we could doubtless develop critical parallels, Whiter for example. But although one can know that one does not know enough, one cannot know what it is that one does not know; and tacit knowledge is founded in the only *epistème* available.

So we now have some notion of what *know* means in this connection, and of what *we* are. *We* who *know* are the possessors of an institutionalized competence. We make mistakes, but on the whole we know that it is better not to confound the senses of the two *lawns*, and we might even say that it was an indication of incompetence to do so; and this condemnation might extend from cases in which it seems to be the semantic quality of the text that justifies the rejection, to others in which we tacitly resist an anamorphosis less obviously open to detailed criticism. The institution has a hierarchy, since competence has to be acquired; and so it rejects not only unqualified material that issues from outside its own limits, but also the efforts of catechumens within. This we do when we examine, say, doctoral dissertations—not without disagreement, but with the sense that agreement is always possible, even if it means calling in a third member of the hierarchy to mediate.[4] With these few words I must leave the whole subject of institutionalized competence, though it is worth many more.[5] The important fact is that if we ceased to behave as if it existed we should be quite useless as teachers and quite incapable, save in what Donne calls "unconcerning things, matters of fact," of deciding upon the value of contributions to the subject. It is, and we have to believe it, *we* who *know*.

The problems inherent in this situation are complicated by the consideration that there are special cases like Shakespeare. I must omit to consider many possible reasons why this should be so and mention only one: Shakespeare is the focus of an inveterate institutional rivalry. Or, the institution Shakespeare is not coterminous with the institution of professional literary scholarship. This is of course true in different ways and lesser measure of other literary institutions, Burns for example, or Blake, or, diminishingly, Wordsworth; but none of these is so solidly founded outside the academy, and in respect of none of them is there so much criticism which has so little to do with *our* sense of what may or may not be usefully said.

Shakespeare has acquired some but not all the characteristic cultural differentiae of a sacred book, and with them has imposed upon his interpreters exceptionally difficult tasks. For these the history of the interpretation of the Bible suggests certain partial parallels. The Roman Catholic Church, for example, has maintained the view that as an institution possessing a valid oral tradition it provides a privileged and authoritative interpretation of Scripture, rather as, I am told, the reading of the Jewish Bible is regulated by the Mishnah. One hothead at the Council of Trent even suggested that the time had passed when it was necessary for anybody to read Scripture at all. But extreme Protestant theology believed that the text, accepted by a grace-illumined mind, was in itself enough; and here the text becomes very "open," as, I am told, the text of the Koran is. It is the presence or absence of a *church*, and the hierarchical rigor of that church, that makes the difference. So within the biblical tradition you have an institutional interpretation full of constraints, and anarchically individual interpretations proposed by independent minds assured of grace and of course hating the institution which claims such privilege and authority. The institution will characteristically be concerned with such matters as canon, and with anathematizing incompetent, that is, heretical or unorthodox, interpretation. The individuals will characteristically do whatever the spirit moves them to do.

Since Shakespeare is, originally at any rate, an English institution, we may expect a good deal of muddle or compromise; and indeed we find a mixture of interpretative traditions, which could, if one had the time or desire to develop the parallel at length, be likened to Roman Catholic, Anglican and all the other Protestant traditions of biblical interpretation down to the extremest forms of antinomianism. Anybody can be directly illuminated by Shakespeare and will claim the right to express his sense of the text.

Consequently we have, in addition to degrees of competence and variations of doctrinal adhesion within the hierarchy, further degrees of antinomian and incorrigible speculation outside it. It may be that a good deal of this lawless speculation derives unconsciously and corruptly from intra-institutional doctrine that has been superannuated, as for instance when entrance examiners are pained to discover that schoolboys think like a Bad Quarto of Bradley. But that is by the way. The real difference between the outside and the inside is marked by the insistence of the outsider that he can say what he likes about Shakespeare and the tacit knowledge of the institution, which he therefore hates, that nothing he says is worth attending to.

We are all familiar with this situation; an obvious but tedious example would be the energetic contempt of all anti-Stratfordians for the academic establishment, and the cruel joy with which they announce in their newsletters that some academic (never one of *us*; usually a stray historian) has expressed some painful doubt about the conventional view. However, I shall briefly illustrate the hostility and lack of communication of which I speak by referring to a book entitled *Othello: Time Enigma and Color Problem*, by Ernest Bloomfield Zeisler, published in Chicago in 1954 in an undated limited edition of two hundred copies. I know nothing of Mr. Zeisler, except that he was kind enough to send me a copy of his book. He is clearly not one of *us*, though; and I do not know whether *we* took any notice of his book when it appeared. My purpose is not to examine the argument of the two essays it contains, but merely to draw attention to Mr. Zeisler's tone. On the question whether Othello was a black man he takes violent exception to the views of some of our institutional colleagues: "Mr. Coleridge's nonsense is so utterly dishonest and vicious that it must be answered in detail," he says; and having done that, concludes that Mr. Coleridge as an arguer has the "razor-sharpness of melted butter." And indeed it must be said that Professor Coleridge was below his best in his comments on this topic. As for Mr. Bradley, he is, like all the rest of us, an "intellectual pygmy" and "a cerebral castrate."[6] It has the ring of a Milton castigating his Catholic opponents.

It would serve no purpose to complain to Mr. Zeisler that we no longer bother our heads about the views of Coleridge and Bradley on this subject. To him the academy is an institution homogeneous, timeless and infamous. Nor is he alone in so believing, for it is only too obvious that a great many people hypostatize our institution in precisely this way, as a sort of transcendental eunuch. But we took no notice of Mr. Zeisler. Institutionalized tacit knowledge assured us that he could be safely ignored, and we no more thought of answering him than the physicists did of responding to Lord Rayleigh's well-formed demonstration "that a hydrogen atom impinging on a metal wire could transmit to it energies ranging up to a hundred electron volts"—a demonstration which, Polanyi assures us, implied a discovery "far more revolutionary than the discovery of atomic fission."[7] In so far as he was one of *them*, Rayleigh ought to have known better; and not to be one of them is to be outside the ranks of the competent.

As I have suggested, the law of tacit exclusion can also operate within the academy, being applied by the more to the less competent. I take, as an instance of this, a totally neglected book called *Caliban: The Missing Link*, published in 1873 by Sir Daniel Wilson, who was a Doctor of Laws and an important professor at Toronto. One could make out a case for this as a book of some importance; so far as I know, it is the first modern reading to attend to Caliban as a Wild Man, relating him to the *homo sylvestris* of Linnaeus, and finding useful parallels in Purchas. The work Wilson began had to be begun all over again, because nobody except Furness, who had a special license to include what all others excluded, paid the slightest attention to Wilson's book.

Why? First because at the time, which was two years before the first edition of Dowden's *Shakspere: His Mind and Art*, nobody, as they say, wanted to know. Dowden does not mention Wilson, nor does Arthur M. Eastman, author of the latest history of Shakespearian criticism. We do not want to know either, though for the different reason that Wilson has nothing to tell us that we don't know already, having access to later scholarship that superseded him without taking any notice of him.

There is, however, a second and perhaps more interesting reason for institutional inattention. Wilson's research into Wild Man was done in the service of a critical discourse, an anamorphosis of *The Tempest*, which tacit knowledge instantly rejected; and now we can see why. He had been reading *The Descent of Man*, and Huxley; and it occurred to him that Shakespeare had, by a purely unconscious process, got there first and created in Caliban, the beast endowed with speech, the equivalent of "the so-called 'brute progenitor of man' of our latest school of science." Assuming that Caliban had as least as much brain as a gorilla, and accepting Huxley's statement that the brain of that animal measures thirty-five cubic inches as against the fifty-five of the human brain, Wilson concludes that "twenty inches is the whole interval to be bridged over"; though that interval contains a qualitative change. "As water at two hundred and twelve degrees passes beyond the boiling point into vapour: so at some undetermined degree in the cerebral scale, between thirty-five and fifty-five, the point is reached at which the irrational brute flashes into the living soul." Intuiting this, Shakespeare created Caliban right, so to speak, on the flash- or boiling-point, and put him on "an imaginary island in the cainozoic world," warm and furnished with abundance of suitable food. Darwin chose Borneo, but Shakespeare remembered the travelers' tales and borrowed for his Mediterranean island certain Caribbean features, even endowing his missing link with a name that is an anagram of "cannibal," which is the same as "Carib." He further gave him certain fishlike qualities because he had a premonition of Darwin on our aquatic origins.

This is the anamorphosis of an infatuated amateur of the science of the seventies. Wilson of course insists that he is discussing an unknowable process, by which the supreme poet could anticipate the supreme biologist; but in fact he is simply fitting the play into a contemporary fashion. The whole thing was tacitly rejected, and for good reason. Now, if we cared to spell it out, we could say why Wilson made such peculiar blunders, and so forfeited the attention some of his inquiries deserved. Despite his reference to Linnaeus, he was incapable of conceiving the Wild Man within a static framework of scientific reference, the only one in which he has a place. The confusion that results from trying to fit the old *homme du bois* into a dynamic evolutionary theory is such that *we* refuse to attend to the attempt; and the assertion that supreme poets can do and can anticipate *everything* is merely to attribute to Shakespeare the omnipossibilism of the heretical individual, which the institution exists to deny.[8]

Henceforth I shall stay with *The Tempest*. The works of Colin Still are probably more familiar, at least by name, than Wilson's, because they were warmly commended by T. S. Eliot and G. Wilson Knight; but in this respect at least *we* regard these distinguished critics as aberrant. Still was convinced that Art resembled the mystery religions not only in the general sense that both provided access to Ultimate Reality, but in the more particular sense that certain very great works of art, notably the Gospels, the *Aeneid* and *The Tempest*, recapitulated with some exactness the ritual of those mysteries. He who would interpret such works therefore must become, in the expression of Aeschylus, *krites enuptiēn*, interpreter of dreams. He must learn the universal language of symbolism, which would give him "the key to every enigmatic utterance in the sphere of art." We note in Still a recurring feature of this kind of interpretation, its absolute inclusiveness; not only will it explain everything, but nothing can be explained in any other way. The academy is by comparison genteel, Anglican, and pluralistic.

Like Wilson, Still postulates that Shakespeare could very well have performed his act of recapitulation in entire ignorance of the rites enacted and the texts cited. The court party of *The Tempest* makes a passage through Purgatory, which constitutes the Lesser Initiation; Ferdinand ascends to the Celestial Paradise (the Greater Initiation) and Stephano and his crew undergo the Psychological Fall. Identifications tend to be peremptory: Miranda is Wisdom, and "if the reader be unconvinced let him ask a Freemason of very high degree (of the rank of Most Wise Sovereign, for example) how far the foregoing argument reflects the more recondite ritual of the Craft. . . ." But explanation also descends to minute particulars. The dogs that are set upon the conspirators have an occult source; even the "Mountayneeres / Dew-lapped" *must* come from a place identifiable as Dante's Mount of Purgatory and Bacon's Hill of Truth. When Sebastian suggests (II.i.87) that Gonzalo might "carry this island home in his pocket, and give it his son for an apple," the reference must be to Avalon, thought to mean paradise as an apple-garden (*aval*, apple, *yn*, island). When Prospero uses the word "revels" he must mean *orgia*; "for nowhere else in his works does the Poet use the word 'revels' in any but its popular and debased sense, as riotous festivity. He must, therefore, have used it on the present occasion with a special and purer meaning." There are also occasions, adds Mr. Still, when the text seems fatuous, and only to be rescued by "drastic interpretation," such as he provides for the foolery about the clothes on the line.[9]

When we reject this interpretation of *The Tempest* we reject some good things, notably some of the detail of the parallel with the *Aeneid*. But we reject it all the same. It is not simply that we can show the detail to be sometimes wrong, though it is so, for example in the passage on the word "revels", or trivial, as in the part about the apple; but rather that it is sectarian to the point of desperation. It is perfectly possible to argue for a Tradition, even a Tradition which establishes some affinity between *The Tempest* and the Eleusinian Mysteries, without going overboard in this way (I think this is the point where Eliot and Knight must have exercised their charity). Mr. Still does not appear to mention *The Magic Flute* in either of his books, but the existence of that work, its analogues with *The Tempest*, and its undisputed Masonic elements, raise issues *we* should probably regard as worth serious attention; but we should want, I think, something much more "scientific," much less dependent on the inexplicable intuitions of Shakespeare. And we should no more ask a Most Wise Sovereign Freemason to interpret Miranda for us than we should ask a Shriner to interpret Stephano.

But whatever we do we shall not accept or even test Mr. Still's thesis, or even invite him to explain all that his total explanation appears to exclude. Unless we belong to a particular sect we simply reject him tacitly, with at least as much confidence as Mr. Wimsatt exhibited in the matter of the lawns.

Let me, in conclusion, repeat that it is no part of my argument that the institution is infallible. The biologists have their Mendel, we our Whiter. The "routinization" of our studies can make it difficult for us, however keenly we feel we need new and perhaps revolutionary departures, to admit the case which challenges our tacit knowledge. But times change, and so do the "paradigms" of that knowledge. Allow me a moment of autobiography. When I began, twenty-seven years ago, to edit *The Tempest* for the Arden series, I looked into Daniel Wilson's book, and, like Mr. Brooke in *Middlemarch*, saw that it would not do. I therefore missed his points about Purchas and the Wild Man, and had to go into it all again. When the edition appeared in 1954 it was reviewed with hilarity by the late John Crowe, who remarked that if the pages on Caliban were representative of the new approach to Shakespeare we might as well head straight for the madhouse and give ourselves up. (I quote from memory, having no intention of looking up *that* review.) A little while ago, in 1974, I was reading a new article on the play which began with a brief account of the conventional views it was about to destroy; the author added a footnote to say that these views were usefully summarized in my introduction, access to which he had perhaps obtained in a late edition.

I speak, I assure you, not out of injured merit, having little pride in my insignificant priority. The point is simply that what a highly respected academician thought extremely silly in 1954 had become tediously conventional by 1974. We must not suppose that in judging our exclusions according to our institutionalized and tacit knowledge we are always referring to the same criteria.

Which conducts me to my last paragraph. There are periodic alterations, sometimes sharp enough to be thought of as quasi-revolutionary but more often consequent upon small changes and adjustments, in the ways in which we judge men or discourses to be competent. But it is upon the current basis of that corpus of tacit knowledge, supposed to be held more fully by those in the upper ranks of the hierarchy, that we allow or disallow criticism or interpretation.[10] Obviously if it comes from a position which denies our competence and privilege, as it does more often than usual when Shakespeare is the text, we spend very little time on it. In general we act, and must act, as if omnipossibilism were a heresy. We may say, with Richards, that the language of the text excludes certain interpretations as impossible (which is sometimes clearly the case, but usually clearly the case only when the error is so obvious and trivial as to leave nothing much to discuss); or, perhaps more often, we may reject an anamorphosis as counter-intuitive—the intuition being, whether we are aware of it or not, institutional in character and founded on a probably unformulated theory of competence.

NOTES

1. W. K. Wimsatt, "Battering the Object," *Contemporary Criticism*, Stratford-upon-Avon Studies, 12, ed. Malcolm Bradbury and David Palmer (London: Arnold, 1970), pp. 75–6.

2. Roland Barthes, *Critique et Vérité* (Paris: Seuil, 1966), pp. 64–5.

3. Michael Polanyi, *The Tacit Dimension* (London: Routledge & Kegan Paul, 1967), pp. 4, 19, 64–5. I have quoted from this short book because Polanyi regards it as providing "a correct summary" of his position (x). But see also the opening section of *Personal Knowledge*, rev. ed. (London: Routledge & Kegan Paul, 1962). Polanyi's theory of "commitment," expounded later in *Personal Knowledge*, is specifically Christian, but has a bearing on the personal effort one makes within a scientific institution, or an institution resembling such an institution in some ways, as ours does. One hopes that this remark could truthfully be adapted to our situation: "While the machinery of scientific institutions severely suppresses some suggested contributions, because they contradict the currently accepted view of things, the same scientific authorities pay their highest homage to ideas which sharply modify these accepted views" (*The Tacit Dimension*, p. 68).

I should add that this point could be made in varying ways by reference to other philosophies of science; see, for example, a fairly recent account of the situation in *Criticism and the Growth of Knowledge*, ed. Imre Lakatos and Alan Musgrave (Cambridge: The University Press, 1970); and Michel Foucault, *Les mots et les choses*, Paris: Gallimard, 1966 (*The Order of Things*, London: Tavistock Publications, 1970).

4. For succinctness I must here omit to discuss the view that agreement is possible only in the branch of the subject called by the French "science de la littérature" and by Northrop Frye "criticism," as distinct from "critique" or "history of taste."

5. By far the best account of "competence" in this sense is Jonathan

Culler's in *Structuralist Poetics* (London: Routledge & Kegan Paul, 1975), Chapter 6.

6. Zeisler, *Othello*, pp. 54, 56, 60.

7. *The Tacit Dimension*, p. 65.

8. Daniel Wilson, *Caliban: The Missing Link* (London: Macmillan, 1873), pp. xii, 21, 25, 36, 72–3.

9. Still first wrote *Shakespeare's Mystery Play* (London: Cecil Palmer, 1923), and then *The Timeless Theme* (London: Ivor Nicholson and Watson, 1936). The argument of the first book is somewhat expanded, and placed in the context of a larger theory of art, in the second, which I have therefore quoted. See pp. 19, 173–4, 189, 206.

10. Here again I must omit to consider the formation of warring parties within the institution, the conflicts, as it were, of theologians and canon lawyers. They are of course important, not only for whatever interest the debates have in themselves, but because in some form they do, in the long run, reach the ears of the parish priest (the instructor in the schoolroom) and affect his pastoral work.

RELIGION OF MAN,
RELIGION OF WOMAN

ROBERT M. ADAMS

". . . a naming of topics on which I would gladly speak and gladlier hear."

Emerson to Carlyle
17 September, 1836

It is, I think, with a sense of lowered horizons and murky atmosphere that anyone who served his apprenticeship to the Caroline divines and the Library of Anglo-Catholic Theology enters on the religious life of the nineteenth century. Lucid and orderly thinking, not to speak of deft controversy, presupposes at least a limited field of preliminary agreement. The further back one has to start in defining and disputing first premises, the less chance there is of getting anywhere in particular; and in the end, no great play is possible between a man with a rapier and a man with a cudgel or pistol. In the earlier age, no man played the game of theology, and few tried to judge it, who did not accept the broad rules of the game and have some appreciation of its fine points. But as the duel gave way to a kind of battle-royal, with everyone brandishing a different homemade weapon, and a loose-lipped public opinion as the arbiter, not much could be expected in the shape of intellectual clarity or distinction. Keble and Newman stood out among

173

their intellectual contemporaries, as they stood apart from the easygoing, pluralist society into which they had fallen, by virtue of their sharp awareness of the older tradition. Newman made the point in brilliant miniature when he said the Tractarian movement, as envisaged, "would be in fact a second Reformation:—a better reformation, for it would be a return not to the sixteenth century, but to the seventeenth."* He meant by this, I think, a return to religion based on evidence, not simply conscience; a religion which did not, in asserting its freedom from papal authority, compromise its own disciplinary and doctrinal powers.

Here one may feel that the extraordinary incomprehension displayed by Kingsley toward Newman was not only individual but historical; apart from being uncommonly wooden in itself, Kingsley's mind was at one with its age in being oriented at an obtuse angle to the entire cosmos of Archbishop Laud. For Laud, as for his age, the question of the true church was all-important, and it was to be decided only on dogmatic, i.e., evidential, grounds. But the creed of "liberalism," as Newman sketched it in Note A to the *Apologia*, neither requires nor admits of sharp doctrinal outlines and distinctions. It is not accessible to evidence. Though it is not necessarily a religion of man, it is a religion of which man's individual conscience is clearly the measure—hence a religion within which dogma plays an insignificant role by comparison with that assigned to conscience. Kingsley and his age thought conscience a sufficient excuse for any possible error of faith, a sure guide to all questions of behavior; and they assumed that assurance about the decrees of conscience was available through the briefest and bluntest form of self-inspection. At the root of liberal theology lay a kind of honesty to uninformed preferences not very different from that so sharply nipped by Professor Trilling

---

° *Apologia*, ed. DeLaura (New York: Norton, 1968), p. 47. Whether the major surgery of the sixteenth century could ever have been performed with the attenuated instruments and conservative instincts of Laudian theology is a question Newman hardly faced.

in *Sincerity and Authenticity*. For Newman, intellectual assurance was an intricate and at best probable deduction from a set of far-ranging positions assumed with regard to the Arians, the Donatists, and the Monophysites, as well as the occasions of the moment. It involved doctrinal justification and consistency, not simply the confident and hasty skimming of one's cerebral cortex.

I do not find the precise phrase "the religion of man" assuming any commanding position, or used to summarize an attitude, before the early twentieth century, when Rabindranath Tagore applied it to one of his lyrical, syncretic celebrations. (And indeed there is a lovely decorum that it should be a Buddhist, writing for Westerners, who first put the phrase at the head of a book. That is certainly where the idea was trending from the first.) But the notion itself can be traced back a long way, first to the French Revolution, then to the English Puritan revolt of 1640, back to the Protestant Reformation, and before that among subtle Greek heretics whose memory is preserved only in the pages of the indignant Irenaeus. Over these many years the concept (it is too vague to be called a "doctrine") has borne many different names, and one would be absurd in suggesting that the early propounders of it had the least intimation of the several shapes it would ultimately assume. Yet as early as 1650 we find Gerrard Winstanley ostentatiously circumlocuting "the great Creator Reason," not only to avoid the too-explicit word "God," but to blur the distinction between the perfect individual man and the deity. That is the same distinction that Ralph Waldo Emerson devoted most of his many pages to eradicating. Professor Abrams has outlined the pedigree of the drift or current as elaborately as need be done for purposes of this essay. His study of *Natural Supernaturalism* (New York: Norton, 1971) culminates very properly in the work of the English Romantic poets. But we need carry the story only a little further to see the ideas of humane, liberal theology move inexorably toward reconciliation with the purely secular philosophy of Bentham and Mill—toward natural naturalism, in fact. The logical Whately, the strenuous Dr. Arnold (to name only two of many) were devout and conscientious men; but in their very emphasis on the qualities of the believer, they tended tacitly to substitute him for the object of belief. They are at least three quarters of the way toward that unitarian declaration of James Martineau which represents the culmination of his argument about *The Seat of Authority in Religion*: "It is in the subjective tincture of our spirits, not in the objective constructions of our intellect, that [Christ's] consecration enters and holds us" (London, 1890, p. 576). The contrast between a tincture and a construction says almost everything.

Perhaps some such diffusion was inherent in the development of Protestantism, as it dwindled from a creed to an ethos to something very little more precise than a mood. The discourses of Emerson, however hazy around the edges and on top, circle back constantly to the infinitude of the private man, his power to be any and all things once he becomes aware of his own divinity. In another culture, out of another set of circumstances, but about the same time, Auguste Comte is found developing his own version of natural supernaturalism in a formula which deliberately unites the structure and terminology of Roman Catholicism with the principles of scientific sociology. It is an amalgam which the philosopher titles "sociolatry," or more pointedly, "the religion of humanity." Michelet, following out the syncretic impulses of philosophes and deists, but basing his views on very different evidence, argued the substantial unity of all religions in a book titled *La Bible de l'Humanité* (1864). About Bergson's "élan vital" and Nietzsche's superman one might well make a question whether they represent religious principles or not, but so far as they place man's highest imperatives in the fulfilling or surpassing of his own nature, they belong among the religions of man. Their common impulse, if not their character, as Mr. Abrams has seen so clearly, is to try to salvage the moral imperatives of supernatural religion without a specific supernatural revelation to underwrite them. There is no need to conflate or equate these and various other formulations assumed by "the religion of man"; their tendency, all too powerful, is to equate and conflate themselves. Neither, for that matter, is there any way of feeling oneself exempt from the condition to which they testify. And yet, when so many streams of thought and feeling pour down into the same basin, one is bound to feel that "the religion of man" or "the religion of humanity" is becoming something of an intellectual and spiritual sink. It is a sink into which the loftiest feelings drain away when they have no prospect of becoming anything more than good intentions, yet retain too much nostalgic appeal to be discarded altogether.

The religion of man—speaking broadly and with occasional exceptions excepted—tends to be Apollonian, rational, progressive, cosmopolitan, and benevolent. Perhaps naturally, it is the "higher" potential of man, the best side of his cultured nature that one invokes—invokes faute de mieux, perhaps, but with the same ends in view as when the supernatural sanctions prevailed. The substitution of *culture* for *cult* marks a shift, if not a clear one, from the qualities of the creed and the ritual to qualities of the individual or community. When the will of God as a distinct, analyzable entity has faded from the world or become blurred, one's best resource is to worship in the soul such traces as may be surmised of the oversoul; one's best hope is that the two may be utterly confused. But the religion of woman, if only because it flowers later and less explicitly than the religion of man, as an extension of it or alternative to it, includes from the beginning something else again.

Comte and Michelet are early theorizers of complementary tendency. Michelet's two books on *L'amour* and *La femme* (1859, 1860) present a theory of the relation between the sexes quite as curious for what it implies as for what it says. Michelet sees woman as a sacred vessel, indeed, but communicating with the Godhead through entirely different channels than man. Her life and her logic center completely on the womb and the reproductive cycle; spiritually and physically, her entire existence depends on her being loved by, and loving in return, one man. Without man she dies, and Michelet assures us, on the curious basis of his modest experience with postmortems, that the brain of an unmarried woman proved to be bone-dry, rock-hard, petrified into a veritable Sahara (*La femme*, Introduction, iv). She is holy, being Nature incarnate and dedicated wholly to Nature; man's first study is to be History, woman's Nature, because his work is to be a creator, a builder, hers is to be a harmony. Each sex is radically deficient in itself, warped and distorted in the absence of the other; each is wholly alien to the other in the first principles of its operation. Woman's thinking, for example, is always perfectly logical and comprehensible, as long as one takes into account the overpowering influence of the menstrual cycle. Because of that constant pressure, she is a lifelong invalid, a perpetual martyr to love; and from that principle of perfect self-surrender comes her only lasting happiness. As she creates babies for man, so she constantly re-creates man himself, regenerating her husband by perpetual acts of trust and submission. It is in her that he finds his beginning and his end. Michelet does not fall far short of saying that it is her divine stupidity that makes her a kind of surrogate-redeemer. Her husband will know what needs to be known about modern science, technology, social and political movements; to all this miscellaneous information, she is beautifully immune. She dominates man by submitting to him, not overawed by his knowledge nor yet mastered by his strength, but in the ecstasy of her own nature. Her highest wisdom is to become his "second self"; her only real thinking is done with her "second brain" (*L'Amour*, p. 182), which discriminates nothing and accepts everything, yearning only for union, unity, love, peace, the fullness of being at one.

These lessons are enlaced with many miscellaneous flowers of rhetoric, ranging from the discreetly erotic to the hazy, pantheistic sublime, with a heavy preference for the sentimental exclamatory. Like many authors of sex manuals since, Michelet in *L'Amour* and *La femme* hangs his lectures on the biography of a prototypical couple, who are married at the ideal age after the ideal courtship, and run through the complete life cycle, with a couple of detour-chapters on the perils of infidelity and the catastrophe of divorce, to the ideal ending in which Eros walks smilingly hand in hand with Thanatos. He assumes the bourgeois family is the ultimate and definitive form of social organization, with the wife as both tyrant and prisoner of that snug unit. It is with special delight that he notes, on the authority of Diodorus Siculus, that in ancient Egypt men swore obedience to their wives; in nineteenth-century France he would order things no differently. For woman in his view is the last—the most lucid and capacious, as well as the most intimate—judge of man. Fractured and debased as he must be by an industrial society that imposes specialization on him, she sees him whole, forgiving yet condemning him from a larger perspective than he can ever know. A fascinating digression in *La femme* (II, x) celebrates the legend of Isis, who even before her own birth was pregnant with Horus, the son who was really no other than his father Osiris, his mother's twin brother, whom it was her mission to restore to his own divine form after his dismemberment. So the story is, or should be, reenacted in the modern world; it is hard to see how togetherness could go further, and in all except the crude utilities of life, it is the woman who covers and encloses the man. From the full male she once married, he is bound to shrink in the course of a lifetime to a puny specialist, a mere lawyer, engineer, or man of business. But the wife is never less than a woman and sometimes a good deal more. She is a natural force, daughter and sister of Nature, Nature herself; she is a flower among flowers; in one of those Michelet metaphors which can be understood to say much or little, she is repeatedly compared to the ocean—free and unbounded, self-purifying, primitive, and unconstrained. One seems to hear in echo the concluding pages of *Finnegans Wake*.

Michelet does not stop short of saying flatly that "Woman is a Religion" (*La femme*, I, vi); or again, and a little more precisely, he says she is an altar before which man bows in homage to a power beyond and above her, of which she is the ikon. And if in the marriage manuals this is exclusively a white religion, there are always the pages of *La sorcière* (1862) to remind us that Michelet recognized it as having a black disguise as well—a disguise so rich and deep that the later century easily adopted it as the reality, only palely masked by "the saint of peace and civilization."

Though Michelet's sentimental rhetoric cloys the modern palate and blurs every subject on which he touches, he strikes one sharp, prophetic discord in his close association of love with death. From one aspect, it is a deeply personal theme in his mind; from another, it is an almost-immemorial association of folklore and myth, as in Dances of Death, earth mothers, sphinxes, vampires, and the nightmares of necrophilia. Michelet feels the presence of death through the woman's readiness to undergo childbirth every time she yields to a man—yields, in other words, to a passion which, even if not brutal, is at least blind. He feels it as well in the practical assurance that his typical wife, several years her husband's junior, will outlive him and so cherish into her last years the memory of a dead lover. These are peripheral contacts, as it were, which Michelet's basic necrophilia sometimes inflates to impressive rhetorical dimensions. But they are enough to cast woman's alliance with nature in an equivocal light, for death too is a natural phenomenon, nothing more so. And they provide a parallel, if not a link, to an equivalent fixation of Comte's. For him too woman must live through man, must be content with the lessons her numb animal-but-spiritual brain can absorb from man's teaching, must devote herself body and soul (but not, emphatically not, mind) to healing and consoling the defective, limited male to whom she has been assigned. The very format of the *Positivist Catechism* (1852; English translation by R. Congreve, 1858), with a priest of the new religion expounding positivist doctrine to his "daughter," mirrors not only Comte's fixation on his own dead saint, Mme. Clotilde de Vaux, but also his social ideal. Woman is on no account to do any work of her own, lest her fibers, both moral and physical, be coarsened. Being in effect "the moral providence of our species" (*Catechism*, p. 33), she is not even to be contaminated by the possession of property. Natural feeling is to predominate in her existence, and women are often joined in Comte's leaden rhetoric with the "proletaries," as two groups which, with the overflowing energy of their untutored hearts, are to construct the new social order under the guidance of the positivist priests. Predictably enough, the climactic manifestation of woman's natural-sacred function is found in "the holy law of eternal widowhood," which forbids her to contract a second marriage under any circumstances whatever.

To be sure, even the docile acolyte of Comte's *Positivist Catechism* jibs momentarily when this doctrine is put before her; but positivism prevails when the instructor shows her how elevating and spiritual permanent widowhood can be. Even if a marriage has lasted only a year, he tells her, the widow will be able to find in it material for meditation and rejoicing through an entire lifetime. (It is one of those unspoken assumptions in which Utopians freely indulge that the survivor of a Comtean marriage will perforce be a woman. We do not hear anything explicit about a "law of eternal widowerhood.") For women, the priest is very assured on the value of absolute, immutable monogamy: "We must consider the institution which prolongs after death the union of husband and wife as quite in keeping with human nature. No intimacy can stand a comparison with theirs" (*Catechism*, p. 325). Not only is widowhood the supreme experience in itself; it sanctifies and spiritualizes a relation which in its first phases might have been contaminated with crass and appetitive elements:

> "Besides, my daughter, our law of widowhood can alone secure for woman's influence its main efficacy. During her objective life, the sexual relation impairs to a great degree the sympathetic influence of the wife, by giving it something of a coarse and personal tinge. Therefore it is that during our objective life, the mother is the principal guardian angel." (*Catechism*, p. 325)

Only when the husband is safely dead does the widow come into her perfection, when she can combine the veneration due to a mother, the attachment due to a wife, and the kindness due to a daughter with the supreme and unquestionable intimacy of a husband who is dead.

Neither Comte nor Michelet was long on a sense of humor; for one thing, they were in deadly earnest because both were relatively radical in their social views, and impressed with their own importance as social therapists proposing massive amelioration of the human condition. Both considered their views of women in the highest degree progressive. Yet in reading them, one has the eerie sense that every concession made to woman's freedom and dignity becomes in their hands a tool for using her as a response to man's needs. She is the "other," defined as what man is not and existing precisely to supplement his inadequacy or support his strength.

Professor Praz, in his long-standard study of the dark erotic fantasies of the nineteenth century (*The Romantic Agony*, 2nd ed., 1951), properly emphasizes the direct line of development from Keats's appetite for extreme sensation to Byron to Rossetti to Swinburne and the self-styled "decadents," with a string of assorted necrophiles, algolagnics, ophiolaters, and kinky types out of Krafft-Ebbing in between. It is a reasonable and persuasive development at which there's no need to do more than gesture here. But even the healers and teachers of the mid-century (men who were to the 1850s and 1860s much what Havelock Ellis, that undeclared but potent moralist, was to be half a century later) seem obsessed with the connection between love and death, and subordinate their definition of woman's "nature" to it. What they celebrate is the instinctual and appetitive side of female existence. Woman represents the fullness of life, the undivided, unspecialized human potential; but her real meaning is death. It is after death that man lives most richly in her; death is the final consummation, in which her continued devotion finally completes his partial and fractured existence. The worship of woman as it develops during the latter part of the century is the worship of an alien principle, redemptive and purifying perhaps but always open toward death, and sometimes receptive of death, eager for death, an active principle of dissolution and decay. The religion of woman complements the religion of man on the surface, but counters it deeply. And yet the one flows imperceptibly into the other on a tide of unbroken feeling that works as well on socialists and liberals, on idealizers of the domestic nest and the family hearth, as on the black romantics.

The mystique of woman that developed during the latter part of the century is too well known to require elaborate description; one sees it vividly in two myths and their variants, the stories of Tristan-Isolde and Salome-John Baptist. Behind both these resurrected fables, or rather contained within them, a miscellany of contrasting energies squabble for predominance. Both stories are latently related to the tale of Orpheus, priest, poet, and musician, torn to pieces by the maenads of Thrace, yet triumphant over death through his music. In Wagner and his several imitators (Maeterlinck, Villiers de l'Isle-Adam, D'Annunzio) the story of doomed lovers becomes a long, lyrical cry in praise of night (instinct, ecstasy, unconsciousness, death) against day (reason, practicality, life-in-the-world). Within these attitudes lies the powerful influence of Schopenhauer's philosophy, newly discovered by Wagner; and within that, the bursting germ of Buddhism, strongly favored by an attitude of disgust at the desolation wrought by Western scientism. The heroes of Wagner and his imitators, even as they possess all the gifts and powers, desire actively and passively nothing—the supreme sensation in the denial of sensation. Tristan drops his sword deliberately in the face of Melot's deadly attack, Pelléas turns his back on the treacherous Golaud, and Giorgio Aurispa allows himself to be drawn voluptuously, consentingly to death with Ippolita. It is sex—not to speak of love in such equivocal cases—that disarms all these masterswordsmen for the battle of life.

Even more striking is the transformation wrought on the figure of Salomé by the late nineteenth century. The Bible, as it sketches her story, is unusually explicit about her motivation in calling for the head of John Baptist. The puritanical prophet had impugned the validity of her mother's second marriage to Herod Antipas, the murderer of her first husband and thus of his own brother. To gain revenge, Herodias prevailed on her daughter to dance before Herod, seduce him into a promise, and thus gain the power to have John beheaded. It is a straightforward little drama of dignity offended and senility imposed upon; and within it the daughter of Herodias plays a role almost entirely passive; she is her mother's agent in everything. The late nineteenth century makes her a recurrent and fascinating enigma largely by a process of subtraction, by removing all the traditional motivations and putting nothing in their place. In Mallarmé she is the fierce and frigid virgin, absorbed in her own ideal or image, reflecting only herself, whatever the mirror in which she looks. She wants the prophet's head on a platter (we are forced to surmise, for she never deigns to explain herself) because he threatens to incarnate and so destroy the icy absolute reverie which is hers alone. Beheading him, as it liberates her from *the other*, liberates him from responsibility to contradictory spheres, a liberation which the severed head, as it bounds free of the humiliating body, cele-

brates with an ecstatic canticle. More mundane and moralistic
—merely perverse rather than nihilist—is Wilde's play, in
which Salomé woos the prophet sexually because he is forbidden fruit. In every other relation, including that with her
mother, she is abrupt and contemptuous. Remote and cold as
the moon which is her emblem, she carries death with her
wherever she goes; and having provoked Narraboth, the young
Syrian guard, to suicide (a rather stagy and facile suicide, one
may feel), she has nothing to say except that there aren't
enough dead men yet. Finally, in Moreau's repeated treatments
of the Salomé theme, so striking that Huysmans assigned one of
them to Des Esseintes so that he could describe it, the princess
is always a shaft of white light in the thick gloom of Herod's
court, a taper of radiant selfishness in a world sick of its own
thoughts and trapped in its own remorse.

Creator and destroyer, but more fascinating in the second
capacity than the first, woman for the late nineteenth century
often stands outside the world of culture—not just the world
of Schumann and Shelley (the museum and drawing-room
world of polite culture, so to speak), but outside all social,
prudential, benevolent, and artificial arrangements. As the
stream through which nature flows—universal, instinctive,
always seeking its own level—woman is both sacred and
obscene, sacred as redeeming man from culture, obscene as
content with a merely appetitive existence that declines inevitably from the high fever of Eros to the low fever of dissolution and decay. Baudelaire marked in a brief sentence a
crucial turning: "La femme est *naturelle*, c'est-a-dire abominable" (*Mon coeur mis á nu*, III). It is in its abruptness an idiosyncratic formulation;* but to generalize it, one need only

---

* Idiosyncratic, and yet Des Esseintes in his flight from the natural-abominable
abandons women altogether in favor of a couple of gussetted, manicured, and
lacqured steam-engines which he finds more spiritual; and Villiers de l'Isle-Adam, in
one of the great early sci-fi's, fantasizes a supremely desirable artificial woman, made
of rubber, synthetics, stainless steel, and several hours of prerecorded conversation.
Produced in. Menlo Park, New Jersey, by Thomas Alva Edison, this fascinating
creature suggests a set of reactions to the American Girl a little beyond the
spectrum of Henry James.

widen the ambiguous overtones of "abominable" through the range implied by the word "fascinating." These demon-daughters of the late nineteenth century may be conventional *femmes fatales*, like Flaubert's stuffed Carthaginian princess; or else cruel ethical idealists like Ibsen's fierce, destructive girls—Rebecca West, Hilda Wangel, Hedda Gabler; or the strident, straight-backed idealists who represented Ireland to young William Butler Yeats. Again, they may be represented by the sacred, instinctive humility of Esther Waters who flows on, uncontaminated by all the passing men who use and abuse her, or she may be figured in the final image of Nana, a dead prostitute in whose festering carrion Zola represents the power of a decay that topples cities and brings down social orders. Woman destroys man by tempting him to heights from which they both know he is bound to fall; she is also the natural flow of things into which, after all his dreams of artifice and eternity, he must be absorbed. Through her and the desire she rouses sounds a distant but irresistible melody, the song of the infinite, eternal void.

Properly to represent the full range of nineteenth-century attitudes toward women would be a task far beyond the dimensions of a paper or, for that matter, a volume; all I've tried to suggest here is the very indefinite way in which the beneficent sanctity of woman accumulated demanding and destructive overtones, how her image as angel of overriding harmony merged imperceptibly into the cloud of apocalypse and the icy, murderous virgin of the ideal. But the more largely we recognize the richness of the spectrum, the more trouble we may seem to be accumulating in making anything of it. These various iridescent fantasies about woman's innate character were never formalized into a coherent body of doctrine; the individuals concerned developed their notions in almost complete isolation from one another; for the few points on which they agreed there were a hundred others on which they disagreed; and the very reference of the pronoun "they" is inchoate and watery. Surely it's an abuse of language to conflate all these various manifestations and cross-purposes under a single catch-phrase as "the religion of woman." As a simple descriptive category, the term is indefensible indeed. But at least it serves to mark a distinct stage in a development that has to be seen as unbroken. For as it had grown out of the religion of man, so the religion of woman, with relatively few tonal changes, transformed itself during the early twentieth century into something very like the religion of sex. This tends to be a masculine phenomenon, based on various mystiques about women; one can trace a central strain of it from D. H. Lawrence and his several epigones in the literature of machismo through Hemingway and Mailer; poets as different as Robert Graves and Dylan Thomas have contributed to it. And nowadays, as everyone knows, the religion of sex extends far beyond literature into subcultures, street-worlds, and commercial enterprises where the therapeutic and spiritual value of promiscuity is an article of faith, and transvestite prostitutes are the supreme martyrs of a new religion of love. Into such curious purlieus we needn't follow it; but its growth can be suggested through reference to the transitional figure of Joyce, who is unusually explicit about all the elements in his personal substitute-religion, and yet hard to grasp because there are so many of them.

The figure of Molly Bloom, for instance, has been subject to critical dispute, mainly because critics have tended to take the graspable part for the elusive whole. Her substantive appearance in *Ulysses* has been delayed till Bloom and Stephen are in the process of being attenuated. Having been established in the first units of the novel as thick and thingly "characters," they are now being subjected to the distorting-mirror of Joyce's art; a stage-direction in "Circe" parodies the effect:

A concave mirror at the side presents to him lovelorn longlost lugubru Booloohoom. Grave Gladstone sees him level, Bloom for Bloom. He passes, struck by the stare of truculent Wellington but in the convex mirror grin unstruck the bonham eyes and fatchuck cheekchops of Jollypoldy the rixdix doldy. (*Ulysses*, Random House, New York, 1934, p. 426)

Bloom and Stephen have been used and used up; they are not only fagged out by the long day's wandering, but exhausted as reservoirs of literary effects. Thus when the two males, who have lost the faith of their fathers yet are wholly alienated from the life of the flesh, celebrate a communion in cocoa and urination, it is made to seem pretty thin stuff. The religion of man, to which they have been reduced and in which they find momentary comfort, is as attenuated as their own inadequate lives. Long ago in the novel the *Ubermensch* was disposed of as a mocking phrase of Mulligan's. Bloom is still Everyman, but he is increasingly Noman as well—transparent, ephemeral, the mere stencil of a person. Stephen is still as isolated and sterile in the labyrinth of his futile mind as he was in "Telemachus." Like the heavenly wanderers to which they are likened, Bloom and Stephen pass one another briefly, distantly, without any real contact, before swinging off into the deep cold of intergalactic space on their separate orbits.

Molly on the other hand is a heavenly body complete and perfect in herself, a "humid nightblue fruit" of another species. Obscene and sacred, living in her sexual cycles not her mind, feeding the desires of all men and indifferent to them individually, she combines them all in the texture of her seamless erotic fantasy. She thus exemplifies that alien, abstract power which makes of woman not a person or a personality, nor even a heroine (we feel immediately how alien all these terms are to Molly Bloom), but a cult-figure.

On these terms the ballad of little Harry Hughes and the Jew's daughter, which Stephen chants to Bloom, and on which he delivers a condensed commentary, takes on special meaning:

"One of all, the least of all, is the victim predestined. Once by inadvertence, twice by design he challenges his destiny. It comes when he is abandoned and challenges him reluctant and, as an apparition of hope and youth, holds him unresisting. It leads him to a strange habitation, to a secret infidel apartment, and there, implacable, immolates him, consenting." (*Ulysses*, p. 676)

The application to Stephen himself as "victim predestined" is obvious enough to have been discussed for a long time, but it works only on a very impersonal level. Neither Molly nor Milly Bloom has challenged Stephen or led him anywhere; neither shows any intention of personally immolating him. Stephen's "destiny," as he had foreseen in the *Portrait*, was "to live, to err, to fall, to triumph, to recreate life out of life" (Modern Library, n.d., p. 200). He is going to do this, not with Molly Bloom as a person, but with the spirit which she, momentarily and for purposes of the particular novel *Ulysses*, embodies. Woman as sewer, woman as falling angel, woman common and precious as the dirt of which our earth is made (her pattern is gravity's rainbow)—these attitudes all tend to invest woman, simply by virtue of her sex, with holy and fearful attributes, before which man can only immolate himself, consenting.

And what is true of Molly in *Ulysses* is confirmed in striking measure by ALP in the *Wake*. Here she is contrasted rather broadly with the death-dealing and socially "adjusted' critics and faultfinders who cause the quick to be still; whereas the very thought of her, Shem's little mummy, causes him to lift the lifewand and make the dumb speak. She is not simply influenced by the tides of her glandular life, she is herself nothing but a flowing and a circulation; and it is in the final completion of her cycle that the novel ecstatically culminates. She becomes the ocean, as Molly becomes the earth; and though the effect of the transcendence is weaker, because she has hardly pretended to be a character, the redemption she brings is no less clear. It is a redemption which involves throwing away the quarrelsome logic and endless guilt of the masculine mind to live in the formless flux of appetite which leads from one identical cycle to the next and ultimately (if that word has meaning in a cosmos where time has no measure) to the void.

A few years ago, before the *Wake* was so well read, some effort used to be put into the thesis that Joyce's view of woman was distinctly medieval. It involved, to be sure, the traditional medieval combination of Mariolatry with the *saccum stercoris* view, but essentially the comparison was as factitious as the notion that Joyce's esthetic views were dutifully elaborated from the *Summa Theologiae*. His esthetics came in fact from Oscar Wilde with a modicum of cosmetic camouflage from the Schoolmen; and his view of women came from the late nineteenth century, where he could have learned to worship and despise, to condescend and to abase himself, quite as extravagantly and inconsistently, as from any medieval clerk. The proof of the pudding, as always in Joyce, is in the *Wake;* what emerges there is not any particular role or combination of roles that woman can assume, but a vision of the female principle, attuned to the cosmos and to the void cradling the cosmos, as uneasy man can never be. That is the religion of woman as it carried over nearly halfway into the twentieth century. One distinctive if somber shape it has taken lately may be noted as a female counter to the predominantly male "religion of sex." Woman is to be thought more sacred than man because she is attuned to nothing at all—she suffers more than man and for less overt reason, therefore better represents the general condition. But that is another story, only now gathering toward the formulation which will render it, in turn, obsolete.

CULTURE AND ITS MINISTERS

RICHARD HOGGART

> For hundreds of years the cultural heritage of mankind was passed on, like a property, to a few heirs. Only slowly did the idea grow that culture, regardless of how it may be defined, is the property of no one.   (Minister of Culture, France)

> Socialist multinational art performs a new social function differing from that of former ages in content and aim.
>   (Minister of Culture, USSR)

> Culture defines the originality of the people in terms of its historic roots, and its readiness to face the future. Our culture is thus our identity card in the community of nations.
>   (Minister of Culture of a
>   New African State)

Among the governments of the world, and virtually right across the world, the last decade has seen an increased interest in "culture" and in the role of the state in "promoting cultural development" which is unprecedented.

In 1970, when UNESCO held a world conference of Ministers of Culture—the first ever held—it found itself host to more ministers and their high officials than it had imagined in even the most optimistic forecasts. True, there were very few artists; but the conference was, in the terms by which ministerial conferences are assessed, exceptionally successful—chiefly, I think, because it allowed all these people (who by and large did not know one another) to take stock of common, new problems.

By now it would be difficult to find a sovereign state which does not have a Minister of Culture or someone with a similar position, whatever his title. The British still balk at the title "Minister of Culture," but for years now they have had a "Minister with Special Responsibility for the Arts." Inevitably, they are self-conscious about it: at the Venice Conference the then Minister confided to the assembled Plenary session: "I will let you into a secret—in my country we have no clear idea what culture means." Which baffled most of his hearers, until they decided it was "typical British humour and understatement." He was right, however, if patronizing; and many of his listeners were in the same boat without always knowing it.

Like Britain, the United States doesn't have a Minister of Culture; but it has arrangements for supporting the arts on a scale hardly thinkable ten or fifteen years ago. Among the nations which don't balk at the title, one thinks first of France and Malraux; and then of all the new nations which, no matter how poor they may be, appointed a Minister of Culture very quickly after their formal incorporation as sovereign states; or of the Eastern European countries where the minister of culture is likely to rank high in the supreme governing body.

If you go on to ask why "culture" has become such a magic word to so many governments you are led into a thicket of contradictions, contradictions not only between countries but within the same Ministry or even the same Minister. Obviously, any unraveling of the main strands will do less than justice to the complexities and interweavings. Still, some main lines are predominant in some countries, some in others; I will discuss three of those strands.

There is, first, the idea of culture as the acquiring of individual virtue. This is, among official attitudes, by far the most disinterested strain, marked by a benevolent, a missionary or a paternalistic spirit. After democratization, the vote, literacy, there is culture; and that too must be spread; culture is a sort of silver-plating.

There are some less attractive variants of this first group of official attitudes. These others lack benevolence, are mainly defensive and developed in reaction to feeling threatened. They feel threatened by what they regard as masses of disaffected, rootless workers with their insistent transistors and insistent bodies, peeling on beaches. So they produce a modern variant of the sour nineteenth century phrase "we must educate our masters." The new form, "we must cultivate our masters," means passing on to "the masses" the idea and the practice of high culture—so that they become quieter. It is also felt that "cultivation" and the more and more sophisticated techniques of modern industry are related and support each other. The need to "spread culture" is, in this view, a necessary concomitant of prosperous modern life. The Minister of Culture of one of the very few wealthy Asian nations can say: "Long considered a luxury, culture is (today) generally understood as being essential for social and economic development. . . ."

The second main group of official attitudes sees culture as an ideological underpinning, as a support to the prevailing ideology. To people who hold this view culture, properly interpreted, leads inevitably to their state's present form. Therefore, the role of the artist is to reflect, embody, celebrate, and justify that interpretation:

> The art of socialist realism truthfully reflects in its various forms the exploits of the people in building the new society, disseminates among the peoples the noble ideas of revolutionary humanism and internationalism, calls upon them to struggle actively for peace and friendship among peoples, and educates in them a feeling of patriotism and a deep sense of civic duty.
>
> (Minister of Culture, USSR)

This implies set arts and fixed roles for artists. Art forms are preeminently channels for known truths, not answers provisionally arrived at after experiment. The assurance is considerable, because the categories are fixed:

> Alongside the development of painting, graphic art, sculpture, and decorative-applied art, monumental art glorifying the historical exploits of our people has, owing to the care lavished on it by the state, made particularly spectacular progress in recent years.
>
> (Minister of Culture, USSR)

The artist works in known forms and utters known truths. The notion of an artist as both inside and outside his society at the same time—personally engaged with his culture as he experiences it, not as it is interpreted to him by others, and therefore led also to try to stand outside that culture and all ready-made interpretations of it—this notion is, in a strict sense, almost inconceivable. People from other societies may talk about the "subordination" and "castration" of the artist in these circumstances, and in their own terms that makes sense. The Communist official will reply in his own terms too, and dismiss such talk as individualistic, bourgeois nonsense. Before that stage is reached, it is useful for Westerners to have realized the total alienness of their attitude to Communist thinking.

It is important at this stage not to confuse methods with principles. The methods of censorship at all levels in Communist countries may be and often are brutal and horrifying; but the principles which are being protected by those measures are regarded as self-evident and indisputable. In this view, the artist does not have a privileged relation to the truth. He is the spokesman or celebrant, through a particular set of forms, of ineluctable truths decided elsewhere and by other processes. His individual views, therefore, are of no particular importance or interest.

I remember one occasion when a Western European artist, shocked by a nasty instance of intellectual censorship by an Eastern European Government, canceled an agreement to perform in that country. It seemed his one sanction. Perhaps he thought that he might shock the Ministry of Culture into seeing the error of its ways. If so, he misread the situation. The Vice-Minister for culture, who handled the matter, was much more shocked than the Western European artist. He was furious that some self-important peacock of an individual had thought he had any grounds, right, or status to put his nose into what were, manifestly and only, matters of governmental decision: someone, battling for a compromise, tried to explain to him that Western artists like to see their artistic and moral integrity as one, and therefore would not happily practice their arts in a situation in which they felt their consciences compromised. The Vice-Minister was outraged. He raised his voice very high and shouted with total conviction, "So much *shit!*" And there the matter ended.

Whatever the calls for détente, this attitude is not likely to change substantially during our lifetimes. Here, the ideological barriers to change are as strong as those against, say, abortion in a very devout, traditionally Roman Catholic country. Add to that the internal political dangers of a relaxation of government controls over art, and you realize that any changes which might encourage the idea of the right and freedom of individuals to speak and write on major matters according to their consciences will be insignificant. Such changes will usually be the result of some particular political need of the moment—and so ad hoc, and liable to be withdrawn when the need changes—rather than part of an alteration in the basic position. A profound change in policy is highly unlikely.

The third main strand in official attitudes is based on the idea of culture as national identity. This is the strongest drive of all; cultural development is assumed here to be politically

195

crucial. So a Minister of Culture of a new nation can typically say (it is a basic theme): "We can never hope to build a nation if we are not united by a common culture."

Naturally, this drive is especially strong in Africa and Asia. It is even stronger among those nations that feel that their sense of identity as peoples was subverted or destroyed by Western colonialization. The aim is to get back to what they once were, or think they were, to get back over the deep ditch cut by colonialism, to reconnect with their roots so that the good sap flows again:

> In a country which has successively seen seven languages and seven different cultures, and in which a score of political regimes have done their utmost to reduce the natives to the rank of second-class inhabitants and destroy even the memory of their predecessors, "national culture" is scarcely an adequate term to use.
>
> (Minister of Culture, Tunisia)

The complications here are enormous—especially since so many of the ruling groups in the new nations have only a vestigial or nostalgic memory of their own cultures. They are products of the Sorbonne or the London School of Economics or, the younger ones, of Cal. Tech. or Harvard Law School. The tension between their acquired Western culture and their original, native culture can be great.

> When we come to speak of our own values, we find ourselves following patterns derived from our imported cultural requirements. Thus we are always, or almost always, somewhat apart from the mass of our people, since nothing in our intellectual and cultural background predisposes us to have an insight into their concerns or to understand their deep-seated aspirations.

> It is therefore time for us to turn to the people to hear the message of our cultures, handed down by word of mouth from generation to generation, so that we can adapt them to our present-day life without allowing ourselves to be disconcerted by

their diversity. What we have to do instead is to lay hold on
the similarities—a sustained effort to adapt and to return to
the fountainhead—since we, the intellectual elites, have been
nurtured by foreign cultures rather than by the realities of our
native African soil.

(Minister of Culture,
New African State)

But, and it is a very big *but*, the rulers themselves, the present
rulers—be they Normaliens or alumni of MIT or ex-lance-
corporals—want to stay in power. Yet they rule over newly
created societies, many of which have never before been unified. Some of these new nations were formed by the departing
colonial powers, drawing straight lines on a map or carving
intricate, or politically and economically significant, new
boundaries. They include people who have been historically
divided on tribal lines and have sometimes been hostile towards
one another, people who may well speak quite different languages which may not yet have orthographies.

Thus we come to the real rub. The search is not only for
national identity. It is also, and even more strongly, for national
unity. The Minister of the new African state spoke of the need
not to be "disconcerted by [the] diversity of cultures" in
each new nation, and of the need to "lay hold on the similarities." That is the heart of the matter. There has to be a center
round which the similarities can be made to accrete. Which
culture, which language shall be chosen as the official culture
and language of the new nation? The answer is usually pragmatic: the culture and language of the ruling group, of the
president and his henchmen.

And what history will the nation have? There may very well
be no national history but only the histories of different tribes
—and those probably oral—(there are few written histories,
and those are often produced by offbeat colonizers and their
missionaries). In the years immediately preceding liberation, the
beginnings of a national self-consciousness may have been

197

forged through the act of kicking out the colonizers. Usually, however, the "national" history is a selective compound of events and figures, and is set into a frame which tends to justify the present setup and the present ruling group. As with the Communist states, all things move ineluctably to the present happy state of affairs, to a people who love the president and the one party.

It then becomes the duty of the Minister of Culture to illustrate, spread, and reinforce that history. In that effort songs, stories, verses, dances, the full range of oral and craft traditions are given an increased and all-embracing symbolic significance. So the Minister of Culture has a key role. In all this (and no matter how vivid one's interest in the differences between cultures) the spirit begins to flag under the barrage of claims that this or that culture has a mystical hold on the truth, a beauty to which no other culture—least of all those of the technological, corrupted West—can aspire. The simplest of local apothegms are held to capture deep truths with all the power of Shakespeare. Sometimes one feels like making a case for the holy perfection of Yorkshire culture and the imaginative power of its idiomatic sayings.

I have described this pattern only in terms of new nations. But a variant of it can be found in some old but relatively small nations which are now caught in the hegemonic embrace of a super power. With them the rediscovery of the *exact* nature of their traditional national cultures—in these cases, there really has been a long-standing *national* culture—is part of their assertion of their own identity against Big Brother outside. I think of Ceauşescu's Rumania or of the immense Polish interest in "national cultural values" which is expressed regularly in resolutions presented by that country to the UN General Assembly and the UNESCO General Conference.

All three strands of the huge, new, official interest in culture which I have described share these qualities: they assume the responsibility of the state for more than material matters; they express a search for some kind of cohesion or harmony in societies, in a period when religious cohesion is regarded as no longer possible or not desirable; and they imply that "culture" is at bottom a very serious and probably a directly political matter.

It may be useful now to approach the subject from a different angle. In non-governmental discussions, the word "culture" is commonly used with a wide range of meanings. We may say that these meanings cluster round two main poles, the esthetic and the anthropological: one conceives culture as having to do primarily with art forms, their creation and appreciation; the other defines culture as "the whole way of life" of a people (a way of life of which art objects are admittedly a significant part). Similarly, one can often recognize two main impulses behind the widespread contemporary drive to "spread" culture, to make it available. These are, respectively, the "handing-on" or "transmission-belt" approach and the "process" or "inner change" approach. With the first, it is assumed that one is giving something, with the second that one is helping to make something happen. The first tends to put very great importance on access to "the high arts" and their wider appreciation by those who have previously been denied that opportunity; the second seeks above all a certain kind of change in the individual consciousness, the arriving at a certain temper of mind, a certain "fineness" of spirit (a fineness which may certainly have been acquired in the course of learning to respond to "the high arts").

If we examine the three main official approaches to culture in the light of the preceding assumptions we see that both types of assumption are present in official thinking, though nowhere in a pure state. The simplest combination might seem to be the esthetic plus the transmission-belt views: that is, "culture" equals the high arts; and "cultural development" equals transmitting them. But no one holds that combination of views in quite so neat a form.

The combinations are, instead, roughly like this. One group of nations—let us call them the developed, mixed-economy, free-enterprise, open group—certainly tend to see "culture" as having primarily to do with artistic forms and objects. Their approach to the business of spreading culture often looks, at first glance, like a fairly pure transmission-belt form. One sees this in particular, for example, when they discuss "the role of the mass media in cultural development." Television is not seen as a new kind of communication which can create new forms and new relationships with audiences. It is seen as a channel through which we send existing good things. But the attitudes of this group are rarely as simple as that. Listen a little longer and you almost always discover that, behind the apparently simple pattern "known good goods→channel of transmission," there lies—though not always consciously—the idea of culture as *process*, the enormous, awe-inspiring idea that in the last resort the aim of culture is to refine, elevate, and *free* the individual and his independent consciousness.

The attitudes of a second group of nations—who may be called the developed socialist group—combine some of the elements above and leave one element very severely alone. They talk predominantly about culture as certain art forms and styles, almost entirely inherited from the pre-Communist period and on the whole fixed and hardly subject to modification. But they also talk about the beauty and distinctiveness of their respective cultures and cultural values in a clearly anthropological way; and they want "their peoples" to appreciate those values (though they are then talking about the appreciation of attitudes identified by authority, not of a continuous process or a becoming). They therefore overwhelmingly see the attempt to spread culture in its transmission-belt form. One is passing something on, not causing something to happen, least of all to the individual.

The new nations, by contrast with both the other groups, put the main emphasis in their definitions of culture on the anthropological aspect. They naturally give very great weight to their artistic traditions, but to those traditions seen as significant expressions of the idea of culture as a "whole way of life." It is the whole way of life of "our people" which gets the main attention. The spreading of culture is less a matter of individual self-fulfillment as an immersion in, a dyeing in the vat of one's traditional culture. There is no suggestion of a movement towards an independent critical self-awareness (or toward the free play of informed opinion which the existence of such individuals can set off). It is rather as though people were expected, separately or—preferably—in known groups (family, village, sub-tribe, etc.), to become linked umbilically to the one great mother.

All of this makes the planning of large-scale cultural conferences particularly interesting. Two years after the Venice World Conference which I mentioned at the beginning, UNESCO arranged a similar conference for European ministers of culture only. Its most important theme was "access and participation," how one makes it possible for more people to approach the arts and also actively to take part in them. This is very much a "developed area" approach, though in its simpler forms (and we did not hear many subtle formulations at the European Ministers' Conference) a very out-of-date one. The more important theme of *freedom* to create and to appreciate was not seriously discussed.

But when, later, a similar conference was prepared for Asia, "access and participation" played a lesser role, seemed not quite relevant. The assumption was that you couldn't propose to give or increase access to an element in which most people were assumed to be still immersed anyway, from which they had never been separated.

One heard, instead, much about the existence of diverse, living, local, oral cultural traditions and of the importance of using the new mass media in such a way that they linked on to those traditions and strengthened them instead of swamping and destroying them. The chaos of life in the huge new cities of the developing world lay like a nightmare reality or an even worse portent behind these debates. And of course one heard much about cultural identity and unity but very little about upon what particular historical bases—in any one nation —that identity and unity should be established.

In its turn, the Conference of African Ministers in late 1975 put enormous emphasis on the African cultural personality as a whole and (even more than the Asian Conference) on the search for cultural unity within each particular new state. The generals and their lieutenants have learned that language in some sophisticated forms.

In the face of all these more or less impure elements in the official interest in culture, one is bound to wonder why those of us who live in developed, open, non-paternalistic, non-centralized, non-authoritarian societies should welcome official support for cultural development at all. Aren't the officials bound to get things wrong, both the definitions and the consequent actions? Isn't *any* difficulty or shortage for artists preferable to *any* state intervention, no matter how hedged in with saving clauses or how apparently well-intentioned it might be? Wouldn't it be better for governments to put their money into indisputably useful activities such as cancer research or practical development aid?

This is a good, strong argument. Sometimes, especially after seeing at close hand a particularly gross or silly example of state intervention, I have felt like settling for that position; and all the time one side of me would *prefer* to be able to settle for it.

But still, I usually end by thinking there are certain things apropos culture which "public authorities"—I prefer to say "public authorities" rather than "governments" because public authorities can be non-governmental, and help to culture is usually better given in that way—can usefully do. But before we discuss these possibilities we really have to ask what definition of "culture" we are working under. What exactly might an open, developed society justifiably mean by "cultural development"?

It is tempting but hardly adequate to take refuge in that favorite English formulation: "We don't like definitions or abstractions. So we won't try to define culture, art, etc. But we can recognize them when we see them, and that's the important thing."

Of the three different general definitions of culture assumed by officialdom which I described above, the third—culture as state-formation—clearly doesn't fit the kind of society I am now talking about. It is too centralist, too authoritarian, too closed, too anthropological, and too collective. In developed, open societies the high level of education and of communications, the existence of multiple cross-currents of opinion, the stress placed (no matter how much it may be subverted by the great power-blocs in a society) on the freedom of the individual to make up his own mind—all put such societies well past the point at which they could or would promote a unitary, traditional, national culture.

The middle definition—culture as ideological underpinning—is even more obviously inapplicable and against the nature of open societies. Yet one can argue that, at another level, such societies (and indeed all societies, no matter how "advanced" they may be) do promote a more or less generally acceptable version of both the national culture and the national ideology. The whole mythology of the "American way of life" as put forth by schools and the media is a good instance of that.

Still, the official definition of cultural development in these societies tends to be, as we saw much earlier, more esthetic than anthropological, more or less Arnoldian, to stress rather heavily certain particular forms of "high culture" but also to pay implicit due to the idea of cultural development as a process within the individual and within society, a refining and "uplifting" process.

In short, this approach has habitually given a dominant role to certain fixed forms (the high arts) in stimulating and validating a desired process. Clearly, no definition of the cultures of these societies which omitted their achievements in music, literature and the visual arts would be an adequate one. Yet the role of those arts in the whole matter of cultural development has been regarded in too fixed a way by official thinking. They have been seen as constituting a pantheon to which a much larger-than-usual audience is now to be admitted, for their own greater good.

There are changes under way here. It has been easy for cultural analysts over the last twenty years or so to show the inadequacy of the above assumptions about culture, their unconsidered or ill-considered, social-class foundations (the high arts of the high bourgeoisie); and generally and rightly to argue for a greater pluralism in forms, styles and sources.

The result is that today you would have difficulty in finding anyone in the field—a "cultural administrator" or "cultural entrepreneur" or "cultural animator"—who did not try to practice considerable pluralism, who was as ready to give funds to street theater as to opera, to the newest pop group (so long as he had been convinced that it was at one musical frontier or another) as to a symphony orchestra, or to a study of the strip cartoon as to one of poetry.

All of which is a far cry from the neatly interlocking set of artistic and social assumptions which guided most such disbursers of public funds a couple of decades ago. The difficulty about changing these assumptions, however, is that as often as not the baby has gone out with the bath water. There are, to change the metaphor, deep ditches on both sides of the road towards cultural development—and by now a great many people, having climbed out of the highbrow right-hand ditch with cries of release and salvation, have fallen just as heavily into the populist left-hand. So now they insist that everything is as valuable as everything else, that only cultural snobs and culture vultures would try to "make distinctions" or introduce, into any discussion of aims for the use of the public funds available, the dread word "standards."

Someone will in turn react against that position, and probably soon; a reaction is by now overdue if we are going to understand better what we really might justifiably mean by support for cultural development in open societies. But for the present, if you like a vigorous but unpopular argument, you need only go to one of those frequent conferences of cultural planners and criticize cultural egalitarianism and populist leveling.

If I think of the art I know best, which is literature, it seems to me that this art asks for two kinds of disposition in its readers.

The first is a readiness to learn to respond to the medium itself. This begins as a love free of ulterior purposes—the sort of fascination, with words and all the intricate objects into which they can be shaped, which makes someone a poet rather than a politician. Without this love of language itself one isn't, though one might be engaged in all sorts of useful and interesting things, engaged with literature, with the art, at all.

The second disposition is a readiness to be, so far as is possible, disinterestedly involved in the exploration of human experience. I mean willing to be introduced to experiences outside those which merely confirm our own ways of seeing things. This disposition is much less valued or encouraged throughout the world than we in the West like to assume. It means trying to stand outside ourselves and our societies and entertaining possibilities we would probably, for our peace of mind, rather not entertain. It means feeling unsupported by the rigid and firm "truths" of any group at all. It requires from the reader some of those qualities which should be required from the writer himself in the face of the experiences he is trying to capture. I know of no fully adequate words for these qualities but I will call them here radicalism and honesty.

Without "the gift of language" no one is likely to write well. But the gift can be wasted and frittered away. Without radicalism and honesty toward the total business of exploring-experience-through-language, no one is likely to produce a work of literature.

The authentic marks of literature, the signs that we are in the presence of creative art, rather than of some other activity such as instruction, exposition, domination, persuasion, flattery or amusement, is the presence of those two quite inseparable qualities. The search for radicalism and honesty toward experience compels the same attitudes toward language. But it may—and perhaps more often does—work the other way round; a love of language demands the effort at radicalism and honesty before the use of language; and from that moment you are concerned not only with the words in themselves but with the experience the words are seeking to capture. Dishonest words show a dishonest handling of experience; the attempt to be honest toward experience drives one to remake the language and the forms.

By now we are fully involved with the matter of standards, with making distinctions (even if we do not actually lay them out point by point, but rather express them by closing a particular book at page three, or by recognizing that a certain poem has nothing to give us). We are a long way past the point at which categories such as "high art" and "low art" can seem useful, since we can by now recognize that what sometimes professes, by its forms and tones, to be high art may be dead toward language and experience, inauthentic, unconvinced and unconvincing. And we may find, in work conventionally assigned to other levels of "brow," signs of just that authenticity. At this point we are beginning to stand up in the middle of the road; we have crawled out of both the right- and the left-hand ditches.

The most important aspect of those qualities essential to the creation of art, those qualities which are therefore essential to a well-founded justification for encouraging "cultural development," is one many of us simply take for granted. Yet over large areas of the world it is not only *not* taken for granted, it is not even recognized or admitted. Nor are there indications that readiness to admit it is growing. This is the assumption that the effort to arrive at an open, discriminating, individual consciousness (whether in an artist or in those who respect his work) is a good thing in itself, that the individual has nothing more important to address himself to than this kind of moral effort. For this assumption means that the arts, though they need not directly concern themselves with "moral striving" and though they do not in themselves necessarily make any one of us, artists and audiences, one whit better morally, are nevertheless the purest of all human activities, the freest expression of the human interest in the meaning of experience, in trying to see life fully and straight by capturing and ordering it in language or some other medium. If that almost impenetrable phrase, "beauty is truth, truth beauty" means anything, it means something like this.

On this view one is overwhelmingly assuming, in any talk about "cultural development," the worthwhileness of an internal process, one which begins with the person and assumes that a worthwhile sense of community can only be reached by moving out from that secured base in the individual consciousness. At this point one is saying something extraordinarily demanding; and one has reached the only indispensable foundation for the encouragement of cultural development. The rest is propaganda or entertainment.

But still, in what we like to call "free" societies, shouldn't people be left to find out such truths for themselves? Yes, ideally. But in fact no societies are free; all societies deform. The authoritarian society deforms as an act of policy. It is not therefore likely to provide antibodies to its own planned deformations. Open societies deform because of their inherent drives; but they can sometimes be persuaded to encourage activities which try to counteract those drives.

Open societies, by their built-in technological thrust, by their reduction of most aspects of life to forms of consumption, by the way their systems of communication—from education through newspapers to television—support these characteristics, such societies concentrate choices, seek to narrow and homogenize taste in goods, styles, attitudes, in art forms and in responses to experience as much as in motor cars or soft drinks. All this affects company directors as much as truck drivers. We are not talking about a dispossessed working class.

One *can*, however, introduce a social-class point. In such societies, for all their "freedom" and "openness," there is still less opportunity for many people to become imaginatively and intellectually aware than there is for others. I do not mean— though it is true, but is a result rather than a cause—that many people, and especially young people, cannot afford to go to the opera or theater. I mean rather that a great many forces ensure that it is harder for a working-class child to break out of the centralizing and narrowing spiral of choice than it is for one who has been brought up in a home with books, one where television is sometimes switched off, or one who has been to a school where the weight of predominant attitudes did not dismiss the idea of a drama group or a voluntary painting class or a discussion group, or one who can reasonably expect to go on to university.

On the basis of all this—on the argument for the *possible* liberating power of the arts, and on the fact that all societies, if left to their own devices, tend to limit rather than liberate— one can found the case for public intervention in favor of cultural development. The basic assumption must be that most of us have more potential than we, whether we are looking at others or considering ourselves, are led to believe. So public authorities must contribute, not so as to provide a glazed sugar-coating over "the masses," but so as to help break up the very concept of "masses" itself; they must gamble on the inherent possibilities of all people and work towards opening up, widening, increasing, choices. Well-conceived initiatives of this sort almost invariably show that most of us have more imaginative and intellectual energies than a market-research, consumer's profile would suggest or could even begin to admit. Such profiles or prophecies, in the nature of the setup, tend to be self-fulfilling. Like sleepwalkers, we tend to go where we are led in the half-light.

But, to rephrase an old chestnut, how can we know what we like to do till we see what it is possible to do? This is a far more adequate motto for public officials than that even hoarier expression of a "dilemma," about whether one should "give the people what they want" or "give them what they ought to have." This false contradiction has served the marketeers of taste immensely well; and it has scared away, or made tongue-tied, many public authorities who wished to use public money to help broaden opportunities. After all—the opponents of public intervention say—isn't it obvious that, respect the arts as we all may, the major instruments of communication do precisely "give people what they want." Don't the viewing and reading figures prove it? Isn't it just as obvious, they go on, that the very idea of giving people what they *ought* to have is an elitist, patronizing, paternalistic, do-gooding relic of authoritarianism and not to be indulged in at any cost?

That false dilemma still has horns strong enough to impale a lot of people. The providers do not "give people what they want" in anything other than a very simple and limiting sense. They do certainly seek out those things which amuse more of us more of the time than others, and then concentrate on providing them. They are not concerned with other things which we, if we were from time to time regarded as belonging to other groupings than that of a great solidified mass, might want and want more intensely and actively. In short, their definition of "want" is based on the assumption that you provide well if you find the least controversial common denominator of current taste; it therefore reinforces the current spectrum of taste and the system which produces it. In the deepest possible sense, it works against change.

Similarly, the formulation "giving people what they *ought* to have" is a falsely reductive one, an instance of cultural slogan warfare. But translate it into something like: helping to make available more and different things than the centralizing and narrowing drive of the market allows; assume that most of us (again, not a "benighted working class" only) can enjoy, respond to a far greater range of intellectual and imaginative experiences than the present achievements of our educational and communication systems would lead anyone to believe. You are then in an altogether different gallery. One very powerful English "communicator" once said that no one who has not run a huge communications instrument has any idea just how low and limited the taste of "the masses" really is. Did he really think that either the reality or the potentialities of his readers—in their day-to-day home lives or working lives—were adequately caught, defined, illustrated in the particular frame of assumed attitudes found daily in the great mass instrument he was responsible for? Apparently he did. He too, incidentally, was generally regarded as a "very cultivated" man.

The range of things we might appreciate is far wider than he, or any other of the highly placed operators of modern society, can allow themselves to believe. If they did come to accept this premise, they would then be hung up on the appalling question of *choice*. If "potentials" are the starting-point, if one cannot decide what to make available from a simple feedback of numbers, by the gross test of the existing common denominators of taste, how on earth *can* one decide *what* to offer? At this point we are at last facing a real but useful dilemma. Most successful experience in this area confirms that

CULTURE AND ITS MINISTERS

a good rule of thumb, one which works from the assumption that most other people are inherently no less sensitive than we are, is to choose between possibilities not out of some cultural-pyramid theory ("leading people onward and upward from brow to brow") but on the basis of how far things excite and challenge and move those particular people who for the moment have to decide. They may sometimes fall on their faces, and should be able to recognize when they are being self-deceptive or self-indulgent. But serious enthusiasm is a better general guide than either patronage or cynicism.

All of which leads to the argument that public authorities should make experiments of a sort and to a degree which commercial authorities cannot dare to make—experiments with ways of increasing "access and participation," and experiments with no-strings ways of helping artists. Add the public authorities' role in supporting performances of those arts (opera, ballet, symphony orchestras, etc.) which require a larger capital outlay and larger recurrent expenditure than audience receipts are likely to bring in, and there is basically little more the public authorities should do; except thereafter to keep well off the grass. I would, however, be inclined to add this qualification: that if the public authorities had to choose between either encouraging artists directly or trying to promote greater appreciation of the arts generally, I believe they should choose the latter. It is safer for all concerned. Almost inevitably, direct official support for artists causes artists themselves insensibly to acquire inhibitions against being *too* shocking, too way-out. Better to help audiences grow, so that artists get their support obliquely, from sufficiently large, free, critical and responsive publics.

Still—to double back at the close—some public authorities do try to help experimentation.

I wonder if those in authority are wise and brave enough to encourage the showing of experimental art and new interpretations of the classical tradition. All really great art disturbs our thoughts and feelings and shows one something of the truth of the human condition. There are those who see a political risk here. But governments must take this risk if men are to be free to become confident, creative and responsible citizens!

It was a British Minister speaking. The rhetoric is certainly plummy and the generalizations rather facile, but the occasion was a large ministerial conference, and in them one does not expect close analysis. And when one thinks of what is *usually* said on such occasions and of what is *actually* done in many countries in the cause of "cultural development," a statement like that—and the fact that it is to some slight extent practiced in a few countries—is a refreshingly good fact in an almost overwhelmingly naughty world.

BEYOND MODERNISM, BEYOND SELF*

DANIEL BELL

> It dsrkles, (inct, tinct) all this our funnaminal world. . . . We are circumveiloped by obscuritads.
>
> James Joyce
> *Finnegans Wake* (p. 242)

Modernism: The Substructure of the Imagination

A single cultural temper, mood, movement—its very amorphousness or protean nature precludes a single encapsulating term—has persisted for more than a century and a quarter, providing renewed and sustained attacks on the bourgeois social structure. The most inclusive term for this cultural temper is *modernism*, a word that sums up what it is: the self-willed effort of a style and sensibility to remain in the forefront of advancing consciousness.

Irving Howe has suggested that the modern must be defined in terms of what it is not, as an "inclusive negative." Modernity, he writes, "consists in a revolt against the prevalent style, *an unyielding rage against* the official order." But this very condition, as Howe points out, creates a dilemma: "Modernism must always struggle but never quite triumph, and then, after

° This essay continues and enlarges with literary evidence an argument I began on sociological grounds in my book *The Cultural Contradictions of Capitalism* (New York: Basic Books, 1976). It begins, therefore, and repeats a theme sounded in that book, and develops the argument in the spirit, if not necessarily the intentions, of Lionel Trilling in his *Beyond Culture.*

In this essay, as in my previous book, I owe an intellectual debt to Steven Marcus with whom I taught a number of the books discussed, especially the novels of Dostoevsky, Gide and the writings of Nietzsche, though I know he will not agree with some of my interpretations. But I am grateful for the fact that friendship overrides politics in these matters.

a time, must struggle in order not to triumph."[1] This is true, I think, and explains its continuing adversary stance. But it does not explain the "unyielding rage," or the need to negate every prevalent style including, in the end, its own.

Modernism, seen as a whole, exhibits a striking parallel to a common assumption of the social-science masters of the last one hundred years. For Marx, Freud, Pareto, the surface rationality of appearances was belied by the irrationality of the substructures of reality. For Marx, beneath the exchange process was the anarchy of the market; for Freud, beneath the tight reins of ego was the limitless unconscious, driven by instinct; for Pareto, under the forms of logic were the residues of sentiment and emotion.

Modernism, too, insists on the meaninglessness of appearance and seeks to uncover a substructure of the imagination. This expresses itself in two ways: one, stylistically, as an attempt to eclipse "distance"—psychic distance, social distance, and esthetic distance—and to insist on the "absolute presentness," the simultaneity and immediacy, of experience. The other, thematically, insists on the absolute imperiousness of the self and sees man as a "self-infinitizing creature," intent on going *beyond*. Beyond what? Beyond everything. Both aspects derive from significant changes in the character of social life in the nineteenth century. Both react against the classical conception of art, which was reaffirmed in the eighteenth century by Lessing.

In his *Laocoön*, published in 1766, Lessing sought to establish the proper boundaries of the arts, especially in painting and poetry. He held that confusion of purpose, such as poetical painting or descriptive poetry, leads to esthetic disaster. The temporal and the spatial defined the distinctions of the different arts, and each genre could realize its intrinsic limitations only by obeying that distinction.*

---

* Lessing wrote: "I argue thus. If it be true that painting employs wholly different signs of imitation from poetry—the one using forms and colors in space, the other

Modernism is a response to two social changes in the nine-teenth century, one on the level of sense perception of the social environment, the other of consciousness about the self. In the world of sense impressions, there was a disorientation of the sense of space and time derived from the new awareness of motion and speed, light, and sound, which came from com-munication and transport. The crisis in self-consciousness arose from the loss of religious certitude, of belief in an afterlife, in heaven or hell, and the consciousness of an immutable void beyond life, the nothingness of death. In effect, these were two new ways of experiencing the world, and often the artist him-self was never wholly aware of the disorientation in the social environment which had shaken up the world and made it seem as if there were only pieces. Yet he had to reassemble these pieces in a new way.

For the second half of the nineteenth century, an ordered world was a chimera. What was suddenly real, in molding the sense perception of an environment, was movement and flux. A radical change in the nature of esthetic perception had sud-denly occurred. If one asks, in esthetic terms, how modern man differs from the Greeks in experiencing environment or emotions, the answer would have to do not with the basic human feelings, such as friendship, love, fear, cruelty, and ag-gression which are common to all ages, but with the temporal-

---

articulate sounds in time—and if signs must unquestionably stand in convenient relation with the thing signified, then signs arranged side by side can represent only objects existing side by side . . . while consecutive signs can express only objects which succeed each other . . . in time.

"Painting, in its coexistent compositions, can use but a single moment of an action, and must therefore choose the most pregnant one, the one most suggestive of what has gone before and what has to follow.

"Poetry, in its progressive imitations, can use but a single attribute of bodies, and must choose that one which gives the most vivid picture of the body as exercised in that particular action.

"Hence the rule for the employment of a single descriptive epithet, and the cause of the rare occurrence of descriptions of physical objects. I should place less confidence in this dry chain of conclusions did I not find them fully confirmed by Homer, or rather had they not been first suggested to me by Homer's method. These principles alone furnish a key to the noble style of the Greeks, and enable us to pass judgment on the opposite method of many modern poets. . . ."

Lessing, *Laocoön: An Essay upon the Limits of Painting and Poetry* (reprint edition, New York, 1965), pp. 91, 92.

spatial dislocation of motion and height. In the nineteenth century, for the first time, man could travel faster than on foot or on an animal, and gain a different sense of changing landscape, a succession of images, the blur of motion, which he could never have experienced before. Or one could, first in a balloon and later in a plane, rise thousands of feet in the sky and see from the air topographical patterns that the ancients had never known.

What was true of the physical world was equally true of the social. With the growth of numbers and density in the cities, there was greater interaction among persons, a syncretism of experience that provided a sudden openness to new styles of life—a geographical and social mobility—that had never been available before. In the canvases of art, the subjects were no longer the mythological creatures of the past or the stillness of nature, but the promenade and the *plage*, the bustle of city life, and by the end of the century, the brilliance of night life in an urban environment transformed by electric light. It is this response to movement, space, and change which provided the new syntax of art and the dislocation of traditional forms.

In modernism the intention is to "overwhelm" the spectator so that the art product itself, through the foreshortening of perspective in painting, or the "sprung rhythm" of a Hopkins in poetry, imposes itself on the viewer in its terms. In modernism, genre becomes an archaic conception whose distinctions are ignored in the flux of experience. In all this there is an "eclipse of distance," so that the spectator loses control and becomes subject to the intentions of the artist. The very structural forms are organized to provide immediacy, simultaneity, envelopment of experience. The control of experience has moved from the spectator, who could contemplate the picture, the sculpture, or the story, to the artist, who brings the viewer into his own field of action. The eclipse of distance provides a common syntax for painting, poetry, narrative, music, and becomes a

common structural component—a formal element—across all
the arts.

The sense of movement and change—the upheaval in the
mode of confronting the world—established vivid new conventions and forms by which people judged their sense perceptions and experience. But more subtly, the awareness of
change prompted a deeper crisis in the human spirit, the fear of
nothingness.*

The sense of death had pervaded the Middle Ages. But with
the rise of rationalism men began to experience a new feeling
of possibility. By the end of the eighteenth century, the belief
in hell, which had had such a strong grip on the human imagination after Origen was excommunicated in the third century
for suggesting that *all* persons could be saved, had slowly de-
clined.† In German romanticism there was also a momentous
break with the centuries-old conception of an unbridgeable
chasm between the human and the divine. Men now sought to

° In the section that follows, and in the remainder of the essay, I deal with that
aspect of modernism which takes the *self* as the criterion for judgment. Certainly I
do not intend to present modernism as a monolithic entity. As I indicated earlier
(and it is a theme which is expressed in my *Cultural Contradictions of Capitalism*),
modernism can be seen through two different prisms: as an experimentalism in
syntax and form (e.g., Mallarmé, Eliot, Joyce, Proust), and, thematically, as a form
of rage or what Quentin Anderson has called "the imperial self." What is striking,
though, is that both aspects represent a break with the past through the disruption
of mimesis and the "rational cosmology" introduced by the Renaissance—which
was not so much modern as a return to classical antiquity. In the *Cultural Contradictions of Capitalism* (see Chapter 2), I have discussed the revolution in syntax
and form through the prism of the "eclipse of distance." In this essay, I deal primarily with the thematic attacks on bourgeois society.
† See D. P. Walker, *The Decline of Hell* (London, 1964).
  As Mr. Walker writes: ". . . by the fourth decade of the 18th century the
doctrine of eternal torment for the damned was being challenged openly, though
seldom, and . . . in the 17th century a few attacks on it, mostly anonymous, had
appeared. This is not true of preceding centuries." (p. 3)
  But even when theologians began to question the doctrine, they felt that such
knowledge was too dangerous for the masses. "This double doctrine is seen even
more clearly in Thomas Burnet's *De Statu Mortuorum*. Burnet is more firmly
opposed to the eternity in hell, and argues against it at great length. But he
cannot reach absolute certainty on the point, and very strongly advises that only
the traditional doctrine should be divulged to the common people. Indeed, Burnet
sees a tradition of esoteric and exoteric truth from Scripture and the Fathers on-
wards, and terms such as *veritas arcana*, as opposed to *veritas vulgaris*, run like a
refrain through his book." (ibid., p. 6)

cross that gulf, and as Faust, the first modern, put it, attain "godlike knowledge," to "prove in man the stature of a god," or else confess his "kinship with the worm."

In the nineteenth century, the sense of the self comes to the fore. The individual comes to be considered as individual, with singular aspirations, and life assumes a greater sanctity and preciousness. The enhancement of the single life, its pain and fear assuaged, becomes a value for its own sake. Economic meliorism, antislavery sentiment, women's rights, the end of child labor and cruel punishments, education for all, were the social issues of the day. But in the deeper metaphysical sense the idea of progress and the vision of material plenty became the basis for the idea that men could go beyond necessity, that they would no longer be constrained by nature but could arrive—in Hegel's phrase—at the end of history.

For Hegel—as the play unfolds in his *Phenomenology**—the drama of life is seen as the movement of consciousness from a primal cosmic unity through time to eternity, a passage from essence to existence to essence which parallels, on a metaphysical level, the Christian drama of paradise, the fall of man and redemption. In the phenomenology of time, man passes out of nature into history. Nature is physical necessity, ineluctable and invariant. History is the unfolding of rationality, man's self-conscious activity in gaining greater control over his own destiny. History is the succession to nature, subject to its own laws. At the end of history—the end of constraint —is freedom. Freedom is the end of necessity and of history, the beginning of man's unbounded ambition as a singular self.

Despite this mesmerizing glimpse of material abundance and self-aggrandizement, there is also present in Hegel, and this is

---

* The *Phenomenology* is written almost literally as a drama, with each scene cast in three moments or acts. It is this dramatic form which gives the work its vividness and peculiar tension. By recasting history as drama, one is thus able to transform the past into a present. Thus, there is in Hegel, too, the sense of the "absolute presentness" of time.

what gives him his radical thrust, a different sense of man's destiny: the nagging awareness of finitude as the finite fate, an ultimate barrier to the self, the final extinction of all self-consciousness—nothingness, death.

In the romantic conception of love, passion transcended death and achieved the unity of selves in a beyond.[2] But Hegel could not be put off by petty mythologies. Modern man was incapable of the consolations of religion in its Christian form or its heretical variants, such as the Manicheanism of the myth of passion. The unhappy consciousness, of which Hegel writes, is the realization of a divine power beyond man for which he must strive. The deepest nature of modern man, the secret of his soul, is that he seeks to reach out beyond himself; knowing that negativity—death—is finite, he refuses to accept it. The chiliasm of modern man, the mainspring of his life drive, is the megalomania of self-infinitization. In consequence, the modern hubris is the refusal to accept limits and to continually reach out; and the modern word is *beyond*—to go always beyond, beyond morality, beyond tragedy, beyond culture. It is in this sense that modern culture is anti-institutional and antinomian, driven by "unyielding rage" to apocalyptic anger.

Few men can live in a state of permanent exaltation or permanent crisis. (Even Zarathustra came down from the mountain.) The early radical vision of Hegel petrified in the conception of the perfect rationality of the State. The early theological writings gave way to the metaphysics of right. But the tap roots which Hegel reached could not be easily shut off. The left-Hegelians sought to "naturalize" the Master. Strauss and Bauer opened up an attack on Christianity. Feuerbach tried to replace theology, the concern with God, with anthropology, the centrality of man. In Marx, the vision of freedom was equated with plenitude, and an end to the division of labor which separated man from his work. It is curious that nowhere in Marx's writings, as is not true of Hegel, is there confrontation with the idea of death. Marx was not apocalyptic, but eschatological. A new kingdom would arise—in this he returned to the earlier Christian view—and man would come into his own at the end of time. Freedom and abundance would provide happiness. In Marxism, there is thus a permanent optimism about history, and this is the source of its renewable appeal.

But the dark stain of Hegel's vision could not be erased. Implicit in his mythos of rationality was the conclusion that rationality itself, the search for absolute knowledge, ends in the contradiction of limitless ends. Man might achieve material abundance, but the unhappy consciousness knows that rationality is futile, that the body will decay, that time has no end. It is this theme, the unyielding rage against man's fate, which defines the self, and its unceasing search for a victory over death.

Three writers whose work was enormously influential in the last quarter of the nineteenth century and the first quarter of the twentieth had a similar vision. In Dostoevski, Gide, and Nietzsche, one finds the "modernist" attack on rationality, the suspension of social and religious morality, and the preoccupation with limitless ends—the struggle against finitude. While Proust's and Joyce's experiments with time may have had the deepest effect on the forms of modernist literature, the attitudes of Dostoevski, Gide, and Nietzsche towards the self, and their definition of a personal style of life, were powerful influences on the sensibility and imagination of modern culture.*

---

* Any choice of representative figures is debatable. In the direct lineage of ideas, one might choose Bakunin and Kierkegaard to exemplify the dark side of Hegel. Hegel's writings came to Russia in the 1840s with a mighty impact, principally through Belinsky, and heavily influenced by his circle. The emphasis on negativity in Hegel became the cornerstone of Bakunin's philosophy. One can delight in destruction, Bakunin said, in a famous phrase, because in the last analysis it is creative. Kierkegaard, also in the 1840s, accepted the "absurdity" of rationalism as self-contradictory, in explaining the problem of man's limits and limitlessness, and he claimed that one could come to terms with existence only by the leap of faith. But Bakunin's influence was only fitful and marginal, and Kierkegaard came to public notice, at least in the English-speaking world, only in the 1940s and 1950s. Dostoevski, Gide, and Nietzsche, as I think the subsequent discussion will show, developed in different ways the major implications of Hegel's early, radical thrust.

For a discussion of Hegel's influence on Russian intellectuals, see Martin Malia,

The theme of Dostoevski, if one reads the *Notes from the Underground* paradigmatically, is an attack on the idea that the world is ordered and has purpose, including the revolutionary purpose of changing society. His particular target was the Crystal Palace, that symbol of man's progress which opened the great 1851 exhibition in London, displaying the works of industry that promised, as one historian has put it, "utopia around the corner."*

To this dream Dostoevski sardonically replies: "We have only to discover these laws of nature, and man will no longer have to answer for his actions, and life will become exceedingly easy for him. All human actions will then, of course, be tabulated according to these laws, mathematically, like tables of logarithms up to 108,000 and entered in an index. . . . [Then] new economic relations will be established, all ready made and worked out with mathematical exactitude so that every possible question will vanish in the twinkling of an eye, simply because every possible answer to it will be provided. Then the 'Palace of Crystal' will be built. . . ."

Against the utilitarian notion that the pursuit of rational self-advantage has made man more civilized, Dostoevski savagely retorted: "The only gain of civilization for mankind is the greater capacity for variety of sensations—and absolutely nothing more. And through the development of this many-sidedness man may come to finding enjoyment in bloodshed. In fact this has already happened to him. Have you noticed that it is the most civilized gentlemen who have been the subtlest slaughterers?"

Reason, Dostoevski insists, satisfies only the rational side of

---

Alexander Herzen and the Birth of Russian Socialism (Cambridge, Mass., 1961). For Kierkegaard's thought, see *The Concept of Dread* (Princeton, 1944) and the *Journals* (Oxford, 1938).

° On the opening of the Crystal Palace, Thackeray wrote a "May-Day Ode": "As though 'twere by a wizard's rod/A blazing arch of lucid glass/Leaps like a fountain from the grass/To meet the sun! . . . God's boundless Heaven is bending blue,/ God's peaceful sunlight's beaming through,/And shines o'er all!" Quoted in John W. Dodds, *The Age of Paradox* (London, 1953), p. 469.

man's nature, while *will* is a manifestation of the whole life. "And although our life, in this manifestation, if it is often worthless, yet it is life and not simply extracting square roots." And life? It is, says this splenetic man, "malignant moans," moans which "express in the first place all the aimlessness of your pain, which is so humiliating to your consciousness."

At the end of all quests for certainty is only the finality of death. And this is why one needs to concentrate on striving and continual striving, rather than on any end itself. "Perhaps the only goal on earth to which mankind is striving lies in this incessant process of attaining; in other words, in life itself, and not in the thing to be attained, which must always be expressed as a formula as positive as twice two makes four, and such positiveness is not life, gentlemen, but the beginning of death. Anyway, man has always been afraid of this mathematical certainty, and I am afraid of it now."

If all that exists is "life," how should one live? The average man lives only for the moment. ("When workmen have finished their work . . . they go to the tavern, then they are taken to the police station—and there is occupation for a week.") For the man of sensibility, however, there is either "nothingness" (and mathematical certainty is a form of nothingness) or suffering. "In the 'Palace of Crystal' it is unthinkable; suffering means doubt, negation, and what would be the good of a 'palace of crystal' if there could be any doubt about it? And yet I think man will never renounce real suffering, that is, destruction and chaos. . . . suffering is the sole origin of consciousness. Though I did lay it down at the beginning that consciousness is the greatest misfortune for man, yet I know man prizes it and would not give it up for any satisfaction."[3]

So, in Dostoevski's view, one accepts life, but life as suffering and with it the consciousness of death. In Gide—the man who can almost be credited with inventing the term "restlessness"—there is a different path, the return to nature.

Modern society, as Rousseau was the first to see, was a movement from nature to culture, the imposition, so to speak, of a second nature on an original human nature. The social order does not come from nature. It is a convention, ratified in the social contract. A social order, necessarily, involves constraint, and a sense of time; of the past, the present, and the future; of actions and consequences; of guilt and retribution. Man in the state of nature lives solely by impulse. He lives from day to day, knows only the present and has no foresight. "His desires do not exceed his physical needs, the only goods he knows in the universe are nourishment, a female and repose; the only evils he fears are pain and hunger. I say pain and not death because an animal will never know what it is to die; and knowledge of death and its terrors is one of the first acquisitions that man has made in moving away from the animal condition."[4]*

Great books renew the myths of mankind, and the books of Gide, as Wallace Fowlie has written, renew the myth of Narcissus. For Gide, the effort was to strip away convention—the religious and social morality imposed on original nature—and to find the authentic self and to be responsible only to that self. To do so, he says, one must first acknowledge naked desire.

In his first book, *Les Nourritures Terrestres*, Gide attacked science, the bourgeois life, and the nation. In his second book, *L'Immoraliste*, he sounds the note of emancipation. Man realizes his authenticity in the release from social constraints—to dare the forbidden, to live by his nature.

In his long convalescence from a debilitating illness recounted in *L'Immoraliste*, "after that touch from the wing of Death,"

---

* One can also point out that Rousseau, in this way, is actually picturing the condition of childhood, or infancy—in the emphasis on food, a woman, rest; on the present and the lack of futurity. The act of coming into civilization—the encounter with others, and the problems of competition, envy and dominance—is, then, the act of growing up. One can read Hegel in a similar, ontogenetic way, in which the original cosmic consciousness is the autistic condition of the infant, and the diremption of the world into the dualisms of spirit and matter, nature and history, is the first separation of the child from the mother, and the beginning of the distinction of self and other.

the "miscellaneous mass of acquired knowledge . . . that has overlain the mind gets peeled off . . . exposing the bare skin— the very flesh of the authentic creature that has lain hidden beneath it. He it was, whom I thenceforward set out to dis- cover—the authentic creature, 'the old Adam,' whom the Gospel had repudiated, whom everything about me—books, masters, parents, and I myself—had begun by attempt to suppress. . . . Thenceforward I despised the secondary creature, the creature who was due to teaching, whom education had painted on the surface."

The excitement of impulse, of the exploration of the senses, lures him. "I confess that the figure of the young king Athalaric . . . attracted me. . . . I pictured to myself this fifteen-year-old boy . . . rebelling against his Latin education and flinging aside his culture, as a restive horse shakes off a troublesome harness; I saw him preferring the society of the untutored Goths to that of Cassiodorus—too old and too wise—plunging for a few years into a life of violent and unbridled pleasures with rude companions of his own age, and dying at eighteen, rotten and sodden with debauchery. I recognized in this tragic impulse toward a wilder, more natural state, something of what Marceline used to call my 'crisis.' "

Gide's crisis is his sexuality, and this is resolved, in North Africa, by his acceptance of his homosexuality. "The society of the lowest dregs of humanity was delectable company to me. And what need had I to understand their language, when I felt it in my whole body." When his wife taxes him with the desire to have people exhibit some vice, Gide replies, "I had to admit that the worst instinct of every human being appeared to me the sincerest."

One has to live in the present. "Memory is an accursed in- vention." And one's life, not any objects, must be a work of art. "A land free from works of art; I despise those who cannot recognize beauty until it has been transcribed and interpreted. The Arabs have this admirable quality, that they live their art, sing it, dissipate it from day to day; it is not fixed, not embalmed in any work. . . . I have always thought that great artists were those who dared to confer the right of beauty on things so natural that people say on seeing them: 'Why did I never realize before that was beautiful too?' "[5]

Both Dostoevski and Gide, as one can see from their major novels, are also preoccupied with murder. Murder is the power to take a life, but also the power, in fantasy, to prevent one's own death. When a child first becomes aware of the terrors of death, the first reaction is solipsistic, to deny death: it will never happen to me; when I turn around the world does not exist. The basic defense against that anxiety is a fantasy of omnipotence, to be able to suspend time and the world. But what happens when one omnipotence meets another, when the reality principle intrudes? Most people accept their limitation and seek to find some consolation or explanation for their final fates. But the fantasy persists too, for it is the necessary, stubbornly rooted "magical" defense against fate. In short, the will to murder is a deep compulsion in human beings, one part of the defense against the anxiety of nothingness. And nowhere is this more evident than in modernism.

For Raskolnikov, in *Crime and Punishment*, the world is divided into the meek and the strong, those who will accept their fate and those who will rail against it and control it. He must prove to himself that he is one of the extraordinary persons, and he commits a murder out of the need to test himself, to convince himself that he has the power to transgress the law. It is a crime of will, but one which merges the unconscious impulses with its intellectual defense. It is the monstrousness of reason.

In *The Possessed*, Pyotr Verhovensky has no such doubts. He is a man who has a secret power, whose arrival has been "heralded," and from whom the revolutionary group expects "extraordinary miracles." He murders Shatov to eliminate a revolutionary competitor. When the corpse is thrown into the pond, Verhovensky speaks to the fellow-conspirators he has involved in the murder: "The highest responsibility is laid upon each of you. You are called upon to bring new life into the party which has grown decrepit and stinking with stagnation. Keep that always before your eyes to give you strength. All that you have to do meanwhile is to bring about the downfall of everything, both the government and its moral standards. . . . The intelligent we shall bring over to our side, and as for the fools, we shall mount upon their shoulders. You must not be shy of that. We've got to re-educate a generation to make them worthy of freedom. We shall have many thousands to contend with. . . ."[6]

By placing his act in the stream of history, Verhovensky seeks to eliminate any self-guilt. It is the oldest of all the techniques of revolutionary self-justification. The Anabaptists at Münster in 1533–1535 thought themselves to be in a state of grace, for the eschatological moment had come, and all commandments, and therefore all sense of sin, had lapsed. Consequently, murder was possible and even necessary. It was the "last" act of violence, to end all violence. In the same way, revolutionary movements have sought to demonstrate that "the cause" is more important than the individual, and no guilt attaches to any act, even murder, committed in the name of the cause. More than any other novelist, Dostoevski dramatized this interplay of murder and revolution when history is the source of a new omnipotence.

Gide too tried to separate retribution from sin, but he explored this solely on the level of personal morality. In *Les Caves du Vatican*, Tafacadis, without any explanation, hurls a complete stranger out of a train, and kills him. This *acte gratuit* occurs in several earlier Gide novels as well. An *acte gratuit* is an apparently motiveless action, but for that very reason, says Gide, it is the freest action of all, the one that separates man from beast, because it has no personal—hence limiting—motive.[7] Man performs such an act with the whole of his personality, with all his characteristics. It is, uniquely, an act of personal omnipotence, and it goes beyond morality, beyond society.

In Western consciousness there has always been tension between the rational and the nonrational, between reason and will, between reason and instinct, as the driving forces of man. A basic triadic distinction was made by Plato, who divided the soul into the rational, the spirited, and the appetitive. Whatever the specific distinction, rational judgment was superior in the hierarchy, and this order dominated Western culture for almost two millennia.

Modernism dirempts this hierarchy. It is the triumph of the spirited, of the will. In Rousseau, the passions guide intelligence; the heart has its reasons which the mind can only understand later. In Hegel, the will is the necessary component of knowing. In Nietzsche, the will is fused with the esthetic mode, in which knowledge derives most directly ("apprehended, not ascertained," as he says in the first line of *The Birth of Tragedy*) from intoxication and dream. What is central to modernism is the derogation of the cognitive.

"Schopenhauer has described for us," Nietzsche wrote, "the tremendous awe which seizes man when he suddenly begins to doubt the cognitive modes of experience . . . when in a given instance the law of causation seems to suspend itself." It is this radical assault on the cognitive which Nietzsche led, under a banner proclaiming the authenticity of experience.

In the classic view, the stoic conception of life, truth freed a man from hubris and allowed him, by understanding the limits of life, to achieve *sophrosyne*—the state of spiritual calm. Socrates (this "despotic logician") held that knowledge alone makes man virtuous. He not only lived by that "instinctive scientific certainty" but he died by it. As Nietzsche wrote: "The image of the dying Socrates—mortal man freed by knowledge and argument from the fear of death—is the emblem which, hanging above the portal of every science, reminds the adept that his mission is to make existence appear intelligible and thereby justified."

But life cannot be justified intellectually, for the cognitive is too devitalizing. It lacks the intoxication, the Dionysian frenzy which is at the root of all impulse, and its taming leads to a loss of creativity: "Every culture that has lost myth has lost, by the same token, its natural healthy creativity. Only a horizon ringed about with myths can unify a culture."

"Throughout the book," Nietzsche wrote later, in a backward glance, "I attributed a purely esthetic meaning—whether implied or overt to all process: a kind of divinity if you like, God as the supreme artist, amoral, recklessly creating and destroying, realizing himself indifferently in whatever he does or undoes, ridding himself by his acts of the embarrassment of his riches and the strain of his internal contradictions."

"Only as an esthetic product can the world be justified to all eternity," Nietzsche wrote in a battle cry as potent for the intelligentsia as Marx's proclamation of the class struggle was for the working class. If an esthetic product is a work of art, art requires illusion—and makers of illusions!—and the esthetic mode is therefore superior to all other modes of conduct. "We have art," Nietzsche says, "in order not to perish of the truth."

Theoretical man, the Socratic rationalist, "finds his highest satisfaction in the unveiling process, which proves to him his own power." But understanding kills action, for in order to act we need the veil of illusion. Art and life, Nietzsche declared, "depend wholly on the laws of optics, on perspective and illusion; both, to be blunt, depend on the necessity of error."

The Christian view of life, entirely moral in purpose, relegates art to the realm of falsehood, but in the Christian doctrine there is a "furious, vindictive hatred of life implicit in that system of ideas and values." Morality, in Schopenhauer's view, which Nietzsche endorsed, is "a mere fabrication for purposes of gulling: at best an artistic fiction; at worst an outrageous imposture."

To find himself, man must return to nature, to become the Dionysian man: "Here archetypal man was cleansed of the illusion of culture and what revealed itself was authentic man, the bearded satyr jubilantly greeting his god. Before him cultured man dwindled to a false cartoon."

Only in frenzy and the release of impulse will man find himself transformed, and realize the secret of life and power. "If one were to convert Beethoven's 'Paean to Joy' into a painting, and refuse to curb the imagination when the multitude prostrates itself reverently in the dust, one might form some apprehension of the Dionysian ritual. Now the slave emerges as a free man; all the rigid, hostile walls which either necessity or despotism has erected between men are shattered . . . as though the veil of Maya had been torn apart and there remained only shreds floating before the vision of mystical Oneness. Man now expresses himself through song and dance as the member of a higher community; he has forgotten how to talk, how to speak, and is on the brink of taking wing as he dances. Each of his gestures betokens enchantment; through him sounds a supernatural power, the same power which makes the animals speak and the earth render up milk and honey. He feels himself to be godlike and strides with the same elation and ecstasy as the gods he has seen in his dreams. No longer the *artist*, he has himself become a work of art: the productive power of the whole universe is now manifest in his transport, to the glorious satisfaction of the primordial One."[8]

In this proclamation of the autonomy of the esthetic—indeed, in the argument that only as an esthetic product can life be justified—Nietzsche declared war on the most profound tradition of Western culture. The writers of the Old Testament, as any religious Jew knows, had a horror of the esthetic because of the implications of its claims. For if the esthetic was autonomous, it was not bound by moral law, and anything was possible in its search for experience lived to the highest peak as art. The history of esthetic movements, from the Sodomites on, bears witness to this fear. The idea of the rose growing out of the dung heap (and who cares if life is a dung heap so long as a rose is produced?), of cruelty and torture as forms of refined debauchery, of perversion and pederasty as products of exhausted lechery—these are all examples of the claims of the "exquisite sensibility" in the name of the autonomous esthetic. In the modern characters of Sanine, or des Esseintes, or "O"—in the novels of Artzybasheff, Huysmanns, and Pauline Réage—one finds the claim to exemption from the moral law. For if the esthetic alone is to justify life, not ethics, religion, or communal sharing, then morality is suspended and desire has no limit. Anything is possible, then, in this quest of the self to explore its relation to sensibility. *Anything.*

The emphasis of modernism is on the present—and the future—but not on the past. The repudiation of the past encourages the hubris of thinking that only present judgment counts. The past has no authority, nor does any of its works or figures. Like the doctrine of progressive revelation, the grace of art, like prophecy, recurs in each generation, and this becomes the source of an antinomianism by which conscience, or the self, rather than law or tradition, becomes the guide of judgment and of the moral canon.

But if one is cut off from the past, one cannot escape the terrors of the future, and the final sense of nothingness that it holds. Faith is no longer possible, and art, or nature, or impulse can erase the self only momentarily in the intoxication or frenzy, or dissolution of the Dionysian act. But intoxication always passes, and there is the cold morning after, which arrives inexorably with the break of day. This inescapable awareness of the future, this eschatological anxiety, leads inevitably to the feeling, the black thread of modernist thought, that each person's own life is at the end of time.

Nietzsche, before his madness, had the premonition that "our whole civilization has been driving, with a tortured intensity that increases from decade to decade, as if towards a catastrophe." And Yeats, in his image of the "widening gyre," had foreseen that "things fall apart . . . anarchy is loosed upon the world." Erich Heller has observed: "Yeats' 'artifice of eternity' and Nietzsche's 'aesthetic phenomenon' are blood relations of the Apocalypse. They spring from the same source as the ancient belief that the world is doomed unless it is transfigured in a final act of salvation."[9]

Beyond Modernism: The Erasure of Boundaries

Traditional modernism, in Frank Kermode's term, sought to substitute for religion or morality an esthetic justification of life; to create a work of art, to be a work of art, this alone provided meaning in man's effort to transcend himself. But in going back to art, as is evident in Nietzsche, one uncovers the taproots of impulse; the problem for the artist is to both acknowledge and tame his Dionysiac rage.

The very search for the roots of self moves the quest of modernism from art to psychology, from the product to the producer, from the object to the psyche. Freudianism, in its uncovering of the unconscious, is a halfway house between art and neurosis. It seeks to explain both, as a compromise between instinct and reality. But in the realm of modernist culture, which is subversive of all restraints, a compromise is a frail structure, and in the 1960s a powerful current of postmodernism developed which carried the logic of modernism to its farthest reaches. In the theoretical writings of Norman O.

231

Brown and Michel Foucault, in the novels of William Burroughs, Jean Genet, and to some extent Norman Mailer, and in the porno-pop culture (more vulgar and more brassy) that is played out in the world of drugs, rock music, and oral sexuality, one sees a culmination of modernist intentions.

There are several dimensions to the postmodernist mood. Against the esthetic justification for life, postmodernism substitutes the instinctual. Impulse and pleasure alone are real and life-affirming; all else is neurosis and death. In a literal sense, reason is the enemy and the desires of the body the truth. Objective consciousness defrauds, and only emotion is meaningful.

Traditional modernism, no matter how daring, played out its impulses in the imagination, within the constraints of art. Whether demonic or murderous, the fantasies were expressed through the ordering principle of form. Art, therefore, even though subversive of society, still ranged itself on the side of order and, implicitly, of a rationality of form, if not of content. Postmodernism overflows the vessels of art. It tears down the boundaries and insists that acting out, rather than making distinctions, is the way to gain knowledge. The happening and the environment, the street and the scene, not the object or the stage, are the proper arena for life.

Extraordinarily, none of this is completely new. There has always been an esoteric tradition which has sanctioned participation in secret rites of release, debauch, and total freedom for those who have been initiated into secret sects through secret knowledge. Gnosticism, in its intellectual formulations, has provided the justification for the attacks on restraints that every society has imposed on its members. Yet in the past, this knowledge was kept hermetic, its members secret. What is most striking about postmodernism is that what was once maintained as esoteric is now proclaimed as ideology, and what was once the property of an aristocracy of the spirit is now turned into the democratization of the cultural mass.* The gnostic mode has always beat against the historic, psychological taboos of civilization. That assault has now been made the platform of a widespread cultural movement. Whether it will remain cultural, or also assume political form, is one of the questions confronting society in the next decades.

The modern temper did achieve an extraordinary gain in human consciousness. What was won is the view that, as Edward Shils puts it, "every human being simply by virtue of his humanity is an essence of unquestionable, undiscriminable value with the fullest right to the realization of what is essential in him."[10] Against this ideal there has always been a realization that desires, no matter how intense, cannot be achieved (though they may be demanded) the moment they are experienced. The limiting condition has been the existence of scarcity. On the one hand there was the economic fact that, on the material level, there were never enough goods to satisfy all the diverse wants of men. On the other, there was the psychic fact that discrepant impulses (oedipal, incestual) necessarily had to be repressed. This conception of restraint "is a tradition," as Shils writes, "with the longest history in the moral repertoire of mankind."

In the nineteenth and twentieth centuries, two developments in social and intellectual history undercut this notion of restraint. One was the economic performance of the society, beginning in the middle of the nineteenth century, which seemed to promise sufficient economic abundance to satisfy every material need of man. This was the foundation of the

---

* By the cultural mass, I mean not the creators of culture, but those who provide the market for culture. Most of these are also transmitters of culture, who work in higher education, book publishing, magazines, broadcast media, theater, cinema and museums, as well as the fashion world and who, thus, often influence and shape the diffusion of cultural products within their own large milieu, as well as often producing the popular materials for the wider mass-culture audience.

socialist ideas of the future. Scarcity, in this conception, was the root of all evil, since the scrambling for scarce goods led to inequality, exploitation, and the institutionalization of privilege. It was the source of distinctions between persons. With abundance, the competitiveness induced by scarcity would be eliminated so that all conflict arising out of competitiveness, such as war, would be abolished.

The second was the idea of "self-consciousness," the conception, first in Hegel and Marx, that men could gain rational insight into their history, and later in Freud, that men could gain rational insight into themselves. These aspects of Marx and Freud—the idea of abundance and the uncovering of the mechanisms of consciousness—are the intellectual bridges to the postmodernist ideas.

Marx himself, unlike Fourier, never had any clear notion of the nature of man's future. He assumed that man was "emergent," that as he gained new powers and a new sense of control, new wants and new needs would arise. For this reason, he felt that he could not predict what man would be like at the "end of history." Freedom was unbounded. All he said was that the elements which divided man, principally the division of labor —between mental and physical work, town and country, male and female—would be overcome, and some sense of a unified whole would emerge.*

Freud was never that optimistic. As he put it in *Civilization and Its Discontents*, the fulcrum of his metapsychological thought, life would always consist in an "irremediable antagonism" between the demands of instinct and the restrictions of civilization. Freud did acknowledge that the most imperious drive of man, "what decides the purpose of life," is the pleasure principle. "The liberty of the individual is no gift of civilization," he wrote. "It was the greatest before there was any

---

* Yet what is equally clear is that we will never overcome scarcity—if not the scarcity of goods, then the scarcities of time and of information. This is an argument developed in my book, *The Coming of Post-Industrial Society* (New York: Basic Books, 1973), pp. 456–475.

civilization." Yet necessarily the pleasure principle is at "loggerheads with the whole world." The development of civilization imposes necessary restriction. In consequence, between the processes of civilization and the libidinal development of the individual there is a basic similarity. Both involve sublimation, displacement, reaction formation. The anal eroticism of the young is transformed into a sense of order and cleanliness. Restraint is a condition of social life.

For Freud, frustration and differentiation are necessary aspects of individuation and growth. An infant at the breast is autistic. He does not, cannot, distinguish his ego from the external world. He learns to do so by the initial frustrations of his life, by the separation of the mother from himself, in his screams for help. "In this way there is for the first time set over against the ego an 'object' in the form of something which appears outside. . . ." The distinction of self and other, the creation of distance, is a necessary condition for health.

Health, in the psychoanalytic sense, as Philip Rieff has pointed out, requires an attitude of "ironic insight" on the part of the self toward all that is not the self. "Psychoanalysis as a science carries an authentic alienating implication, from the breaking of the bondages of the past (advocated on the therapeutic level) to the critical appraisal of moral and religious beliefs (on the level of theory)."[11]

The major problem for Freud, though, was not restraint of impulse. Beyond civilization there is a greater threat to life, the most deep-rooted and ineradicable of all threats—the death instinct. In his early clinical work, Freud had assumed that the death instinct was a component of sadism and an extreme form of such displacement. In his later writing, he thought that it was part of the instinct of mastery and domination. But at the end of his life, he saw the death instinct as an independent, almost reified force. He saw the drama of existence as a cosmic battle between Eros and Thanatos—life and death battling for the dominion of the world. Thus, while civilization represses instinct and subdues life, it has a wider, sweeping function in the service of life. As he was to conclude in *Civilization and Its Discontents*:

> The inclination to aggression is an original self-subsisting instinctual disposition in man, and I return to my view that it would constitute the greatest impediment to civilization. . . . *civilization is a process in the service of Eros*, whose purpose is to combine every single human individual, and after that, families, then races, peoples and nations into one great unity, the unity of mankind.[12]

In the end, Freud advocated a reconciliation with social and cultural authority, provided that authority is rational and reasonable. One does so by establishing and maintaining critical distance between a person and an event, between a person and a doctrine, so that the individual is not swamped by them. In the unconscious, Freud wrote, there is no sense of time, and the terrors we originally experience lurk below, constantly, with all their primal intensity, breaking through at times to overwhelm us in all their fury. The definition of maturity is the ability to interpose a time interval between past and present, to allocate experiences to their proper time frame. Against the external controls and coercions of law and historic codes, men will learn to regulate themselves, in accordance with their own rationally determined individual needs. But life has to consist of boundaries and of balance, otherwise one is hamstrung from without and destroyed from within.

In an essay published in 1925, Freud wrote of the appetites of men: "The throne [of civilization] rests upon fettered slaves. Among the instinctual components . . . the sexual instincts, in the narrower sense of the word, are conspicuous for their strength and savagery. Woe, if they should be set loose! The throne would be overturned and the ruler trampled under foot. Society is aware of this—and will not allow the topic to be mentioned."[13]

And then Freud asks: "But why not? What harm could the discussion do?" And he notes, it is "consequently left to the individual to decide how he can obtain, for the sacrifice he has made, enough compensation to enable him to preserve his mental balance." Freud favors an open discussion, but comments upon the attitude of psychoanalysis, which he feels people have misunderstood: "Psychoanalysis has never said a word in favour of unfettering instincts that would injure our community; on the contrary it has issued a warning and an exhortation to us to mend our ways."

The writer who has gone furthest in arguing for the unfettering of all instinct, the herald of the postmodern mood, is Norman O. Brown. As Leslie Fiedler noted some years ago: "Only Norman O. Brown . . . has come to terms with the aspiration to take the final evolutionary leap and cast off adulthood completely, at least in the area of sex."[14] Brown's is the fullest theoretical statement of the aspirations of a generation in revolt against the past, a past represented essentially by the cult of reason. His is the most savagely stated argument that all of man's cultural ideals are illusory, and that the only salvation for life is spontaneous, unbridled instinct.

Norman O. Brown is a classicist who had written two earlier books on Hesiod and Hermes. Impelled to seek the sources of human nature and culture because of "the superannuation of the political categories which informed liberal thought and action in the 1930s," he wrote *Life Against Death* (1959), an essay on the psychoanalytical meaning of history, and *Love's Body* (1966), an aphoristic collection which foretells the end of history.[15]

In his "Apocalypse" Brown echoes the opening lines of Rousseau in the *Social Contract*: "The human mind was born free, or at any rate born to be free, but everywhere it is in chains"; and, as he adds in chiliastic fashion, "now at the end of its tether." Speaking in pentecostal tongue, he announces his prophecy: "Freud is the measure of our unholy madness, as Nietzsche is the prophet of the holy madness, of Dionysius, the mad truth." To Dionysius he will also add Christ, but in a manner heretofore known only in gnostic literature.

Brown, like all utopians, begins with the implicit assumption that man can be free only in a world of abundance. But he assumes that scarcity has already been abolished, or—though this is never clear—that men should begin to act *as if* scarcity had been eliminated. The materialist utopias of the nineteenth century had promised a plethora of goods; the psychological utopias, such as Fourier's, had promised the end of all restraints. Brown's proclamations are the complete realization of all that Fourier, on the philosophical level, had only barely glimpsed.[16]

Like the Christian and the Hegelian drama of history, Brown begins with the notion that at the start there was paradise, a cosmic undifferentiated unity of self with other, which psychoanalytically is the child at the mother's breast. The fall, or the diremption, is the introduction of culture, the restriction of instinct. Culture is a "diseased reification," a precipitation of body metaphors erected into a thing, and working against the deepest instinctual impulses of man. For Brown, culture is thus analogous to original sin in Christian doctrine. He writes in *Life Against Death*: "Neurosis is not an occasional aberration . . . it is in us, and in us all the time . . . or, to put it another way, the doctrine of the universal neurosis of mankind is the psychoanalytic analogue of the theoretical doctrine of original sin." As Lionel Abel comments, "History has no other content than neurosis . . . what we call history is nothing other than the sequence of events motivated by, or symptomatic of, man's illness. . . . Man is sick; moreover he is a sickness unto death."

Brown believes that the antagonism between instinct and culture, between the pleasure principle and the reality principle, is total. Culture and history, like each who participates in them, are neurotic since they are products of repression. Both culture and history impose a sense of time and psychic distance on men. As the Arab philosopher Al-Ghazzali once wrote, to think of tradition is already to destroy it, since the nature of such an involvement and embodiment must be un-reflective. What Brown seeks to do is to destroy consciousness, to enthrone the primary process in the hierarchy of action, to make each man not an artist (for that still involves some distance and control) but a dreamer. Instinct, not knowledge, is the means of gaining mastery over the self. Only by the dissolution of the self in the body can man acknowledge his life instincts and blot out the death instinct—or the sense of death —which awaits him. Thus Brown chooses the Freud of the pleasure principle and rejects the Freud of civilization. But to the primal Freud, Brown adds a Dionysian Christ. There is to be a rebirth, a new man, and Brown sees this as the esoteric meaning of the Christian resurrection of the body. As in Hegel, there is a quest for the reunification of the divided self. In the fall of man, there was the dismemberment of the first man, Adam. The resurrection of the second man, Christ, but a gnostic Christ, reconstitutes the lost unity. Thus, Brown brings back to the poetic and mythic level what Christianity had transmuted to the theological and Hegel to the metaphysical: the transmutation of the "unfortunate" fall.

How does one know all this? The classical, Platonist view, as I indicated earlier, had set up the hierarchy of three faculties of knowing: the rational, the spirited, and the appetitive. Plato believed that knowledge was gained through the dialectic, the questioning of all propositions, in the contemplative mode, as one moved from becoming to being. For Hegel, however, the knowing process is a willing process. It must not be supposed, he says, that man is "half thought and half will, and that he keeps thought in one pocket and will in another, for that would be a foolish idea." They are not two faculties, for "will is rather a special way of thinking, thinking translating itself into existence." What is practical contains the theoretical: "the will contains the theoretical in itself. . . . An animal acts on instinct . . . and so it too is practical, but it has no will, since it does not bring before its mind the object of its desire."[17]

For Brown, knowledge is carnal knowledge. One knows from the wisdom of the body. He asserts this aphoristically in *Love's Body*:

> Speech resexualized: overcoming the consequences of the fall. The tongue was the first unruly member. Displacement is first from above downwards: the penis is a symbolic tongue, and disturbances of ejaculation a kind of genital stuttering. . . .
>
> Speech resexualized. Sexual potency, linguistic potency abolished at Babel and restored at Pentecost. At Pentecost, tongues of fire, a flame in the shape of a male member. . . .
>
> Knowledge is carnal knowledge, a copulation of subject and object, making the two into one. *Cognito nihil aliud est quam coitio quaedam cum suo cognobili*—"Sex becomes not only an object of thought but in some sense an imaginative method of comprehension." Polymorphously perverse sexuality, in and through every organ of perception. . . .*

Brown begins his quest by accepting the dichotomy between the death instincts and life instincts as fundamental to man. But Brown identifies reality with the death instincts, which he equates with repression, and pleasure with the life instincts, which he identifies with unalloyed, unrestricted Eros.

There are no compromises, no halfway houses, either of rational balance or even of art. Art, "if its object is to undo repression," is in that sense "subversive of civilization," for art goes back to the unconscious and taps its roots. But art, because it imposes an external order, is in the end a sublimation. And sublimation for Brown is only another form of neurosis. "The path of sublimation, which mankind has religiously followed at least since the foundation of the first cities, is no

---

* *Love's Body* is largely a pastiche of quotations which Brown has made into his own. Individual passages in the above quotations are from different writers, but for the purposes of exposition one can assume that in each case the voice is Brown's.

way out of the human neurosis, but on the contrary leads to its aggravation."

The only valuable things "in psychic life are the emotions." Ideas are forms of repression. "All psychic forces are significant only through their aptitude to arouse emotions." And again: "All Freud's work demonstrates that the allegiance of the human psyche to the pleasure-principle is indestructible and that the path of instinctual renunciation is the path of sickness and self-destruction."

Just as Marx seeks to overcome the division of labor which separates man from his own work, so Brown seeks to overcome the division between mind and body, and more, the differentiation between men that occurred in some mythical moment of the past—the primal crime when sons become estranged from their fathers. To overcome biological specialization and human fragmentation, to erase biological and historical fate, to restore the primacy of instinct—this is the aim of the resurrection of the body.

But what kind of instinct? Instinct, too, especially the sexual instinct, has been shaped by the ordering pressures of civilization. Proceeding from an early undifferentiated stage, sexual instincts become organized orally, move to an anal stage, which is a basic bodily repression, and finally become focused in the genital organs. In the values of civilization, the genital is the highest orgasmic form of pleasure. But Brown asks, is not the genital a specialized form of the division of labor itself, concentrating all pleasure in a single organ of the human body, rather than in the body itself? "It is part of the tyranny of genital organization," Brown writes, quoting Blake, "that its slaves are blind, and see not tyranny but natural necessity."

If the eroticism of the body is what men must admit, then pleasure must be suffused throughout. Genital man is to become polymorph perverse, able to experience the world in all senses and through all orifices, to recover, in effect, in unlimited subcoital intimacy, the pleasures of childhood.

Brown writes:

> At the mother's breast, in Freudian language, the child experiences that primal condition, forever after idealized, in which object-libido and ego-libido cannot be distinguished; in philosophical language, the subject-object dualism does not corrupt the blissful experience of the child at the mother's breast. . . . If therefore we think of man as that species of animal which has the historical project of recovering his own childhood, psychoanalysis suggests the eschatological proposition that mankind will not put aside its sickness and its discontent until it is able to abolish every dualism.

Spinoza had wanted to acquire "a body which is fitted for many things," but that is only possible, Brown writes, if we can "recover the body of infancy." As Kai Erikson sums it up:

> Birth and death and copulation are all fragments of the same act, and what man seeks in his restless comings and goings is somehow to combine the fragments of his everyday existence into the unity of experience from which they were once torn. Thus man hopes to possess both penis and vagina, he seeks both potency and castration, he yearns for both life and death, youth and experience, action and passivity; he wants to be both man and woman, mother and child, subject and object; he seeks identity in a posture between the artificial halves of every division; he is transvestite, hermaphroditic, androgynous, polymorphous. And he seeks this position not because he wants to escape his nature but exactly because this *is* his nature.[18]

What this is, of course, is William Blake *redivivus*, and from Blake the mystical tradition of the oneness of all. Blake's appeal to the androgyne is derived largely from Jacob Boehme, who wrote that "Adam was a complete image of God, male and female, and nevertheless, neither of them separately, but pure like a chaste virgin." The creation of selfhood shatters the primal man and relegates him to the realm of law and sin. While Hegel regards Adam's transgression as a *felix culpa*, Blake's sense of the world's heaviness demands a return to the pre-fall state itself:[19]

> ... wherever a grass grows
> Or a leaf binds, the Eternal Man is seen,
>   is heard, is felt,
> And all his sorrows, till he reassumes his ancient bliss.

All of this is couched in the eschatological language of the apocalypse: "The fulfillment of prophecy is the end of the world. Figures are always figures of last things. . . . The unconscious is to be made conscious; a secret disclosed; a veil to be rent, a seal to be broken; the seal which Freud called repression."

What is the meaning of all this? It is a program to erase all boundaries, to obliterate any distinction between the self and the external world, between man and woman, subject and object, mind and body. "The boundary line between self and external world bears no relation to reality. . . . Separateness, then, is the fall—the fall into division, the original lie. . . . To give up boundaries is to give up the reality principle [which] is a false boundary, drawn between inside and outside, subject and object; real and imaginary; physical and mental."

And where does it all lead? In a breathtaking sweep, to the promulgation of a new religion, the worship of the body of Christ, the oneness of man, in the most literal sense of the word. Nietzsche used Dionysius to break down the Christian belief in humility. Brown uses Dionysius to break the seventh seal. "Dionysius, the mad God, breaks down the boundaries; releases the prisoners. . . ." And what returns? "Christ is the second Adam; these two are one; there is only one man. . . . If we are all members of one body, then in that one body there is neither male nor female; or rather there is both. . . ." And in that realization one breaks out of the cave "in which like Plato's prisoners, most of us spend our mortal lives," and come onto that sea of the unconscious, that oceanic feeling in which there is "one sea of energy or instinct; embracing all mankind, without distinction of race, language or culture; and embracing all the generations of Adam, past, present, and future, in one phylogenetic heritage; in one mystical or symbolic body."

And beyond the mystical body? For that, too, like the world, is only metaphor. Beyond the mystical body is *nothing*. "The world is the veil we spin to hide the void. . . . Admit the void; accept loss forever."[20] Since in the end there is only nothingness, Brown insists that life, in an ultimate sense, can consist only of the dissolution of the self in "love's body."

In perceiving the world, we ask: what is true and what is false, what is real and what is unreal? In the everyday, ordinary, commonsense view of things, the world is an *either/or*, in which the boundary lines are distinct and judgments are made in binary fashion. Yet the entire thrust of social science, particularly in the nineteenth century, has been to discount appearances, and to insist that truth lies in some underlying reality which negates perception.

Social science has even sought to erase the distinction between primitive and scientific thought. It used to be argued—this was the thesis of one of the most influential books in anthropology fifty years ago, Lévy-Bruhl's *Primitive Mentality* —that the savage mind was prelogical, irrational, and childlike, "although normal under the conditions in which it is employed."[21] But in the writings of Claude Lévi-Strauss, this argument is questioned. The classification systems of "primitive" thought, such as totemism, or kinship arrangements, or categorization of plants and animals, are for Lévi-Strauss as valid as contemporary science; the one is a function of "concrete," or perceptual thought, the other of abstract thought. These are, he writes, "two distinct modes of scientific thought. These are certainly not a function of different stages of development of the human mind but rather two strategic levels at which nature is accessible to scientific inquiry."[22] To the extent that Lévi-Strauss is right, the distinction between primitive and advanced thought is erased.

Psychologists and historians of art have insisted that vision is only a convention, since what appears to be real is a stylistic precept. And pychiatrists have argued that normality is only a statistical mode. Freud himself did much to blur the lines of arbitrary sexual distinctions. Even in the biological separation of male and female, impulses of one or the other kind mingle in each person, and the dominant traits sometimes shade off into the opposite when the barriers are down. The line between normal and abnormal behavior is equally hard to draw with firmness, since in each person there lurk neurotic impulses, more or less well controlled. To this extent behavior is seen as a continuum rather than marked off in either/or categories.

Despite all these questions few persons have gone so far as to erase the lines completely, and fewer still have reversed the order of truth by arguing that madness (assuming it can be defined) is a superior way of exploring reality. But that boundary was crossed by the French philosopher Michel Foucault and, following him, the influential British psychiatrist R. D. Laing.

Foucault is a historian of madness.[23] In his books, which have been widely read in France, Foucault argues that madness is a form of knowledge which the emerging bourgeois culture could not understand, and therefore the mad, who once were allowed to wander about, were shut up in asylums and confined; the "ship of fools" which once traveled from town to town became the hospital. In the Renaissance, Foucault writes, in the shift to the secular world, madness displaced the medieval obsession with death. "Up to the second half of the fifteenth century, or even a little beyond, the theme of death reigns alone. The end of man, the end of time bear the face of pestilence and war. . . . Then in the last years of the century this enormous uneasiness turns on itself; the mockery of madness replaces death and its solemnity."[24]

Yet madness retained the eschatological power of death, a reminder of the chaos and absurdity of existence, rather than the nothingness of the beyond. The sensibility of the Renaissance was preoccupied with occultism, Cabala, witchcraft as means of interpenetrating time and existence. But it is the "age of reason" which, challenged by madness, confines it to the asylums and madhouses in which the misfits, the deluded, and the obsessed are sequestered in a separate place, and distance, spatially distinct, is enforced.*

While Foucault is primarily writing history, he does so with *parti pris*. Madness, he says, is not only a form of knowledge, but reason itself has no superiority over unreason. Madness is "a monologue" which reason does not deign to listen to. In Freud, as Steven Marcus points out, the dialogue is restored. But Foucault believes that madness is a superior metaphysical and occult power which can transcend the beyond. In Freud's view, the primary process, the dreams and nightmares of the mind, are distortions of reality which have to be interpreted, but Foucault sees them as primary truths. Madness, he says, is a confrontation with the "liberty" and violence in our own psyche which we fear and suppress and which we refuse to face. The same theme is echoed by Norman O. Brown. "It is not schizophrenia but normality that is split-minded," he writes; "in schizophrenia the false boundaries are disintegrating." And in a phrase which is the essence of the new psychiatry, Brown declares: "Schizophrenics are suffering from the truth."[25]

R. D. Laing regards schizophrenia as a form of "futurism"

---

* "There must have formed, silently, doubtless over the course of many years, a social sensibility, common to European culture, that suddenly began to manifest itself in the second half of the seventeenth century; it was this sensibility that suddenly isolated the category destined to populate the places of confinement." *Madness and Civilization*, op. cit., p. 45.

in which a brave internal cosmonaut is venturing into an unknown psychic world. "The process of entering into *the other* world from this world is as natural as death and giving birth or being born. But in our present world, which is both so terrified and so unconscious of the other world, it is not surprising that when 'reality,' the fabric of this world, bursts, and a person enters the other world, he is completely lost and terrified and meets only incomprehension in others."[26]

For Foucault, the prophets of the age are de Sade, Nietzsche, and Antonin Artaud, for in these men "the work of art and madness" are at first united, but art is eclipsed when madness emerges as the superior truth. "Artaud's madness does not slip through the fissures of the work of art; his madness is precisely the *absence of the work of art*. . . . Nietzsche's last cry, proclaiming himself both Christ and Dionysius, is not on the border of reason and unreason, in the perspective of the work of art . . . it is the very annihilation of the work of art. . . . Madness is no longer the space of indecision through which it was possible to glimpse the original truth of the work of art, but the decision beyond which this truth ceases irrevocably, and hangs forever over history."[27]

From the time of Hölderlin and Nerval, Foucault writes, the number of writers, painters, and musicians who have "succumbed" to madness has increased. There is, of course, no way of proving or disproving the statement. But it is clear that in the serious as well as the psychedelic culture of today, the preoccupation with hallucination—crossing "the doors of perception"—has been a central feature. "Surely it is not the lucidity and logic of Robert Lowell or Theodore Roethke or John Berryman which we admire," writes Leslie Fiedler, "but their flirtation with incoherence and disorder. And certainly it is Mailer at his most nearly psychotic, Mailer the creature rather than the master of his fantasies who moves us to admiration; while in the case of Saul Bellow, we endure the

theoretical optimism and acceptance for the sake of the delight-
ful melancholia, the fertile paranoia which he cannot disavow
any more than the talent at whose root they lie."[28]

I have taken Brown and Foucault as representative figures for
a twofold reason: intellectually they have pressed the logic of
modernism toward its most radical theoretical conclusions, and
sociologically they have sounded a note which became expressed by the cultural mass, and in more extreme form by the
porno-pop culture of the day.* This cultural mode for a time
became intertwined with political radicalism, and its theoretical
aspects have been obscured. Whether a political radicalism
spreads depends on the ability of a government to solve pressing economic and social problems. But the postmodern mood,
touching deeper springs of human consciousness, and deeper,
more restless longings than the overt political search for community, is only the first act of a drama that is still to be played
out.

When we return to the postmodern mood—the effort to
erase all boundaries—we come in a sense full circle to the
problem of the self. All transcendental religions have as their
aim the dissolution of the self in at-oneness with God. But
except for some momentary mystical or exalted experience,
this possibility lies only at the end of time.

Gnosticism denies the self as being created by God. It de-
taches the "alien" self from the created world and eclipses time
by asserting the immediacy of a "real" world, which can be
apprehended through secret knowledge, in the "beyond." But
the postmodern mood denies the self as a being created by

* What is most striking sociologically is the extraordinarily rapid spread and intense
public preoccupation with the polymorph perverse—with the public display, in
motion pictures, of fellatio and cunnilingus, so much that what was once
obscurely hinted at in Edward Albee's play *Tiny Alice* is enlarged on the screen
in hard-core pornographic movies such as *Deep Throat* and *The Devil in Miss
Jones*, and portrayed so casually in a slick movie for the cultural mass such as
Shampoo. It would be difficult to find a similar period in Western history (with
the possible exception of the time of Messalina) when sexuality was so open, vulgar
and commercialized.

history or culture. By insisting on the reality of the primal, erotic, diffuse, and polymorph-perverse undifferentiated instincts, it obliterates the line between body and mind, physical and spiritual, self and other. Where the early gnostic movements had sought to absolve the self from the world of theology, the postmodern temper dissolves the self in the realm of psychology. To that extent, while the quest is similar, we have moved through different layers of cultural experience, from the heavens through nature and art to the psyche. But with this difference: while *gnosis* is hermetic and given only to a few, the undifferentiated psyche—or instinct—since it knows no sense of time or culture, is accessible to all. It is in that sense, too, that a once esoteric quest becomes exoteric; and this poses the problem of culture—the definition of the symbolic meanings of experience—in a new, problematic way.

The postmodern temper, looked at as a set of loosely associated doctrines, itself goes in two directions. One, inevitably, moves onto an even more esoteric plane; and its logic is clear. A hundred years ago, Nietzsche proclaimed that the idea of a redeemer or a transcendental vision had lost all power to move men—that God is dead. Man himself was only a halfway house between the animal of the past and the superman to come. Today one finds among the French structuralists a kind of negative Hegelianism: not an *Aufheben* to a higher rationality, but a *Niedergang* to the thesis that "man is dying." Foucault sees man as a short-lived historical incarnation, "a trace on the sand," to be washed away by the waves. The "ruined and pest-ridden" cities of man called soul and being will be "de-constructed." It is no longer the decline of the West, but the end of all civilization. Much of this is modish, a play of words pushing a thought to an absurd logicality. Like the angry playfulness of Dada or Surrealism, it will be remembered as a footnote to cultural history.

But the postmodern temper, moving in another direction, does carry a much more significant implication, not of the esoteric, but as the doctrinal justification for an onslaught on the values and motivational patterns of "ordinary" behavior, in the name of liberation, eroticism, freedom of impulse, and the like. It is this, dressed up in more popular form, which is the importance of the post modernist doctrine. For it means that a crisis of middle-class values is at hand.

The bourgeois world-view—rationalistic, matter-of-fact, pragmatic; neither magical, mystical, nor romantic; emphasizing work and function; concerned with restraint and order in morals and conduct—had by the mid-nineteenth century come to dominate not only the social structure (the organization of the economy), but also the culture, predominantly the religious order and the socialization system which instilled "appropriate" motivation in the child. It reigned triumphant everywhere, opposed only in the realm of culture, by remnants of an aristocratic and Catholic spirit that disdained its unheroic and antitragic mood, as well as its orderly attitude towards time.

The last hundred years has seen an effort by antibourgeois culture to achieve *autonomy* from the social structure, first by a denial of bourgeois values in the realm of art, and second by carving out enclaves where the dandy, the bohemian, and the avant-gardist could live in contrary style. A hundred years later, both efforts have been completed. In doctrine and cultural life-style the antibourgeois has won.

Baudelaire's thesis that poetry is a secret form of knowledge and Nietzsche's argument that life could only be justified esthetically were doctrinal battles against the belief that religion should justify life or that society should determine the form and content of art. By the turn of the century the avant-garde had succeeded in establishing a "life-space" of its own, and by 1910–1930, the eras of Apollinaire and Breton, it was on the offensive against traditional culture. The triumph of modernism represented a victory for the autonomy of culture. In the culture today, antinomianism and anti-institutionalism rule. In the realm of art, on the level of doctrine, no one opposes the idea of experiment, of boundless freedom, of sensibility rather than intellect as a principle of art, of impulse rather than order, of the imagination completely unconstrained. There is no longer an avant-garde, because no one in the culture is on the side of order or tradition.

Herbert Marcuse calls this "repressive desublimation." By this he means that the society does not feel threatened by such unrestraint, and the indulgence of such permissiveness is only a device of the established order to tame (or, in the sociological argot, to "co-opt") the avant-garde. In the immediate sense this may be true. But to see it in this limited way is to misunderstand the subversive consequences of these changes for the morality, if not legitimacy, of Western Christian and bourgeois society.

The traditional bourgeois organization of life—its rationalism and sobriety—has few defenders in the serious culture; nor does it have a coherent system of cultural meanings or stylistic forms with any intellectual or cultural respectability.* What we have today is a radical disjunction of culture and social structure, and it is such disjunctions which historically have paved the way for the erosion of authority, if not for social revolutions.

The larger problems are those of authority and legitimacy in the polity, and of religion in the society. Common to both is the idea of coherence, that the meanings, mundane and transcendental, of one's life experience should cohere in some intelligible pattern. What modernity has done—in its drive to enhance experience, in its repudiation of tradition and the past, in its sanction for the new and the idea that the individual could

---

* What is equally true, as I argue in my *Cultural Contradictions of Capitalism*, is that the capitalist system, half undercuts the traditional bourgeois life—of sobriety and delayed gratification—by the furious promotion of hedonism and pornotopia. What I have been concerned with in this essay is the role of modernism in high culture—in its radical extension of the self—in destroying dialectically the individualism of bourgeois life.

remake his self in accordance solely with desire—is to disrupt that coherence in the name of an unbounded self. The radicalism of postmodernism now drives the individual into the beyond. But it is highly unlikely that—as history has repeatedly shown—except for a hermetic few, the cultural mass can live, since its exists in a mundane world, in that beyond. And even the daring moment of trespass—the polymorph perverse state of androgyny—becomes only a vicarious frisson of the voyeur.

Whatever the further searches of the esoteric few, it seems clear that most of contemporary society is weary of those experiments and seeks—in the political religions of Maoism for community or in the new cults for the dissolution of the self—for some new coherence. The difficulty in the West is that bourgeois society—which in its emphasis on individuality and the self gave rise to modernism—is itself culturally exhausted. And it, too, now exists in a beyond.

NOTES

1. Irving Howe, *The Idea of the Modern* (New York, 1967), p. 13 (my italics).

2. This is explored in Denis de Rougement's *Passion and Society* (London, 1940; revised edition, 1956), particularly his discussion of the Tristan and Isolde myth.

3. All the quotations are from *Notes from the Underground* in *The Short Novels of Dostoevski* (New York, 1945), pp. 137–152.

4. "The Second Discourse," in Rousseau, *The First and Second Discourses*, edited by Roger D. Masters (New York, 1964), p. 116.

5. All quotations are from André Gide, *L'Immoraliste* (New York: Vintage Books, 1958); pp. 42–43, 55, 133, 137, 134–135.

6. *The Possessed* (New York: Modern Library, 1936), p. 617.

7. See the discussion in Enid Starkie, "Gide," in *Three Studies in Modern French Literature* (New Haven, 1960), pp. 162, *passim*.

8. All citations are from the Golffing translation, *The Birth of Tragedy* (New York: Doubleday Anchor, 1956), pp. 22, 93, 136, 9, 42, 10, 53, 23–24, in sequence.

9. Erich Heller, "Yeats and Nietzsche," *Encounter*, December 1969, p. 64.

10. Edward Shils, "Plenitude and Scarcity," *Encounter*, May 1969, p. 44.

11. Philip Rieff, *Freud: The Mind of the Moralist* (New York, 1959), p. 330.

12. Sigmund Freud, *Civilization and its Discontents*, Standard Edition (London, 1961) vol. 21, p. 122 (italics added). Previous quotations from pp. 76, 95, 97, 66.

13. "The Resistances to Psychoanalysis," in Standard Edition, vol. 19, p. 219.

14. Leslie Fiedler, "The New Mutants," in *Partisan Review*, Fall 1965, p. 518.

15. There is, in addition, the essay "Apocalypse: The Place of Mystery in the Life of the Mind," in *Harper's*, May 1961. For two useful interpretive essays, see Richard Noland, "The Apocalypse of Norman O. Brown," *The American Scholar* 38, no. 1 (Winter 1968–69), and Lionel Abel, "Important Nonsense: Norman O. Brown," *Dissent*.

16. For the role of Fourier as a forerunner of the psychological utopias, see my essay, "Charles Fourier: Prophet of Eupsychia," in *The American Scholar* 38, no. 1 (Winter 1968–69).

17. Hegel, *The Philosophy of Right* (Oxford, 1942), pp. 225–27.

18. Kai T. Erikson, "A Return to Zero," *The American Scholar*, p. 140.

19. For a discussion of the *felix culpa* and the subsequent debate, see Herbert Weisinger, *Tragedy and the Paradox of the Fortunate Fall* (London, 1953).

20. The quotations in this section are taken, except where otherwise noted, from Brown's two books. *Life Against Death* is noted as L/D; *Love's Body* as L/B. In sequence, beginning with the quote on carnal knowledge, on page L/B, 251, 249; L/D 307, 7, 57; L/B, 127; L/D 51–52; L/D 48; L/B 219, 217, 143, 148–149; 161, 83, 84, 88–89; 261, 260.

21. Lucien Lévy-Bruhl, *Primitive Mentality* (London, 1923), p. 33.

22. Claude Lévi-Strauss, *The Savage Mind* (London, 1966), p. 15.

23. *Madness and Civilization: A History of Insanity in the Age of Reason*, written in 1961 and published in New York in 1965. His *Les Mots et les Choses: une archéologie des sciences humaines* (Paris, 1966) was a best-seller in France. In addition, Foucault has written two books on mental illness and personality and also a study of the presurrealist writer Raymound Roussell.

24. *Madness and Civilization* (Tavistock edition, London, 1967), p. 15.

25. *Love's Body*, p. 159.

26. R. D. Laing, "The Schizophrenic Experience," in *The Politics of Experience* (New York, 1968).

27. *Madness and Civilization*, p. 287.

28. "The New Mutants," *op. cit.*, p. 524.

ON *THE MIDDLE OF THE JOURNEY*

QUENTIN ANDERSON

The Middle of the Journey, published in 1947 and reissued in 1976, is Lionel Trilling's only novel. It seems likely that there would have been others had this one been given the place it deserved in our literature and the history of our culture. We are not yet, I think, prepared to acknowledge the accuracy of the picture of ourselves it affords. I am convinced that the novel constituted an attack so grave and inclusive on the pieties of middle-class radicalism that what it made apparent simply had to be ignored, elided. Direct denial would have been too painful. The chief of these pieties resulted from our confusion of the aims of the American Communist Party with the belief that the world could be remade in accord with our personal demands. This was but one case of a persisting American habit of appropriating political ideas as narcissistic supplies for a self which demanded nothing less than imaginative possession of its world—a habit we have enshrined in celebrating Emerson, Thoreau and Whitman. The habit or impulse is with us still, although its ideological forms have varied; members of Trilling's own generation have in fact strengthened it considerably by occupying the center of the stage in American intellectual life. Defensive reactions to *The Middle of the Journey* are likely to recur.

It is significant that both on the occasion of the novel's first appearance and on that of its reissue the English found easier and more direct ways to praise it; in the United States it had a rather modest critical recognition. The writer of the original dust jacket used the term "comedy of manners" to describe the book, but this blurs the fact that much of its comedy consists of the attempts of Trilling's characters to deny the actuality of the very distinctions between classes and cultural perspectives to which their Marxist theory commits them.

It is a fact of the highest importance that the thirty years following the book's initial appearance have not discernibly changed the situation it describes. It is no wonder that the political liberalism of Trilling's novel is still largely unpalatable in the United States. The English continue to take it for granted that ideas have a clear relation to intellectual groups as well as the social classes which adopt them—English identity is achieved in matters relating to politics and art *after* one has willy-nilly accepted the fact of one's social origin and the social milieu—perhaps a very different one—that one has come to occupy. It follows that the term "comedy of manners" is still marginally usable in England. It helps one to be a liberal to recognize a certain fatality, a measure of the socially given, as well as the possibility of valuable novelty when one is acknowledging the existence of other people. The socially given is the ground against which the novelty may be seen. But it is hard for Americans, born like gods of their conception of themselves, to accept the idea of class or intellectual milieu except as a way of talking about others with whom one has no connection, or about aspects of ourselves we wish to deny. When we adopt a radical stance we are Emersonian to the bone—our selfhood is anterior to its history. In particular, self-definition after the romantic model in which phases of one's growth are marked by recorded experience as in Keats's letters or Wordsworth's *Prelude* is a rarity among us. To say these things is to posit an historical foreground for *The Middle of the Journey* which the novel does not undertake to provide, and I must attempt to sketch this in after I have suggested what the novel puts before us, and why it has prompted a strong defensive reaction.

Rereading the novel in the current year I felt that the Second World War, the holocaust, and all the other conflicts and cultural upheavals that succeeded these have not carried Americans past the kind of political awareness they had at the time the novel takes place, that of the Spanish Civil War. It is not a "political novel" in the sense that one is involved in the events of that war and that period. It is a novel about the relation of a discernible spectrum of middle-class Americans, readers of *The New Republic* and *The Nation*, who occasionally read the *New Masses*, to the convictions and passions they think of as political; about their relation, putting it most generally, to their ideas.

This question is pervasive in Lionel Trilling's work, both in fiction and in criticism; the positions we take, whether in politics or art, both define and express the desiring, judging, willing self. The failures on the part of ostensible liberals to recognize the immediate bearing of ideas on the self comprise the adverse judgments in *The Liberal Imagination*; in that book they are regarded as failures to recognize the variousness, complexity and difficulty of the human situation which literature is best fitted to enable us to perceive. That literature could be caught up into the realm of the "autonomous self," that Blake could be read for what Trilling called his "tyrant dream," or that literature itself could be hypostatized as distinct from actuality and aggregated into a substitute world, was a perception the culture later forced upon Trilling. This perception informed much of the major work he did after 1950, the year in which *The Liberal Imagination* was published. Art can no longer illumine our judgment in the same way if it has been set apart from the occasions of individual perception and choice on an actual social scene.

It is with a self in literal and exemplary extremity that *The Middle of the Journey* begins. John Laskell's illness has brought him near to death. For a period of days he embraces a negation of will, a pleasure he afterwards recognizes as involving a denial of guilt and responsibility. The first realized moment of the novel's fictional present is Laskell's experience of panic on a suburban railway platform when he finds that his hosts are not there to meet him. His recent absorption in nonbeing is felt for the threat it had been, and he responds in utter, and, at that moment, uncomprehending, terror. The steps in his resumption of will thereafter become conscious, and carry him quite beyond the sense of the world he had had before falling ill. These changes in Laskell's sense of things are associated with what had happened before he took the train with Gifford Maxim. Maxim had stayed on that train in pursuit of his own project, the resumption of a life above ground; he is returning to a world he had abandoned in order to carry on "special and secret" work for the Communist party. Maxim too has come to the surface in terror, but it is a terror which persists and has a basis in the fact of political murders. While ruminating over a break with the Party he has been ordered to Moscow and the prospect of annihilation; he is seeking to establish a public identity so that it will be less easy to murder him without public uproar. Laskell responds with shock and disgust to the fact that Maxim has broken with the Party, and that he is entertaining what Laskell believes to be fantasies about the likelihood of his assassination, which Laskell and the Crooms, his hosts in rural Connecticut, have been taught to regard as reactionary inventions. For Arthur and Nancy Croom and Laskell—people of the "near future"—Maxim has been a figure of the "far future." Laskell has habitually imagined Maxim as flanked by two looming figures: those of suffering humanity and of youthful revolutionary power, both facing future historical perspectives, and both characterized in their male sexlessness by that "blind brooding look," that "lack of personal being" which, as Trilling writes, are "given by men to the abstractions they admire."

Laskell's voluptuous surrender of a personal will, of guilt and responsibility during his illness, has become a curious and valued experience, an episode recalled by a man for whom it has enhanced the complexity of being an agent in the world. It is this experience of his that sensitizes him to a kind of demand —also frighteningly inclusive—that Nancy Croom is making on the future: that the future must realize, as Trilling puts it, "the promises" made to the "well-loved child" of the middle classes. The crucial difference between Nancy and Laskell is of course that she has quite unconsciously projected her demand outward upon the world and given it the name current in her circle—the future, the shape of things inevitably to come. She mistakes a deep need of her own for historical necessity. She is for that very reason capable of enormous cruelty. She does not experience her actions or those of her circle on a scale appropriate to the business of living with others—she is all too often tacitly saying what she says outright when Laskell steps on her flowerbed: "Step out of the cosmos, John." Nancy's political passion inhabits the region described by Wordsworth in his account of his own love affair with a total rationalism, the political future planned by Godwin in *Political Justice*.

> This was the time when all things tending fast
> To deprivation, speculative schemes—
> That promised to abstract the hopes of man out of his feelings,
> To be fixed thenceforth
> For ever in a purer element—
> Found ready welcome. Tempting region *that*
> For Zeal to enter and refresh herself,
> Where passions had the privilege to work,
> Without ever hearing the sound of their own names.

It is one of Trilling's peculiar distinctions to have long ago perceived the quality of the personal relations enjoyed by those who inhabit the region of abstract zeal. His John Laskell makes a succession of discoveries which bear on this: the first of these is that the Crooms feel that his interest in his near approach to death is retrograde; that for them death is a reactionary idea. Laskell is resentful of the Crooms' failure to respond to his experience of illness, and this leads him for a time to withhold the news of Maxim's break with the Party. When he does tell them what Maxim has done they are covertly angry with him, and strangely resistant to any discussion of what it means or how it can have come about. Laskell understands after an interval that they give the Party a fixed and secure place in their imaginations. For him the Party, the "Movement," the Future itself, have simply fallen away; he finds himself unable to imagine that anything lies ahead which is less qualified, less a question of discrimination and choice than what he now confronts. There is then no future which lies beyond personal hope and desire.

It is tempting to rehearse Laskell's other discoveries, but these are the pleasures of the novel, and I limit myself to what seems essential here: Laskell's ensuing struggles with Nancy Croom and Gifford Maxim. Trilling's hero comes to his conviction that Maxim is telling the truth about being in mortal danger on evidence that he cannot offer anyone else. His evidence is the fact that Nancy Croom in her intransigence has made an attempt to destroy Laskell's sense of himself in defense of her imperious inner demand which she has externalized as historical fate. She attacks him as a "romantic," a man tied to the past and to his memory of his dead lover. This is not direct evidence of Maxim's danger; it is evidence that passions commensurate with political murder are indeed to be found among the members of the Communist Party, and it wholly convinces Laskell that Maxim is telling the truth. The climax at the end of the book is a lesser one. It arises out of a conflict between Laskell and Maxim, who has reappeared on the scene, and whose new-found religiosity has turned him into an intolerable spiritual bully. In the end Laskell sees both Maxim and the Crooms as incapable of "ideas in modulation," which is to say that they cannot bear the right use of any idea; they are unaware that neither in politics, morals nor art can ideas be thought of apart from the emotions they inspire and the actions they lead individuals to take.

I quote from Trilling's new introduction to the novel: "So far as *The Middle of the Journey* had a polemical end in view, it was that of bringing to light the clandestine negation of the political life which Stalinist Communism had fostered among the intellectuals of the West. This negation was one aspect of an ever more imperious and bitter refusal to consent to the conditioned nature of human existence." In what I have said of the novel I have of course emphasized the central figure's growing awareness of that refusal in the other characters of the book, and in doing so I have tried to bring out the burden of personal consciousness that John Laskell is led to assume. That that burden is of the very order that Lionel Trilling's criticism assumed—with the important proviso that the criticism has an incomparably wider reach and variousness—is clear. My thesis here connects what is essential in the fictional character and the critic himself: a burden of consciousness I should describe in the full and old-fashioned sense of the word as political, as of the middle ground of human life on which we encounter, to quote the new introduction once more, "opinion, contingency, conflicts of interest and clashes of will and the compromises they lead to."

Trilling's absorption in the art and culture of the last three centuries could be plural and various because he was himself single and complete; a judging self who held himself responsible for the articulation of his passions and his ideas. He seemed to stand curiously alone, almost as if the single judging self had become the one thing we did not know how to refer to. I belive this to be the result of a wide and pervasive shift in our sense of the world. The great novels, poems and structures of thought created in the nineteenth century were made by persons who themselves attributed a measure of authority and potentiality to the single self that balanced their interest in the works these selves made or enjoyed. The very fact that a Keats, a Marx, a Dickens had existed filled the scene with a sense of the makers as well as the things they had made. Ideas, poems, novels and the newly apprehended powers of the self to make such things existed together in the minds of both their creators and those of their audience—an audience which lived in the very first human century in which a strenuous effort to distinguish and celebrate individual human powers over against a scene called society had ever been made. Yet nowadays when we are considering art or politics our attention is chiefly directed to formal patterns, structures, or the homologous schemes of social science. We do not pay a commensurate attention to the kinds of human subjects who pursue these patterns in a nexus of social relationships. What could be more fabulous for us than the relation of a Carlyle, a Dickens, or a George Eliot to their readers? We are far more interested by patterns in the romantics than we are in Wordsworth's observation that rationalism offers a refuge for abstract and irresponsible zeal, and we have not, as I have insisted, paid any attention to Trilling's urgent warning that the characteristic political mode among intellectuals masks our impulses from our awareness. Curiously enough our fiction is full of figures who, like Pynchon's Oedipa Maas, are simply overwhelmed by patterns, as if the thing we do most enthusiastically as literary and cultural critics showed a frightening and even apocalyptic side to us in our fiction.

No character of the order of John Laskell, who assumes the full burden of moral and cultural judgment now seems a fictional possibility. Among students of literature the pursuit of patterns without any concern with their meaning in personal and political actuality is ascendant. Harold Bloom, clutching a doll father named Freud, soars into an empyrean in which poems snarl at each other. The romantics are found to have been far more absorbed in linguistic undertakings than in their personal plight or the conviction that their poetry had an office in the world. Scholarship now has the habit of excising the historical past: we get Blake without the Duke of Wellington, Wordsworth without the French Revolution, Keats without his marvelously direct sensuousness or his capacity to confront mortality—such bodiless figures may all be entrapped in the prison of language built in France and Switzerland.

Carl Woodring speaks of the English romantics as undertaking the staggering job of judging the whole natural order in their own persons, and it is surely one source of Trilling's lasting concern with these poets that they too assumed a personal reponsibility for the interpretation and judgment of their times. Indeed, the readiest way to explain Trilling's political position to students of literature is to juxtapose Wordsworth and Keats with Emerson, Thoreau and Whitman, so often miscalled romantic.

In Americans the impoverished imagination of the human subject takes the form we call American individualism. Those three American writers are classic instances of the denial of conditioned human reality. They strongly deprecate the idea that their lives have crucial and determining phases of growth; they neither acknowledge a personal history nor aspire to have one and they cannot countenance the notion of historical determination in general. They do not think of their relations with other people, whether familial or social, as in any way constitutive of their personalities, and they are equally concerned to deny that the bisexuality of the species is one of its defining characteristics. Emerson and Thoreau cannot admit death into their imaginations, and Whitman, as we know, struggled to reduce death to one of the pulses of organic existence and rob it of any meaning for individuals. This much denial demanded a corresponding quantity of affirmation. What I have elsewhere called the imperial self stood both above and below society; below in that it was passive before the welter of presented appearances, and avoided the plane of action with and upon others; above in that it claimed an imaginative possession of the whole upon which it had renounced the power to act directly.

The only way in which such a self can conceive of political action is through a wholesale execution of its inward fiat. This explains the apocalyptic violence of Emerson's response to the Civil War. It is upon this very ideological and emotional fact that *The Middle of the Journey* focuses, and if our three American worthies do indeed represent an earlier stage in the history of American individualism, this is the connection I would make between American Stalinism and Emerson, Whitman and Thoreau. But whether that connection be valid or no, the kind of massive denials we find in Trilling's fictional characters and in these three writers has the same effect. To make an imperial claim for the self is to cancel out ideas in modulation, to mask your own impulses from yourself, since you do not exhibit them openly where they can be felt and where they must encounter the proposals of others directly.

In an account as brief as this I must put to one side any attempt to suggest how Americans came by this impulse to universalize the self and consider solely the effects that seem to follow from it. In general the formula is: the more one claims for the unconditioned self the more one becomes subject to large abstractions. Or we may put it, the larger one's claim for an impersonal scheme the more nakedly one's hidden desire for apocalypse shows. This, in America, appears to have been the commonest form of the refusal of the conditioned character of human existence of which Trilling speaks in his introduction.

Once we have understood that an hypertrophied self is the wholly necessary complement of the claim to a wholly sufficient comprehension of politics or art, we are in a position to see that that claim to sufficiency cancels the middle ground on which limited human lives are led and actual persons encounter one another. If we can get it through our heads that the masked will can do no more than exfoliate its hidden desire we may be able to get on with the business of facing up to the actuality of the relation of desire to idea. To repair or make good our denial of the desiring, willing, judging human subject is to make possible once more the politics of liberal democracy. There could be no more fundamental error about Lionel Trilling's politics than that of the critic who wrote in 1971: "In its moral tendency this criticism contributed to a cultural malaise—the symptoms were premature resignation, social passivity, and relentless privatism." It was not Lionel Trilling who abandoned the politics of liberal democracy—in fact, regarded as a proposal about politics his novel taught us more about the necessary conditions of that politics than any other document of its time. It was Trilling's contemporaries who, by their refusal of the human condition, and their love affair with an authoritarian politics which served their personal needs rather than those of the community, proceeded to charge Trilling with disloyalty to apocalypse. The quality of a democracy is to be measured not simply by its formal extension of rights to all, but by the capacity of its citizens to extend recognition to the full personhood of their fellow citizens. Our love of pattern and abstraction does not help us to extend this recognition, and it is disabling rather than useful when we are struggling with immediate questions like the impersonal power of such structures as oil companies and banks.

LIONEL TRILLING, 1905–1975*

STEVEN MARCUS

When Lionel Trilling died at the age of seventy in November 1975, a figure of great importance was removed from the world of literature and ideas. It isn't often that intellectual distinction of such magnitude occurs in a scholar or critic of literature. There is even something restrictive and slightly misleading in referring to Trilling as a scholar and literary critic. Though he was both, he was also clearly much more. Nevertheless, he had started out in what seemed to be the conventional way. His first book, published in 1939, was an intellectual biography of Matthew Arnold. He followed this in 1943 with a critical study of E. M. Forster. Both of these books received the large measure of praise that was their due.

It was not until 1950, however, that Trilling began to acquire the wider recognition he would subsequently enjoy. In that year he published his first collection of essays, *The Liberal Imagination.* This volume contained discussions of such writers as Sherwood Anderson, Wordsworth, Henry James, Mark Twain, Kipling and F. Scott Fitzgerald, and such topics as psychoanalysis and literature, the little magazine in America, and manners, morals and the novel. Diverse and wide-ranging as these concerns may have been, the essays were in fact remarkably connected and unified. The collection had indeed a hidden agenda—it was a running argument with Stalinism in both its political and cultural forms. Although Trilling understood himself to be a liberal, he used that word here in a slightly Aesopian sense and with a variety of meanings that shifted according to their context. His essential understanding of his subject, however, can be gathered from this passage that comes at the end of the Preface to that volume:

"It is one of the tendencies of liberalism to simplify, and this tendency is natural in view of the effort which liberalism makes to organize the elements of life in a rational way. And when we approach liberalism in a critical spirit, we shall fail in critical completeness if we do not take into account the value and necessity of its organizational impulse. But at the same time we must understand that organization means delegation, and agencies, and bureaus, and technicians, and that the ideas that can survive delegation, that can be passed on to agencies and bureaus and technicians, incline to be ideas of a certain kind and of a certain simplicity: they give up something of their largeness and modulation and complexity in order to survive. The lively sense of contingency and possibility, and of those exceptions to the rule which may be the beginning of the end of the rule—this sense does not suit well with the impulse of organization. . . .

"The job of criticism would seem to be, then, to recall liberalism to its first essential imagination of variousness and possibility, which implies the awareness of complexity and difficulty. To the carrying out of the job of criticizing the liberal imagination, literature has a unique relevance, not merely because so much of modern literature has explicitly directed itself upon politics, but more importantly because literature is the human activity that takes the fullest and most precise account of variousness, possibility, complexity, and difficulty."

This is, to be sure, a splendid declaration, one that Trilling himself set great store by. By regarding the excesses and deformations of liberalism as moving toward the extreme end of a continuum, Trilling established a capacious context for criticizing it. And by placing Stalinism within the historical tradition of Western enlightenment and rationality, he found a pertinent way of dealing with it from the perspective of the very tradition of which it was an aberration. Nevertheless, as fine as that passage is, we shall see that Trilling did not continue to adhere to every statement it contains.

But *The Liberal Imagination* was much more than a book of essays with an intermittently overt political interest. To those of us who read it at the time, it was unmistakable that a major figure in modern literary criticism had put in his appearance. Trilling at once took his place beside F. R. Leavis and Edmund Wilson as one of the three or four dominating and decisive presences in the twentieth century critical discourse—that discourse in which literature, culture, history, ideas and values freely and richly mingle. Yet the point of such a comparison almost always turned out to be a demonstration of how different each was from the others, how distinct were their virtues of mind and intellect, how unique a combination of forces was incorporated in each of them.

Leavis was distinctively English, a central figure at Cambridge, founder of a school of criticism, with disciples and enemies, a passionate moralist, a grand polemicist, a true believer in the redemptive powers of literature. Wilson was both distinctively native American and cosmopolitan, already in 1950 a grand old man of letters in the grand old patrician tradition, immensely learned in many languages, purveyor and apostle of modernism to the educated world.

Trilling was something else again. He was in the first place urbane in the strict sense of the word—he was a man of the city, of the metropolis. That city was New York, and the sector of urban culture that Trilling emerged from and partly embodied was the subculture of the New York Jewish intellectuals. That subculture was distinguished by the intensity of its commitment to ideas, its radical secularism and its involvement in the ideological consciousness of modern political life. Trilling united these qualities with those that he acquired during his years of academic and scholarly training at Columbia University.

This combination produced a figure that seemed new and at the time was rather unlikely: an American academic who was also a genuine intellectual in the non-academic sense; a professor of English who could really think, whose writing—elegant and elaborate as it often was—moved to the movement of ideas. And these ideas, one felt, were important. They were generated in the discussion of literature, but they went beyond that discussion and touched consciously upon matters of larger consequence for both the reader and the culture in which the reader was situated.

One felt as well that the essays in *The Liberal Imagination* were helping to generate a new kind of discourse; in them the traditional disparities between English and American ways of discussing both literature and society were being transcended. The specific means of this transcendence had largely to do with the intensity and luminosity of Trilling's mind, with its rigor and flexibility, and with his being able to bring relevantly to bear upon the discussion of literature bodies of thought and theory that had their origins in extraliterary realms—such as history, psychoanalysis and the social sciences. This was certainly not the discourse of the New Criticism—with its narrow focus upon isolated texts—which was then becoming a dominant force in academic life. If it reminded one of anything it was the prose of the great nineteenth century critics and essayists. Yet it was a clearly modern idiom, and it proposed to bring to the discussion of literature a seriousness and cogency that such discussion merits but only rarely finds.

As the 1950's moved on, Trilling's essays began self-consciously to focus upon a number of major themes. These themes, one now can see, constituted the central preoccupations of his intellectual career from the outset. He was concerned, as he wrote in the Preface to *The Opposing Self* (1955), his second major collection of essays, with the idea of the modern self as it has been expressed in the literature of the last century and a half; and at the same time he was equally concerned with a particular characteristic of that self, "its intense and adverse imagination of the culture in which it has its being."

These concerns were articulated with characteristic balance, coherence and dialectical subtlety. On the one hand, the great writers of the modern world, such as Dickens, Dostoevsky, Joyce and Kafka, conceived of "modern culture as a kind of prison," a place in which the modern self finds fulfillment through the experience of "alienation," a contradictory and painful state which is at the same time a "device of self-realization." On the other hand, as opposed to the pain and despair of the life of society, civilization and culture, modern writers tended to project "the experience of art . . . into the actuality and totality of life as the ideal form of the moral life."

It was this set of complex and unstable oppositions that Trilling habitually returned to explore. What he found was always surprising and sometimes alarming. For example, in discussing Flaubert's "despair of culture"—meaning, largely, bourgeois culture—Trilling asks what remains for Flaubert when "culture is rejected and transcended." The answer, "given with a notable firmness and simplicity," he continues, "is that something of highest value does remain—it is the self affirmed in self-denial: life is nothing if not sacrificial."

That last graceful and powerful formulation was subscribed to by Trilling himself, as it had been by the individual who, after Arnold, exerted the second most important influence upon the development of Trilling's mind. I am speaking, of course, of the influence of Freud. That influence was deep, pervasive and radical. Trilling looked to Freud and particularly to Freud's "emphasis on biology" as "actually a liberating idea." It was liberating because "it proposes to us that culture is not all-powerful. . . . We reflect that somewhere in the child, somewhere in the adult, there is a hard, irreducible biological *reason*, that culture cannot reach and that reserves the right, which sooner or later it will exercise, to judge the culture and resist and revise it." This was one kind of reason and one kind of resistance that Trilling unwaveringly continued to affirm.

Yet the importance of Freud for Trilling was also of a more than intellectual kind. The figure of Freud was for him something very close to a moral ideal, or to an ideal of personal character and conduct. Freud's fierceness, boldness, honesty and independence, his sense of tragedy and stoical resistance all served or figured as models for him, models that he re-affirmed in his own person and tried to fulfill in his own existence. Indeed he believed that Freud's dealings with the notions of instinctual renunciation and with the inevitable price that has to be paid for civilization and culture were exemplary. For him they were one of the supreme expressions of the self affirmed in self-denial, of the idea that life is nothing if not sacrificial.

As the years passed, such notions, contemporary renderings of classical humanist aspirations and ideals, tended to be increasingly beset. As what came to be called the sixties rose up into self-conscious and assertive life, such notions were openly, and on a wide scale, declared to be discredited. Trilling prepared himself to meet these challenges in his own way. He undertook amid the pressure of the times to examine yet once more "the adversary intention, the actually subversive intention, that characterises modern writing." The original intention of such modernist writing had been "to liberate the individual from the tyranny of his culture in the environmental sense and to permit him to stand beyond it in an autonomy of perception and judgment." Trilling never faltered in his steady commitment to the ideal of autonomy, but what he now thought he saw taking shape was a factitious or pseudo-autonomy, the adoption of the adversary program on a relatively massified scale.

As he looked back from the mid-sixties over forty-odd years of cultural life, he noted that in the interval "there has grown up a populous group whose numbers take for granted the idea of the adversary culture." He located this development largely, though not exclusively, in the changes in character that had occurred in higher education in America. Forty years earlier, he wrote, "the university figured as the citadel of conservatism, even of reaction." Today, however, he continued —with an irony that seemed for once uncertain—there exists "between the university and reality . . . the happiest, most intimate relation." The adversary project of modernism had become institutionalized, and its adherents now formed a virtual class within the bourgeoisie that was supposed to be its enemy. Because it had become established and so to speak "successful," Trilling rightly wondered how the ideal of autonomy would fare under such conditions of sufferance and prosperity. His view remained skeptical, for he observed that the modernist and adversary culture had now begun to share "something of the character of the larger culture to which it was—to which it still is—adversary."

He did not stop there but went on to confront an even graver difficulty. This difficulty has to do with the dominant part that is played by art in the adversary culture. As he considered this problematical subject, Trilling found himself approaching "a view which will seem disastrous to many readers and which, indeed, rather surprises me. This is the view that art does not always tell the truth or the best kind of truth and does not always point out the right way, that it can even generate falsehood and habituate us to it, and that, on frequent occasions, it might well be subject, in the interests of autonomy, to the scrutiny of the rational intellect. The history of this faculty scarcely assures us that it is exempt from the influences of the cultures in which it has sought its development, but at the present juncture its informing purpose of standing beyond any culture, even an adversary one, may be of use."

These arguments were made in the Preface to *Beyond Culture*, Trilling's third large collection of essays; when that volume was published in 1965 there were indeed some readers who responded as if Trilling had committed a cultural and moral disaster. These arguments do in fact represent a departure from—or at least a significant modification of—some of the beliefs put forward in *The Liberal Imagination*. That work, one may recall, opened with the ringing assertion that "literature is the human activity that takes the fullest and most precise account of variousness, possibility, complexity and difficulty."

The Liberal Imagination had been directed to a generation of readers whose determining experiences had been the political-ideological crises of the left in the 1930's and 40's; this generation had in considerable measure committed itself to a deformed and deforming notion of rationality, to such simplifications and constrictions of it as Stalinism represented. For these readers, Trilling had contended, the experience of literature, had they been open to it, would have acted with salutary force; for literature was no less than a criticism of life, in particular of the life of inadequate rationality to which so many had given themselves. *Beyond Culture* was addressed to the grown-up and growing-up children of those readers. The inadequacies and deformations were now running in the other or opposite direction. Hence the polemical line of discourse that Trilling now took up was essentially aimed at the excesses of irrationalism and self-abandonment that the "success" of the adversary culture had made popular and even *chic*.

But Trilling himself had changed as well. Earlier on he had been a partisan, however qualified, of the modern. By the mid-1960's the qualifications increasingly tended to outweigh the original partisanship. Yet in some other part of himself Trilling had not changed at all. There had always been something in him that responded positively to the proposal made by Plato in *The Republic* to banish poets from the ideal society. Not that Trilling would have endorsed any such banishment himself. What he was responding to was Plato's recognition of the power of art, a power to exert influence on attitudes and behavior. It was a power, he was fond of remarking, that modern dictatorships understood only too well.

Trilling himself responded to this power with exceptional literalness. Part of his greatness as a critic was that he regarded the dramatic proposals made by literature as solicitations directed toward the reader. He ascribed to art a purposefulness that was more than esthetic. He detected in the formal gestures of literature intentions that, were they taken seriously by the reader, would lead to new behavior, to changes in life, to consequences of every kind.

He did not in effect think of literature and artistic representations as primarily symbolic actions or as theoretical and contemplative flights of the imagination—although he was not, to be sure, innocent of such conceptions and of how they can be persuasively applied and/or manipulated. He experienced the radical negativity of some of the most characteristic modernist art and thought, such as Beckett's writings and certain forms of existential philosophy, with uneasiness, ambivalence and finally, I think, with downright dislike—although, once more, he fully appreciated the undeniable power of that negativity.

Here again he took his stand with Freud. *Civilization and Its Discontents* was the text by Freud that Trilling read and taught the most and prized most highly. In that work, Freud raised the question "of whether or not we want to *accept* civilization . . . with all its contradictions," and with all its pains and torments. For Trilling, Freud asked that question with unique force and answered it with equally telling saliency. Trilling's formulation of that answer—the style in which he paraphrases Freud's unblinking acceptance of civilization—is as much Trilling as it is Freud. "We do well to accept it," he writes in summary, "although we also do well to cast a cold eye on the fate that makes it our better part to accept it." As I contemplate, with admiration, that grave and exacting declaration, I also find myself shaking my head in wonderment at what part of it, in the climate of the 1960's, Trilling thought was getting through, or could conceivably get through.

In reaffirming the idea of rational intellect, which he also called "the idea of mind," Trilling realized that he was not supporting anything that could currently be conceived of as glamorous or even attractive. Mind today, he wrote, "must inevitably seem a poor gray thing," and he was under no illusion that it could regain the power and mystique that it had once enjoyed in our culture. In putting forward an ideal and a set of values that even in his own eyes seemed bleak, exigent and yet minimal, Trilling was behaving with characteristic courage. He once wrote that Freud and Nietzsche "thought that life was justified by our heroic response to its challenge." To my mind Trilling's spiritual heroism was in large part bound up with his exigency and his minimalism—his ability to affirm, without illusion, qualities and virtues that his own group, his own culture, his own audience had largely given up on as being at once excessive in their demands upon us and insufficient in the gratifications they return.

During the political and cultural storms of the sixties Trilling continued to sustain himself in these attitudes. As he considered some of the more bizarre lunacies of the New Left or wilder manifestations of the counterculture, he thought he saw in these rapidly fluctuating formations genuine threats to the cultural order that he affirmed, albeit minimally and with a cold, skeptical eye. He tended on the whole to see tragedy in such developments, while others tended to see farce. Others often responded to these phenomena with the usual distancing defenses of literary criticism and placed them in contexts that were literary, symbolic and theatrical. Trilling for the most part did not. To him, these were real events, created by real people, in the real world.

In American academic literary life, it is extremely uncommon to find someone who actually believes in the real world—whatever it may be—and who believes further that literature has some determinate and important relation to that world, to the society and culture out of which it arises and which it helps in turn to form. Trilling's great virtue as a critic of literature and culture was that he never ceased to attend to the social and cultural circumstances out of which art and literature arise and that they serve in part to constitute. His legacy to us, I believe, is the seriousness and directness with which he addressed himself to the verbal and written productions that came to him from the world "out there." It was almost as if, in the face of everything modernity had taught us, he continued with old-fashioned perversity to assert that society really exists and that each one of us is an important part of it.

As the cultural turbulences began to abate, Trilling gathered his forces together for yet one further inquiry into the grimness of the current historical situation. The outcome of this investigation, and his final volume, was a small masterpiece. *Sincerity and Authenticity* (1972) ranges across the culture of the last four centuries of Western history—and deals with such writers as Shakespeare, Molière, Diderot, Goethe, Rousseau, Schiller, Hegel, Conrad and Sartre, among many others—but its subject remains the fate of the modern self, the historical vicissitudes that our individuality and personhood have undergone. That is the book's subject, but its argument—if indeed it has an argument in any conventional sense—is almost impossible to summarize.

What Trilling had come to realize afresh is that the modern Western self, that proud creation of our historical culture, was beleaguered and endangered. It was threatened on the one hand by its old cultural enemies, such as repression, deprivation and alienation; it had to continue to struggle against such forces in order to attain what Trilling referred to as the personal sense of "authentic being," that sense in which an individual modern person recognizes the state of his own positive self-realization. But the modern self was threatened as well by some of its putative new cultural friends, those who would lead us away from repression and deprivation and deliver us, reborn, to a new disalienated condition of authentic existence. Prominent among these are the recent prophets and savants of madness, those who have proclaimed to us in one form or another that madness is an adequate, appropriate and even healthy personal response to a sick, corrupt and exploitative society. It was to such pronouncements that Trilling turned at the end of the book, whose final passage runs as follows:

"Yet the doctrine that madness is health, that madness is liberation and authenticity, receives a happy welcome from a consequential part of the educated public. And when we have given due weight to the likelihood that those who respond positively to the doctrine don't have it in mind to go mad, let alone insane—it is characteristic of the intellectual life of our culture that it fosters a form of assent which does not involve actual credence—we must yet take it to be significant of our circumstance that many among us find it gratifying to entertain the thought that alienation is to be overcome only by the completeness of alienation, and that alienation completed is not a deprivation or deficiency but a potency. Perhaps exactly because the though is assented to so facilely, so without what used to be called seriousness, it might seem that no expression of disaffection from the social existence was ever so desperate as this eagerness to say that authenticity of personal being is achieved through an ultimate isolateness and through the power that this is presumed to bring. The falsities of an alienated social reality are rejected in favour of an upward psychopathic mobility to the point of divinity, each one of us a Christ—but with none of the inconveniences of undertaking to intercede, of being a sacrifice, of reasoning with rabbis, of making sermons, of having disciples, of going to weddings and to funerals, of beginning something and at a certain point remarking that it is finished."

The densities of judgment in that prose—its identification, for example, of "a form of assent which does not involve actual credence"—modulate into the ironic bite of "an upward psychopathic mobility" and then turn once again into that remarkable and moving conclusion in which Trilling is able to evoke with utter conviction and finality what the authentic life of the authentic Christ entailed. Confronted with such a prose and such a text, we see literary criticism becoming something larger, richer and more alive with meaning than it almost ever is. We see, in short, a secondary text—something which began as a commentary on another text—in the very act of turning itself into a primary one, into a work of literature.

He was our historian of the moral life of modernity,. our philosopher of culture. He had adopted for himself what he described as Freud's "patrician posture of simultaneous acceptance of and detachment from life in civilization." In him, literary criticism became an enactment of the autonomy that he esteemed as the high goal and destination of personal existence. His writing embodied and dramatized the self-conscious and self-defining individuality that was at the same time its principal subject. He regarded this individuality as being today everywhere coerced, stunted, distorted and constrained; and he sought to sustain in us his readers an awareness of the value of this unique historical artifact. He came to conceive of the modern self as an endangered species, and he thought that however burdensome and troubling that individuality might be for each of us, it was certainly worth conserving.

In his essay on Jane Austen's *Emma* Trilling wrote: "There is no reality about which the modern person is more uncertain and more anxious than the reality of himself. For each of us, as for Emma, it is a sad, characteristic hope to become better acquainted with oneself." As one reads Trilling's essays, one becomes aware that in him the project of literary critical analysis is at the same time a project of conscious self-examination. Trilling's native pedagogic impulse expressed itself in its clear implicit invitation to the reader to undertake on his own part a similar project of self-scrutinization—to read Trilling's essays was in fact one step in such an activity.

He was our teacher, and I believe that future generations of readers will continue to learn from him as well. They will read his writings and discover that they too have become better acquainted with themselves. The faculty of rational intellect, the idea of mind, that he had once described as a poor gray thing was not so gray after all. In some of the writers whom he most admired—in Hazlitt, Arnold, Tocqueville, Mill, and George Orwell, to name but a few—that faculty, rigorously and pertinaciously exercised, had led to its own self-trans-cendence and to its transformation into literature. In the writings of Lionel Trilling we can observe these same processes at work. Those writings are now a permanent part of our culture's heritage.

BRIEF CHRONOLOGY OF THE LIFE
AND WORKS OF
LIONEL TRILLING*

1905	Born in New York City, son of David W. and Fannie (Cohen), July 4
1921	Graduated from DeWitt Clinton High School, New York City
1923-31	Contributed stories and reviews to *The Menorah Journal*, edited by Elliot Cohen; during this period also wrote reviews for the *New York Evening Post*
1925	A.B., Columbia University
1926	A.M., Columbia University
1926-7	Instructor, University of Wisconsin
1929-30	Editorial assistant on *The Menorah Journal* (part time)
1929	Married Diana Rubin, June 12
1930-2	Instructor, Hunter College (evening session)
1932-9	Instructor, Columbia University
1938	Ph.D., Columbia University
1939	*Matthew Arnold*
1939-45	Assistant Professor, Columbia University
1943-63	Advisory editor, *Kenyon Review*
1945-8	Associate Professor, Columbia University
1947	*The Middle of the Journey* (novel) Guggenheim Fellowship
1948-61	Member of the Advisory Board, *Partisan Review*
1948-65	Professor, Columbia University

* Dates of publication refer to first American edition.

1948   James Lionel Trilling born, July 22
1949   *The Portable Matthew Arnold*
1950   *The Liberal Imagination*
1951-63 Contributed essays to *The Griffin* (after July, 1959, *The Mid Century*). This was the organ of a book club whose editorial board consisted of W. H. Auden, Jacques Barzun, and Trilling who were jointly responsible for the selection of books offered the members. (Some of these essays by Trilling were collected in *A Gathering of Fugitives*.)
1951   Editor, with introduction, *The Selected Letters of John Keats*
        Elected to National Institute of Arts and Letters
1952   Fellow of American Academy of Arts and Sciences
1955   *The Opposing Self*
        Freud and the Crisis of Our Culture
        Hon. D. Litt., Trinity College, Hartford, Connecticut
1956   *A Gathering of Fugitives*
1962   Hon. D. Litt., Harvard University
1963   Hon. LHD, Northwestern University
1964-5 George Eastman Visiting Professor, Oxford
1965-70 George Edward Woodberry Professor of Literature and Criticism, Columbia University
1965   *Beyond Culture: Essays on Learning and Literature*
1967   *The Experience of Literature* (an anthology and extensive commentary)
1968   Appointed member of the Executive Committee of the Faculty of Columbia University
        Hon. D. Litt., Case Western Reserve University
        Creative Arts Award, Brandeis University
1969-70 Charles Eliot Norton Visiting Professor of Poetry, Harvard University
1970-4 University Professor, Columbia University
1970   *The Life and Work of Sigmund Freud* (an abridgement of the three volume work by Ernest Jones, edited with Steven Marcus)
        Literary Criticism (an anthology with commentary)
1972-3 Visiting Fellow, All Souls College, Oxford
1972   *Sincerity and Authenticity*
        Received the first Thomas Jefferson Award in the Humanities, Washington D.C. Jefferson lecture published as *Mind in the Modern World*.

Delivered the first University Lecture, Columbia University
1973   Co-editor, *The Oxford Anthology of English Literature*
Hon. D. Litt., University of Durham
Hon. D. Litt., University of Leicester
1974   Retires as University Professor. Continues part-time teaching at Columbia University
Appointed member of Planning Committee for the National Humanities Center
Hon. LHD, Brandeis University
Hon. LHD, Yale University
1975   Guggenheim Fellowship
Died in New York City, November 5

ABOUT THE AUTHORS

JACQUES BARZUN has been a historian, a cultural critic, translator, and university administrator. Since he retired from his chair at Columbia University in 1975, he has been devoting himself to writing and literary consultancy at Scribners. Among his many books are: *Clio and the Doctors: Psycho-History, Quanto-History and History; House of Intellect;* and *The Use and Abuse of Art.*

GERTRUDE HIMMELFARB was graduated from Brooklyn College and received her M.A. and Ph.D from the University of Chicago. She is Professor of History and Executive Officer of the Doctoral History Program at the Graduate School of the City University of New York. She is a Fellow of the American Academy of Arts and Sciences and of the Royal Historical Society. Most recently she was named a Fellow of the Woodrow Wilson International Center for Scholars for 1976–77. Among the books she has written are: *On Liberty and Liberalism: The Case of John Stuart Mill* (Knopf, 1974), *Victorian Minds* (Knopf, 1968), *Darwin and the Darwinian Revolution* (Doubleday, 1959), and *Lord Acton: A Study in Conscience and Politics* (University of Chicago Press, 1952). Professor Himmelfarb is now working on *The Idea of Poverty: A Historical Study.*

EDWARD W. SAID is Professor of English and Comparative Literature at Columbia University. He is the author of *Joseph Conrad and the Fiction of Autobiography* (Harvard University Press), *Beginnings: Intention and Method* (Basic Books), and the forthcoming books, *Orientalism: An Essay in Criticism* (University of California Press) and *Criticism Between Culture and Method* (Harvard University Press).

STEPHEN DONADIO was graduated from Brandeis University, spent a year in Paris as a Fulbright Scholar, and completed his graduate studies as a Danforth Fellow at Columbia University, where he has taught for the past eleven years in the Department of English and Comparative Literature. Since 1976 he has served as Assistant Editor of *Partisan Review*, and he has contributed numerous articles to that quarterly, *Commentary, The New York Times Book Review*, and other notable publications. Mr. Donadio has recently completed a book entitled *The Conquest of Experience: Nietzsche, Henry James, and the Artistic Will*, to be published by the Oxford University Press in the spring of 1978. He is now at work on a critical and intellectual biography of Henry David Thoreau, a project for which he has been awarded a Rockefeller Foundation Fellowship in the Humanities.

FRITZ STERN received his B.A., M.A., and Ph.d. degrees from Columbia University, where at every phase of his career, he was a student of Lionel Trilling's. He began teaching at Columbia in 1946 and since 1967 has been Seth Low Professor of History. Fritz Stern is the author of a number of books, the most recent of which are *Gold and Iron: Bismarck, Bleichröder and the Building of the German Empire* (New York and London, 1977), *The Failure of Illiberalism: Essays on the Political Culture of Modern Germany* (New York and London, 1972), and *The Politics of Cultural Dispair* (2nd ed., Berkeley, 1974). His reviews have appeared in *The New York Times Book Review, Commentary, Foreign Affairs*, and other distinguished publications. Mr. Stern is now working on a book on contemporary Europe, supported by a grant from the Ford Foundation.

IRVING HOWE is a Distinguished Professor of English at the City University of New York. A co-editor of *Dissent*, he is the author of many books, among them *Politics and the Novel, Steady Worker, Decline of the New, The Critical Point*, and *World of Our Fathers. World of Our Fathers* received the National Book Award for History in 1977.

FRANK KERMODE is currently King Edward VII Professor of English Literature at Cambridge University. He is the author of *The Romantic Image* (1957), *The Sense of an Ending* (1967), *The Classic* (1974), and other books. During 1977–8, Mr. Kermode will serve as the Charles Eliot Norton Professor at Harvard University.

ROBERT M. ADAMS is a graduate of Columbia University. He will be retiring shortly from the University of Southern California at Los Angeles, after being active in the field of education for forty years. During this time, he has written many scholarly books such as *Stendal: Notes on a Novelist* and *Milton and the Modern Critics*. His forthcoming publications are: *After Joyce* (Oxford University Press), a new translation of Machiavelli's *Prince* (Norton), and *Bad Mouth* (University of California Press).

RICHARD HOGGART is currently the Warden at the University of London Goldsmiths' College. He was formerly Assistant Director General (Social Sciences, Humanities, and Culture) UNESCO, 1970–1975, and Director, Center for Contemporary Cultural Studies, University of Birmingham, 1964–1970. Among his books are *Auden: An Introductory Essay*, *Uses of Literacy*, and *Speaking to Each Other*.

DANIEL BELL is a Professor of Sociology at Harvard University. He was, from 1959 to 1969, a Professor of Sociology at Columbia University where, for several years he taught a joint Literature-Sociology seminar, first with Lionel Trilling and Steven Marcus, and then with Steven Marcus. He is the author of many books; the most recent are *The Coming of Post-Industrial Society* (Basic Books, 1973), and *The Cultural Contradictions of Capitalism* (Basic Books, 1976).

QUENTIN ANDERSON, a student of Lionel Trilling's both as an undergraduate and a graduate, is Professor of English at Columbia where he has taught Romantic, Victorian, and American literature. He is the author of *The American Henry James* (1957), and *The Imperial Self: An Essay in American Literary and Cultural History* (1971). His criticisms and essays have appeared in a variety of periodicals over a considerable span of time, ranging from *Scrutiny* and *The Kenyon Review*, to the *Times Literary Supplement* and *Commentary*. Professor Anderson taught at Toulouse and Lille as a Fulbright lecturer in 1962–63; he was a Visiting Professor of English at Sussex in 1966–67, and a Fellow of the National Endowment for the Humanities in 1973–74.

STEVEN MARCUS received his undergraduate and graduate degrees from Columbia University, where he studied with Lionel Trilling. He is at present George Delacorte Professor of the Humanities at Columbia and Chairman of the Department of English and Comparative Literature. He is the author of *Dickens: from Pickwick to Dombey* (1965), *The Other Victorians* (1966), *Engels, Manchester and the Working Class* (1974), and *Representations* (1976). In 1961, he collaborated with Lionel Trilling in editing and abridging Ernest Jones' *The Life and Work of Sigmund Freud*. He is Associate Editor of *Partisan Review*.

INDEX